Indian Nation

New Americanists

A Series Edited by Donald E. Pease

Indian Nation

Native American Literature and

Nineteenth-Century Nationalisms

Cheryl Walker

Duke University Press   Durham and London

1997

This book is dedicated to the two Michaels:

Harper, my partner in life and literature, and

Cunningham, my Indian guide

The Indian is "the first and best blood of America."
—Zane Grey

Lost in this [forlorn modernity] (and its environments)
as in a forest, I do believe the average American to be an
Indian, but an Indian robbed of his world.
—William Carlos Williams

The project of imagining themselves *Homines Americanis* posed unusual problems for the subjects of the new US. . . . The true Americans were American Indians. Iconography inscribed ideology; since the Renaissance, America had been represented not as a pious Puritan or a sturdy white husbandman but as a naked, voluptuous American Indian woman. To legitimate their possession of America's lands, their exercise of political suzerainty and their new national and political identities, Euro-Americans had to refuse that representation, establish themselves as the only true Americans and all other Americans, including that voluptuous American Indian woman, as marginal and hyphenated. —Carroll Smith-Rosenberg

Questions of power remain unresolved
where you have neither identity nor a way of
knowing what "identity" might be.
—Leslie Marmon Silko

[N. Scott] Momaday's self-portrait reveals a child inside, looking out at "Indians," questioning how he can define himself as bi-cultural American. This confusion, this challenge, *is* an Indian identity in America, as much as the call for harmonies in the old ways or tribal integrities. —Kenneth Lincoln

Tribal imagination, experience, and remembrance,
are the real landscapes in the literature of this nation;
discoveries and dominance are silence.
—Gerald Vizenor

Contents

Preface and

Acknowledgments

This book has had a long germination period. I first started teaching Native American literature in the early 1970s, but I knew little then about nineteenth-century Indian texts. *Black Elk Speaks* was a work I deeply admired, so I included it in my survey of American literature and found that the students were equally impressed by it. Over the years I added other works from the twentieth century by such writers as Louise Erdrich, Paula Gunn Allen, and Leslie Marmon Silko. But I still postponed considering nineteenth-century texts.

It was not until I began to team-teach the introductory course in the intercollegiate American Studies Program at the Claremont Colleges that I became aware of nineteenth-century issues in Native American history and nationalism. These led me to formulate some preliminary ideas about "the outsider inside." But when I finally put together my first proposal for a book on minority literature and American nationalist rhetoric, I had grandiose plans to examine not only Native American but also African American, Asian American, Latin, immigrant, and homosexual writers, a range of "outsiders" from both the nineteenth and the twentieth centuries. Needless to say, that project was far too ambitious. As I worked my way through the nineteenth century, exploring material by and about Native Americans as well as the increasingly large body of literature concerning nationalism, it became clear to me that I could not deal adequately with this material in one or even several chapters of a multidimensional project. Ultimately, the project became a book just about Indians. Where possible, I have tried to suggest crosscurrents in subaltern studies, but the focus has remained centered on Native Americans, in the nineteenth rather than twentieth century.

As this brief summary of a twenty-year process indicates, I approach Native American literature as a scholar and a teacher. I am not an Indian, and most of my prior professional work has concerned poetry and issues of gender. Is it, then, inappropriate for me to write about Native American texts? The issues are complex, but I nevertheless believe that they can be addressed usefully by those who are willing to take the time to understand them, even if such people are not Native American themselves.

In support of this position, let me introduce some comments I have found helpful from two recent articles that are part of the ongoing "authenticity" debates that have emerged in this era of multiculturalism. In "Scholarship and Native American Studies: A Response to Daniel Littlefield, Jr.," Arnold Krupat addresses the challenges that have been raised by some Native Americans to the infiltration of the field of Native American Studies by non-Indians. According to Krupat, Littlefield responds defensively to these challenges instead of understanding that (1) not all Indians agree with the challengers and (2) some of the challenges are rhetorical rather than substantive. Krupat's main point is that there is no logical (as opposed to political) reason why non-Indians should be excluded from Native American Studies as long as they do responsible work.

This is not to deny the importance (or the lived reality) of having the experience of being Indian; it is to point to the obvious fact that Indian experience is not always and everywhere the same, nor is it ever unproblematically given to consciousness (nor is consciousness unproblematically represented in writing, etc.). *All* experience must be interpreted, and even people who have the "same" experience—the inverted commas indicate the differences inevitable in any "sameness"—may interpret it differently, reaching very different conclusions. (85–86)

In "The Great Pretenders: Further Reflections on Whiteshamanism," Wendy Rose has given a dramatic firsthand account of her experiences of being challenged by non-Indians who insist that their "research" is more authentic than her own experiences of her culture. She is understandably vexed, for instance, by ethnographers who insist that "basket-hats are no longer worn by California Indian women. Yet, nearly every weekend such women attended the same social functions as I, wearing basket-hats that had been passed down through their families and, more importantly, were still being made"

(406). Rose is angry that "Simply *being* Indian—a real, live, breathing, up-to-date Indian person—is not enough" (413) to guarantee authenticity, as far as white people are concerned. Therefore, her own experience of Indianness is often set aside as simply anecdotal or eccentric in favor of the claims of white people who "do research," or pretend to be "whiteshamans" and cater to stereotypical expectations concerning the way Indians are supposed to think and dress.

But, according to Rose's argument, is authenticity guaranteed simply by possessing Indian blood? The answer here seems to be no; one must continue to live according to Indian customs and keep in contact with the community. Similarly, Rose does not insist that non-Indians stay out of the field of Native American Studies. She says simply: "We accept as given that whites have as much prerogative to write and speak about us and our cultures as we have to write and speak about them and theirs. The question is how this is done and, to some extent, why it is done" (416).

Like Krupat, another non-Indian, I am committed to Native American Studies and happy to be enlightened about my mistakes. Like Wendy Rose, I agree that a non-native scholar should be cautious about contradicting a native person whose experience is rooted in the indigenous culture itself. I hope that this book demonstrates my dedication to accuracy, my interest in revising the historical record most Americans have read, and my continuing commitment to expanding the literary canon.

Of course, there are genuine problems in being an outsider inside, even as a critic. Krupat and Rose help us think about some of the many knotty questions that plague the fields of multiculturalism today. Who should speak and what legitimacy does the speech of those who are not living the experience of oppression have? What is the difference between necessary generalization (e.g., in the abstractions "Indians" or "Euro-Americans") and destructive essentialization? To whom (if anyone) does a culture belong? How does one distinguish between the desire to produce "noncoercive knowledge in the interests of human freedom"—to quote Edward Said (Krupat, "Response," 98)—and the temptation to give oneself greater conceptual latitude in speaking "for others" than one is entitled to?

All these questions belong to the larger category of issues concerning authenticity. In this intellectual environment, questions might even be raised about the Native American authors I treat in this book. Since many of them rejected traditional ways to some degree, are they "real Indians"? Obviously, I think they are (and so do other scholars in the field); what I wish to show is that "real Indians" were of many different persuasions.

A provocative intervention in the authenticity debates is Rey Chow's "Where Have All the Natives Gone?" Chow argues that the image of the native (she is usually speaking here of Asians) is never unproblematic in Western scholarship. As a starting point, she suggests that the gaze of the Western scholar is "pornographic" in the sense that Fredric Jameson uses the term when he alludes to the "mere naked body" uncovered by Western scholars when they take the native as their text. Chow says: "Whether positive or negative, the construction of the native remains at the level of image-identification, a process in which 'our' own identity is measured in terms of the degrees to which we resemble her and to which she resembles us. Is there a way of conceiving of the native beyond imagistic resemblance?" (130–31). In other words, can the "authentic native" ever speak?

Chow takes up two responses to this question, Homi Bhabha's and Gayatri Spivak's. Spivak argues that the subaltern cannot speak in Western discourse (which always co-opts the speaker and translates such speech into its own terms). Bhabha, by contrast, argues that the subaltern has always already spoken, because Western discourse is fractured and framed by its encounter with the Other. Chow finds both of these responses inadequate, however. One is too pessimistic, but the other is too optimistic in its erasure of all struggle.

Instead, Chow proposes that we consider the native as "an indifferent, defiled image" (145–46), silent, unperturbed, framed, resistant.

To insist on the native as an indifferent, defiled image is then to return to the native a capacity for distrusting and resisting the symbolic orders that "fool" her, while not letting go of the "illusion" that has structured her survival. To imagine the coexistence of defilement and indifference *in* the native-object is not to neutralize the massive destructions committed under such orders as imperialism and capitalism. Rather, it is to invent a dimension beyond the deadlock between native and colonizer. (146)

In chapter 1 I will introduce my own approach to "the native" and to Native American texts. As will be spelled out in greater detail there, I have chosen to focus on two forms of discourse—"transpositional" and "subjugated"—which are, in a sense, contradictory. The contradiction is similar to that which Chow suggests in the pairing "indifferent, defiled." I too wish to make room for agency and resistance. I too must deal with images, distortions, and their effects.

Perhaps the only way to avoid being captured by the reductivism of hegemony is by preserving the oxymoron: that is, the contradiction implied by two incompatible discourses within which it becomes clear there are gaps and fissures one cannot dismiss. That aporia, that silence, must give one pause, as Chow suggests when she says: "we should argue that it is the native's silence which is the most important clue to her displacement. That silence is at once the *evidence* of imperialist oppression (the naked body, the defiled image) and what, in the absence of the original witness to that oppression, must act in its place by *performing* or *feigning* [i.e., pretending to serve] as the preimperialist gaze" (134).

In what follows I will periodically examine passages in Native American texts that I cannot "translate," that is, identify and fit into a clear, systematic perspective. In such cases, I will usually ponder several possibilities, as I do with one section of Black Hawk's autobiography which gives "his" views about African Americans. I hope that both my commitment to the struggle to translate (and thus enter into) Native American perspectives, and my willingness to refrain from expressing certainty about such translations, will be seen as part of the weave of Native American scholarship whose basic premises I support and share.

The research I did for this book involved a number of libraries and librarians whom I wish to acknowledge and thank here: the Huntington Library of Pasadena (Peter Blodgett), the Chicago Public Library (Connie Gordon), the Huntington Free Library in the Bronx (Mary

Davis), the Alderman Library of the University of Virginia, the Indiana University Research Library, the Wisconsin State Historical Society, the Chicago Historical Society, the Newberry Library, and the Rare Book Collection of the Honnold Library of the Claremont Colleges. Many people at these institutions took considerable time to answer my questions and search for materials. Special thanks go to Alfred Bendixen, who told me about the Southwest Museum in Los Angeles. Ultimately, their library (and Kim Walters in particular) were the most helpful to me in my search for Simon Pokagon's birchbark document "The Red Man's Rebuke."

I would also like to acknowledge the following people who gave me information helpful in the preparation of this manuscript: Jim Anaya, Jean Smith, Julie Liss, Nathalie Rachlin, Rita Roberts, Héctor Calderón, Stuart McConnell, and my students Sarah Goss and Robin Podolsky. Arnold Krupat, Suzanne Clark, Michael Harper, and Michael Cunningham read the entire manuscript and offered enormously useful advice. This book owes a great debt to the NEH Seminar on Postcolonial Literature given by Albert Wertheim at Indiana University in 1993 and to the Rockefeller Foundation, which made it possible for me to work during 1994 at the Study and Conference Center at the Villa Serbelloni in Bellagio, Italy. People in both places steered me to useful resources and refined my thinking about the issues addressed herein. I gratefully acknowledge the research funds I received from Scripps College (especially the Richard Armour Chair) and the support for scholarly activity provided by Mary W. Johnson. Special thanks go, as always, to my wonderful secretary Nancy Burson.

I would also like to thank here four people who helped me to create a spiritual context that became increasingly precious to me during the writing of this book: Colin Thompson, Homer D. "Butch" Henderson, Peter Farmer, and Coleman Barks.

"And don't forget about us!" my daughter insisted. Ian (sixteen) and Louisa (thirteen) have given me great cause to be thankful and, as Louisa is fond of reminding me, they wish the Indians had won.

The complete text of Simon Pokagon's "The Red Man's Rebuke" (1893) is reprinted courtesy of the Southwest Museum (Ms 745).

1. The Subject of America
The Outsider Inside

American character is a particularly vexed subject, vexed because, on the one hand, we no longer wish to define Americans in terms of certain character traits, modes of behavior, physical types, and yet, on the other, we have never lost the desire to puzzle over the implications of ideas of the nation for a certain conception of the human being understood to represent those ideas. Whether or not we think of ourselves as "typical Americans"—and most of us don't—many of us have had the experience of being so labeled when we travel abroad, causing us to ponder our own understandings of what America is and how we are affected by it. Black Americans find that in Africa they are often considered more "American" than "African American." The children of immigrants, or even those who have themselves emigrated from other parts of the world, discover that they cannot easily shrug off the buffalo robe of "Americanization" when they visit friends and relations from their past. One never feels quite so American as when one is not in the United States. But what does it mean to be an American subject, the representative of certain conceptions about the nation? What aspects of one's identity and one's politics are not simply personal but national? At home we are all exiles. Abroad we seem, strangely, to be heard speaking only of "home."

Even those for whom life in America[1] has been far from ideal, those subjected to a process of identity deformation that is connected in no small way to a conception of the nation as composed of insiders and outsiders, even these have had to think about their relation to national ideology and American subjectivity. The African American playwright Anna Deavere Smith writes: "It seems to me that American character lives in the gaps between us and to the degree to which we are willing to move between those gaps. It lives in our struggle to be together in our differences, even the non-negotiable ones" (8).

Thus, the subject of America must be seen as without a fixed content; rather than being representable as a particular set of characteristics, it becomes a conversation, perhaps, or a set of stories. Similarly, one might say, as Liah Greenfeld does, that "American nationalism was [and essentially is] idealistic nationalism" (449); therefore "nationhood" emerges and reemerges not as a historical entity or an accepted sequence of events but as a counterweight to history, a projection into the future always waiting to be realized. When the subject of America is raised abroad, it is often accompanied by head shakings of one sort or another as the gap is measured between American ideals of justice and equality and American practices seen as unjust and undemocratic. But these friends abroad misconceive the effect of these challenges. Rather than undermining the force of nationalist rhetoric, such grumbling is in fact a principal aspect of the discourse on American character, a familiar feature of what America is and has always been.

Nathaniel Hawthorne was one of those who, even in the nineteenth century, both idealized America and took her to task for a certain wayward individualism. Personifying America in the figure of the adulteress Hester Prynne, who wears the red A (perhaps identifying her territory), he admired its independent spirit but wondered about its memory and its capacity for moral commitment. In "The Custom House" essay that precedes the main text of *The Scarlet Letter*, Hawthorne also reflected on the double nature of America in his reading of the American eagle.

With the customary infirmity of temper that characterizes this unhappy fowl, she appears, by the fierceness of her beak and eye and the general truculency of her attitude, to threaten mischief to the inoffensive community; and especially to warn all citizens, careful of their safety, against intruding on the premises which she overshadows with her wings. Nevertheless, vixenly as she looks, many people are seeking, at this very moment, to shelter themselves under the wing of the federal eagle; imagining, I presume, that her bosom has all the softness and snugness of an eider-down pillow. But she has no great tenderness, even in her best of moods, and sooner or later,—oftener soon than late,—is apt to fling off her nestlings with a scratch of her claw, a dab of her beak, or a rangling wound from her barbed arrows. (23–24)

America is seen here as both the truculent federal eagle (the state), apt to scratch her offspring, and as "the inoffensive community" (the people) deeply connected to Hawthorne's sense of himself. So "America" is power and privilege, the misuse of these through arrogance or selfish inattention, and, as a third component, the silent majority who struggle on despite a less than nurturing environment. In *The Anatomy of National Fantasy,* Lauren Berlant argues that Hawthorne constructs America as "a domestic, and yet a strange and foreign place" (3), a space where the experience of "home" and "exile" inevitably meet.

Hawthorne found it odd that such an inhospitable creature as the federal eagle should attract so many new nestlings wishing to shelter themselves under its wing, but the same is true today. What's more, many writers from oppressed minorities in America have responded to America's hostility or exclusionist practices not by an attack on nationalist rhetoric but by asserting their right to be Americans and their fitness for contributing to the National Symbolic.[2] "I, too, sing America," wrote Langston Hughes,[3] and the commitment reflected in these words has been echoed by Latins, Asians, Eastern Europeans, and many other groups and individuals seeking a home within a nation of immigrants. Alienation often engenders disaffection, but it has also produced attempts to seize the terms of the dominant discourse and redeploy them. Poor, Jewish, and homosexual in a country known for its wealth, its WASPs, and its celebration of the nuclear family, Allen Ginsberg wrote into his 1956 poem on his wildly eccentric experience of national identity a wonderful conclusion: "It occurs to me I am America," he said, and ended, "America I'm putting my queer shoulder to the wheel" ("America," 34).

I offer these thoughts by way of introducing what will strike some as a peculiar project: a book about conceptions of America and American nationalism in nineteenth-century Native American writing. The general assumption in the critical literature has been that Native Americans were the victims of nationalist discourse pure and simple, that they resisted attempts to impose an idea of nation that derived from European models on their native and essentially tribal structures of governance and knowledge, because such ideas obviously threatened many aspects of their cultures. But the truth is more complicated than this view allows for, because by the end of the first third of the nineteenth century, there were several understandings of nation in play among both Euro-Americans and Native Americans. Let me suggest some of them here, though in subsequent chapters I will try to deepen and complicate these preliminary notions.

In his discussion of the evolution of the words "nation," "national," and "nationalism," Raymond Williams clarifies the sense in which Western understandings of nation developed from the seventeenth century onward, during the precise period when Native Americans and Europeans were coming into conflict over this issue in the "New World."

There was from [the seventeenth century] a use of the *nation* to mean the whole people of a country, often in contrast, as still in political argument, with some group within it. The adjective *national*, which is clearly political, is more recent and still alternates with the older *subject*. *Nationality*, which had been used in a broad sense from lC17, acquired its modern political sense in lC18 and eC19.

Nationalist appeared in eC18 and *nationalism* in eC19. Each became common from mC19. The persistent overlap between racial grouping and political formation has been important, since claims to be a *nation*, and to have *national* rights, often envisaged the formation of a *nation* in the political sense, even against the will of an existing political *nation* which included and claimed the loyalty of this grouping. It could be and is still often said, by opponents of *nationalism*, that the basis of the group's claim is racial.[4] (178–79)

Though developed in a European context, much of this is useful for our purposes as well. By the nineteenth century, American rhetoric conceived of the nation as both a political entity, with geographical dimensions and laws, and a people, whose "deep, horizontal comradeship"[5] had to be identified and argued, even racially codified. However, there was great disagreement over who was qualified to be an "American" and what the nature of "America" really was.

Native Americans had not traditionally understood nations as the West came to define them. Nor did race play much of a role in their thinking.[6] In Indian oral traditions the nation originally meant simply the people and the environment they inhabited, an environment without legislated boundaries. William Least Heat Moon tells a story about the Native American sense of "nation" in *PrairyErth (a deep map)*:

The white man asked, *Where is your nation?* The red man said, *My nation is the grass and roots and the four-leggeds and the six-leggeds and the belly wrigglers and swimmers and the winds and all things that grow and don't grow.* The white man asked, *How big is it?* The other said, *My nation is where I am and my people where they are and the grandfathers and their grandfathers and all the grandmothers and all the stories told, and it is all the songs, and it is our dancing.* The white man asked, *But how many people are there?* The red man said, *That I do not know.* (16)

Though strikingly different, such a conception of nation shares some components with Euro-American ideas. Land, traditions, people, stories—these are also part of the national lexicon of Hector St. John de Crèvecoeur, Francis Parkman, and James Fenimore Cooper, white men whose writings served to define the nation for later generations of Americans. But Indians thought of the nation as constituted "in the early days," an era lost in the mists of time. Furthermore, the relations among the various components of the nation were sacred, not political in a European sense. Each component—land, traditions, people, stories—was connected in a deep and mysterious way to the others.

Vine Deloria Jr. and Clifford Lytle describe the difference between Euro-American and Indian ideas of nation this way:

Because the tribes understood their place in the universe as one given specifically to them, they had no need to evolve special political institutions to shape and order their society. A council at which everyone could speak, a council to remind the people of their sacred obligations to the cosmos and to themselves, was sufficient for most purposes. . . . Indians had a good idea of nationhood, but they had no knowledge of the other attributes of political existence that other people saw as important. Most of all, Indians had no awareness of the complexity that plagued the lives of other peoples, in particular the Europeans. (9)

Using these representations of Native American ideas about "nation," we might conclude that there was no real convergence between Euro-American and Native American understandings. According to Benedict Anderson, this "good idea of nationhood" (to which Deloria and Lytle refer) is actually prenational, reflecting a worldview more akin to the unself-consciously coherent sacralized communities that preceded modern political arrangements. It is precisely the fact that such communities "rooted human lives firmly in the very nature of things, giving certain meaning to the everyday fatalities of existence (above all death, loss, and servitude), and offering, in various ways, redemption from them" (*Imagined Communities*, 36) that for Anderson disqualifies them from modern nationhood. Nations, he argues, come into being when the West is desacralized due to the spread of capitalism and print culture, the multiple interrelations between writing, printing, and reading that are enmeshed in the market economy. The nation, then, operates in part as recompense for the loss of the religious certainties that allowed for integration between the self and the cosmos.

If Native Americans had been allowed to continue in their tribes as they had for centuries, it would indeed make little sense to introduce Indian conceptions of nationalism into a discussion of European ones. However, from the seventeenth century onward, traditional ideas had been modified by contact of varying sorts with white people. By the beginning of the nineteenth century, Indian-white relations were well advanced in most parts of the country east of the Mississippi. Furthermore, during the century the United States vastly expanded its empire so that by 1900 all indigenous peoples had been touched by American nationalism, mostly in negative ways.

The responses of Native Americans to white encroachment were varied. Some like the Pueblos first sought accommodation. Others resisted and went to war. The Cherokees were unusual in the degree to which they adopted aspects of white culture into their own national identity.[7] But eventually all were forced to come to terms with the non-native conception of nation represented by America itself. Thus, the nineteenth century was a defining time for both Native Americans and their white counterparts. During this time Americans were actively engaged in the process of constructing a sense of "nationness" through iconography, art, writing, rituals, speeches, institutions, and laws.

What has not been adequately recognized before is that Native Americans also participated in this cultural process, sometimes in order to distinguish themselves from the invaders but sometimes in the interests of revising notions of America to include the tribes themselves. Thus, America in the nineteenth-century was intercultural in significant ways. In this kind of context, as Timothy Reiss puts it, "Cultural categories mingle and float. 'Borders' are more than just porous. Cultures are mutually defining. The fault of European cultures was to believe that they are not" (651).[8]

The mistake that Reiss refers to here may be seen not only in the nineteenth-century essentialism that demonized Native Americans as savages but also in more recent assumptions that Indians took no part in the discussions of national identity. Let me offer three recent examples of the persistence of the idea that Native Americans contributed little or nothing to the development of an American national discourse. In Larzer Ziff's *Writing in the New Nation: Prose, Print, and Politics in the Early United States* (1991)—and let me say here that I have great respect for Ziff as a cultural historian—he articulates the view that print culture in the United States inevitably transformed the experience of immanence in Nature, admired by so many American writers, into fodder for an imperial cultural project destructive of, inter alia, Native Americans. In the chapter entitled "Captive Language," he traces the transformation of Lewis and Clark's journals into Nicholas Biddle's *History of the Expedition under the Command of Captains Lewis and Clark* (1814). Though Lewis and Clark, like Timothy Dwight and Thomas Jefferson in Ziff's earlier examples, were sympathetic to the Indians and admired many features of their culture, literary conventions and print culture itself, according to Ziff, sealed the fate of Native Americans.

The process of literary annihilation would be checked only when Indian writers began representing their own culture. As whites had utilized sign language to commence their dialogue with Indians, so Indians, finally, would come to utilize the conventions of written English to restore dialogue to what *for a century after Biddle's History,* had been in reality a monologue with the Indian's voice supplied by the ventriloquizing culture of the white. (emphasis added, 173)

In truth, Native Americans began to express their views at least as early as the 1830s in texts published in English, some of which went into several editions. (Whether these texts were simply examples of another kind of ventriloquism is a question we must consider in some detail.) Furthermore, their speeches, delivered in many cities throughout the United States, were attended by large crowds and were subsequently both printed and reviewed in newspapers and journals, as examples of Indian oratory. Yet Ziff seems to believe that Indians were effectively silenced until the twentieth century.

Similarly, in *Manifest Manners: Postindian Warriors of Survivance* (1994), Gerald Vizenor (Chippewa)—the champion of postmodern mixed-blood narrators of Indian culture and identity—repeats Ziff's argument, though he takes notice (as Ziff does not) of William Apess's early example of Indian autobiography, in which Apess reflects at various points upon the nations. For Vizenor the production of literature outside the tribal context is inevitably a desecration because such "simulations" (Vizenor's word) present an absence, an absence partly accessed only by what Vizenor calls "trickster hermeneutics." "The stories that are heard [in tribal ceremonies] are the coherent memories of natural reason; the stories that are read are silent landscapes" (96), thus in need of hermeneutic voices.

Against the destructive simulations of nationalist dominance, which he names "manifest manners," postindian warriors create "a counter word culture" (20). "The postindian warriors bear their own simulations and revisions to contend with manifest manners, the 'authentic' summaries of ethnology, and the curse of racialism and modernism in the ruins of representation. The wild incursions of the warriors of survivance undermine the simulations of the unreal in the literature of dominance" (12).

The "postindian warriors" Vizenor addresses (and he has many interesting things to say about them) all come from the twentieth century. He quotes Ziff extensively in creating his argument about the development of nineteenth-century American nationalist rhetoric, the literature of dominance that, Vizenor agrees, attempted to capture the Indian with words. But one struggles to resolve the seeming contradiction in Vizenor's argument between his poststructural contention that everyone—"postindian warriors" and "missionaries of manifest manners" alike—must deal in simulations and articulations of absence (13), and what seems to be a belief in authentic experiences of presence within tribal aural culture where "the shadows of tribal consciousness, and the shadows of names and natural reason are overheard" (96). It remains unclear whether Vizenor believes that nineteenth-century Indian writers had anything to offer in countering American nationalist "manifest manners" or whether, as seems more likely from his argument, postindian literature had to await an opportunity for "the new" that did not arrive until manifest manners had to some extent played its hand.

In my first two examples, Ziff and Vizenor agree that print culture effectively kept Native Americans from entering the cultural conversation during the nineteenth century; they hold out for a twentieth-century counterdiscourse as the beginning of Native American resistance to American nationalist rhetoric. My third example of the persistence of the view that Native Americans contributed nothing to the National Symbolic is *Removals: Nineteenth-Century American Literature and the Politics of Indian Affairs* (1991), in which Lucy Maddox argues that there were *two* discursive communities—Indian and white—but that they never converged. Though her work on Euro-American writers (especially Melville) is fascinating, she too seems to accept the idea that Native Americans were basically out of the national loop.

Maddox begins her study by talking about the problem of bringing Indian and white discourses together, claiming that the eastern Indians, in order to guard the nation, were mainly dedicated to frustrating efforts to construct and enforce laws, while the western tribes frustrated efforts at expansion. Thus, "the nation"—understood as the United States—inevitably developed in opposition to "the tribes." "The Indians, that is, continued to frustrate white America's efforts—

official and unofficial—to include them within the discourse of American nationalism and, concomitantly, within the structures of the country's laws and institutions" (7).

It may well be true that from a white point of view—that is, from the point of view of many Euro-Americans, especially those with political power—there was no available discourse "that seemed able to put *Indians* and *government* together in any precise or logical relation except that of opposition" (8). Though there were some who believed that oppositions "should and would be dissolved in the new nation, as the union became more perfect" (8), their writings on the Indian question almost always took the form of either-or. That is, either Indians would give up their culture or they would be annihilated. "The persistence of the notion that their tribal identity precluded Indian peoples from being or becoming members of a nation—that is, citizens—is reflected in the report of the Commissioner of Indian Affairs in 1856, who noted approvingly that one object of federal treaty-making with the Indians had been the 'gradual abolition of the tribal character'" (10).

Nevertheless, as we will see in subsequent chapters, there were literate Indians—some of whose views were known even in congressional circles[9]—who believed nothing of the sort. Their works, which often argue for Native American citizenship and always engage the hegemonic discourse on the issue of nation, confirm the conclusion of Pauline Turner Strong and Barrik van Winkle, that "the complex imaginings of national identity found among Native Americans call into question some of the basic presuppositions of modern nationalism" (20), especially its emphasis on individualism, singular national identity, and the seamless discursive web. I would add that these texts challenge our notions of American literary history as well.

This book focuses on nineteenth-century Native American writing and its reflections upon nationhood. All the Native American texts it considers are not only postcontact but also multivoiced, reflecting the influence of cultures upon one another. This is not to say that there are no continuities in these texts with earlier conceptions of "the nation" as the tribe and its lands. But such continuities are present along with other conceptions of the nation as "America": a political umbrella, a space of negotiation, and an "imagined community." I use the term "imagined community" not in Anderson's sense of a contentless structure, trailing like a kite string strategic scraps of history, but as a future-oriented (and thus particularly American) dream of shared experience, what Anna Deavere Smith describes as "the struggle to be together in our differences, even the non-negotiable ones."

The device I have chosen to highlight in these Native American texts is the personification of America as an Indian. In the nineteenth century, national personification appeared in works by both Indians and whites and may still be seen in such figures as Uncle Sam and the Statue of Liberty.[10] Imagining the nation as a person was a rhetorical strategy even more common in the nineteenth century than it is today, and, as we will see, sometimes even Euro-Americans chose to personify America in an Indian figure. But my focus on personification here will consider, not the more commonly treated topic of the co-optation of Indian images for white nationalist purposes,[11] but rather Native American usages of this trope and the challenges mounted in their texts to America as home only to whites of European background.

In all of my readings of these complicated texts, I am interested in "the subject of America," but I have in mind as subject both the producers and the products of stories about the nation. The vexed topic of American character—that is, the nature of America itself as a unique entity and the reflection of a belief that there is an American essence in its mirroring as a human individual—will occupy us throughout.

Nationalist rhetoric takes America as its "subject," and we will examine this rhetoric both as it appears in Native American texts and as it provides the background for these texts. In the nineteenth century (especially but not exclusively in its first half), national allegory is perceptible in a wide range of productions. Native American literature is the central focus here, but we will also look at poems, paintings, essays, histories, speeches, and promotional literature by Euro-Americans in order to understand the vision of America against which Native Americans felt they had to argue and which provided the context in which whites responded to Indian claims.

Another meaning of the term "subject" focuses upon the individual: as agent (sovereign subject), as recipient of various forms of pressure (subjected to authority), and as the personification of national themes. We will be alert to places in these texts where "the subject of America" is modeled as a representative individual, "an American subject" in both positive and negative senses. However, in Native American texts such a figure often contests the assumptions about personal agency so typical of Euro-American personifications in heroes such as George Washington.[12]

In Native American national allegory we find instead something that Arnold Krupat has named "the synecdochic self": that is, the individual whose worth is determined not by autonomous acts but by his or her capacity to represent the group, synecdochic as "the part representing the whole." Krupat summarizes as follows:

In any event, insofar as we would attempt to generalize about the Native American self from available studies, that self would seem to be less attracted to introspection, expansion, or fulfillment than the Western self appears to be. It would seem relatively uninterested in such things as the 'I-am-me' experience, and a sense of uniqueness or individuality. More positively, one might perhaps instantiate an 'I-am-we' experience as descriptive of the Native American sense of self, where such a phrase indicates that I understand myself as a self only in relation to the coherent and bounded whole of which I am a part. (*Ethnocriticism*, 209–10)

This differing sense of self has implications for the way personification is used in Native American writing.

Often, in Euro-American texts, one encounters the personification of America in an allegorical context that promises benefits specifically geared to the individual: rights of property, upward mobility, the pursuit of happiness. Even an Indian, such as Sequoyah, could be enlisted (e.g., by T. L. McKenney and J. Hall in their 1842 *Indian Tribes of North America*) as a model American, but this white allegorical usage of an Indian personifies America as a self-made man.[13]

When Black Hawk presents himself as quintessentially a Sauk, when Sarah Winnemucca embodies America in the form of a Paiute woman, or when William Apess uses King Philip as an American personification, they are doing something other than entering the economy of abstract individual personhood underlying industrial capitalism, as some critics have suggested is typical of Euro-American usages of national personification.[14] Instead, Black Hawk, Winnemucca, and Apess offer an interpretation of nationhood as a player in the theater of interpersonal (and intertribal) relations, many and one at the same time. The personification offers a story about how an idealized sense of the nation might operate in certain circumstances. And always in these cases, that story insists upon the subordination of individual desires to the needs of the community.

Some critics have suggested that personification is deep-rooted in Indian culture and, therefore, is inevitably part of Native American literature.[15] However, I will not try to argue this myself, since I am more interested here in the kind of mirroring that occurred between Euro-American and Native American personifications, and the effect of that mirroring gesture on the possibilities present in national discourse.

To begin with, one must acknowledge that Native American *literature* is something of an oddity. Since Indians before contact did not have anything but pictographic writing, written literature emerged, to some degree, as a form of collaboration with the enemy. Larzer Ziff states: "When sign language gave way to interpreted speech, even as the recorded facts and unmediated impressions of the travelers gave way to the written history of the [Lewis and Clark] expedition, so cultural equality gave way to dominance and the process of literary annihilation" (172). Yet, in *For Those Who Come After,* Arnold Krupat revises this point of view by addressing Indian literature itself, arguing that Native American autobiography is always the product of what he calls "original bi-cultural composite composition." However, even he admits that during most of the nineteenth century, the lack of Euro-American forms of writing within most tribal communities meant that "the presence of the grapheme still signified for the Indian the cultural other, the track of the Indo-European snake in the American garden" (30).

I have taken my cue from Krupat's reflections on hybrid auto-biography and from Kwame Anthony Appiah, who, in his excellent book *In My Father's House: Africa in the Philosophy of Culture* (1992), wishes to move beyond readings that either attempt to reify cultural purity in the body of the text or to present textuality itself as the death knell of indigenous cultures. Appiah's outline for productive modes of reading (and teaching) is one that has considerable relevance to my practice in what follows.

First, identify accurately the situation of the modern African [here Native American] text as a product of the colonial encounter (and neither as the simple continuation of an indigenous tradition nor as a mere intrusion from the metropole); second, stress that the continuities between precolonial forms of culture and contemporary ones are nevertheless genuine (and thus provide a modality through which students can value and incorporate the African [or Native American] past); and third, challenge directly the assumption of the cultural superiority of the West, both by undermining the aestheticized conceptions of literary value that it presupposes and by distinguishing sharply between a domain of technological skill in which—once goals are granted—comparisons of efficiency are possible, and a domain of value, in which such comparisons are by no means so unproblematic. (69–70)

If we look to Native American texts from the nineteenth century, we can see that they are in Appiah's sense a product of bicultural encounters. Some Indian writers directly addressed the issue of what role native peoples should play in the development of the new nation. George Copway (Ojibwa), William Apess (Pequot), John Rollin Ridge (Cherokee), and Sarah Winnemucca Hopkins (Paiute) are examples of Indians who were literate and addressed an assumed Euro-American readership, arguing among other things for American citizenship for Native Americans. Other Indians, such as Governor Blacksnake (Seneca), Black Hawk (Sauk), and Red Jacket (Seneca)[16] were not literate, nor did they directly address the construction of American national identity. But in the translations of their words that we do have, they inevitably had to consider the intersection of native and American ideas of nationhood.

It hardly needs saying that a reading of Native American texts from the nineteenth century challenges the ideology of Manifest Destiny in its belief that "America" required the destruction of native peoples. Though, as Carroll Smith-Rosenberg argues, some Euro-Americans (she means males) may have recognized that "the true Americans were American Indians" (482) and therefore felt a need to denigrate racially and sexually marked Others (Indians / women) in order to overwrite their sense of the artificial construction of "American identity" in the first place, Native Americans tended at first to view whites as belonging to another tribe, a tribe that could be accommodated or not in a given situation, as was the case with other rival factions. Even as a sense of American nationalism emerged and began to threaten some Indian tribes, there yet remained available a fundamental sense of parity in which the American nation was seen by indigenous people as essentially a mobile force field where groups might negotiate for particular rights and privileges but which would not inevitably mean the triumph of one and the extirpation of all others. This more humane mode of interaction persists to some degree in Native American writing.

However, there is a second strain of narrative, another "plot," if you will, in Indian texts. Harsher, more contestatory, this mode enlists in the hierarchical ranks of cultural conflict, sometimes for the purposes of condemning the dominant rhetoric but sometimes, as a form of mimicry, reproducing that rhetoric's assumptions. It is tempting to reproduce only the uplifting vision of "a nation among nations," in which—as we now say—different voices might be heard in polylogue, different national identities speaking together harmoniously, or at least contrapuntally, as they did in Iroquois councils. However, to do so is to obscure part of the evidence and to engage in a form of romanticizing that is as problematic as giving Euro-Americans the only voices in the development of a national discourse. As Frederick Turner comments, in "On the Revision of Monuments": "In recent years we [revisionist historians] have been creating a red Ecological Wise Man, who is in some ways as inhuman and fictive as the cunning savage in the bad old books of [William Gilmore] Simms, [Francis] Parkman, and [Theodore] Roosevelt" (116).

Some Native Americans, in the process of becoming literate, took to mimicking the discourse of the whites. But rather than stabilizing their position vis-à-vis the dominant culture, their rejection of their own heritage as often as not began a process of national disestablishment that resulted, in the lives of the Indian authors themselves, in an almost complete loss of psychic balance. An example is George Copway, an Ojibwa and a Methodist minister, who for a time became the darling of the Boston intelligentsia and who published several books advocating Christian assimilation and Native American citizenship. His life went steadily downhill in the 1850s, however. As Donald B. Smith writes: "There can be no question that George Copway, stricken by family tragedy, forsaken by his literary friends, and bankrupt, had begun by the summer of 1851 to lose all touch with reality" (25). Among the bizarre, and highly symbolic, actions Copway undertook late in his life were his stealing of the bones of Red Jacket from a former Indian reservation without telling the Seneca for whom they were sacred, and the kidnapping of young Indian males in order to enlist them in the Union army, a job for which he was paid by the American government. In his case, his desire to assimilate reinforced his position as a subjugated individual, causing him to lose his psychic stability in the throes of taking on the trappings of an alien culture.

In order to clarify the different effects produced by these two versions of national allegory—the egalitarian and the differential—I will explore two rhetorical paradigms; I call them *transpositional* and *subjugated* discourse. Both are forms of mirroring because they double (and thus complicate) the prevailing image of America. However, they do so in quite different ways. Transpositional discourse suggests mirroring in the sense that each entity (person, group, or political unit) might occupy the space of its opposite.[17] The force of transpositional discourse is ethical, because it calls attention to underlying principles of similarity which provide the context for certain kinds of behavior. The mode of transpositional discourse might be said to be utopian because it imagines a world outside history, a world governed by principles of reciprocity.

The second mode I will isolate in these texts I have called subjugated discourse because, unlike its opposite, it calls attention to differences, especially those of power, prestige, and purpose. Whereas transpositional discourse is fundamentally horizontal, subjugated discourse is inevitably vertical, but the placement of entities on the vertical axis is unstable, sometimes presenting Euro-Americans as the superior group and sometimes presenting Indians as deserving the higher position. If transpositional discourse is utopian, and therefore static since it presumes human essence, subjugated discourse is mobile and its appropriate sphere is political. The very instability of its vertices suggests temporality and change. Subjugated discourse may be derogatory in its presentation of Indian culture, or it may be denunciatory in its representations of whites. But it always seeks a transformation of current arrangements.

Why call both positions—derogatory of Indians, denunciatory of whites—by the same name, "subjugated discourse"? The reason for this is that they tend to fold into one another, according to the logic of *ressentiment* in which, as Nietzsche suggested, envy and anger are mixed (see chapter 9 for a discussion of *ressentiment*). Though my intention is to return to these terms in each of the following chapters, in order to see how these models come into clearer definition in the discussions of the texts themselves, I offer here one example of each by way of introduction.

One of the most moving examples of transpositional discourse may be found in the simple words reportedly spoken by Black Hawk upon his meeting as a captive with President Andrew Jackson at the end of the Black Hawk War. The Sauk chief said, "I am a man and you are another."[18] These words do not appear in his autobiography (and may be apocryphal), but even in the first Patterson text of 1833 the incident appears transpositional:

On our arrival at Washington, we called to see our Great Father, the President. He looks as if he had seen as many winters as I have, and seems to be a *great brave!* I had very little talk with him, as he appeared to be busy, and did not seem much disposed to talk. I think he is a good man; and although he talked but little, he treated us very well. . . . He said he wished to know the *cause* of my going to war against his white children. I thought he ought to have known this before; and, consequently, said but little to him about it—as I expected he knew as well as I could tell him. (Black Hawk, Jackson ed., 170, emphasis in original)

Though I have chosen to emphasize the transpositional nature of this passage, the account here given us by the writing team[19] suggests more than one possibility. In some ways, Black Hawk appears naive, trusting the president when he is being treated dismissively. On the other hand, there are strong suggestions of sarcasm in Black Hawk's comment that the president's inquiry hardly deserved an answer ("I thought he ought to have know this before; and, consequently, said but little to him about it—as I expected he knew as well as I could tell him"). In my reading of Black Hawk, both responses (trust and distrust) are typical of the war chief's relations with military leaders. He admired American generals (such as Winfield Townley Scott and General Alexander) even when they were fighting against him. On the other hand, he was not easily intimidated, even by the power of the presidency.

Given the disadvantageous circumstances in which Black Hawk found himself (he was a prisoner of the United States Army), how might his self-possession be explained? Without claiming to be able to reconstitute Black Hawk's point of view, one can usefully bring into the discussion several bits of information. Black Hawk's pride in his Sauk heritage was considerable. He was willing to acknowledge the superior technological strength of white America, but his nation seemed to him equal in many ways to the one of which Jackson was the head and in some ways he thought it superior. Furthermore, this was true of Sauks from early conflicts through the period of the Black Hawk War. In 1804 Captain Amos Stoddard reported that the Sauks "certainly do not pay that respect to the United States which is entertained by the other Indians—and in some instances have assumed a pretty elevated tone" (Nichols, 22). Black Hawk was convinced that his Sauk identity put him on the same basic footing as his captors.

Transpositional discourse, as this example illustrates, emphasizes the essential parity of Indians and whites. Black Hawk sees the president as a mirror image of himself, someone who has seen a great many winters and is "a great brave." Furthermore, he responds to

Jackson's initial silence by mirroring it in his own behavior. He refuses to answer questions that seem to him simply rhetorical. But he continues to see Jackson as "a good man," much as he sees himself.

In fact, the autobiography of Black Hawk repeatedly testifies to the Sauk chief's belief in the principle of reciprocity. This principle is quite consistent with the first view of nation I outlined above in which groups might negotiate or fight to resolve a certain issue but are not understood as occupying essentially different positions on the scale of being. Thus, Black Hawk's autobiography as a form of transpositional discourse refuses the hierarchical model for Indian-white relations that whites such as Captain Stoddard (and Jackson himself) thought appropriate. Furthermore, Black Hawk argues against "politics" in the sense of rhetorical manipulation, a skill he bitterly assigns to his archrival Keokuck.[20] For him, the truth is always the superior argument and does not need embellishment.

In summary, the most important feature of transpositional discourse is its leveling of the playing field. Transpositional narratives are generally reciprocal, egalitarian, ethical, utopian, universalizing, horizontal, and direct (nonpolitical).

Subjugated discourse, on the other hand, is more complicated because one position is always dissolving into its opposite, by which I mean, not that subjugated discourse is always becoming transpositional, but that superiority and inferiority are always changing places and persons. Where transpositional discourse tends to be direct, subjugated discourse is frequently ironic, and its ironic mode can present itself as the "gaze of otherness" Homi Bhabha describes in "Of Mimicry and Man: The Ambivalence of Colonial Discourse," a gaze that "liberates marginal elements and shatters the unity of man's being through which he extends his sovereignty" (129).

As Bhabha suggests, one may see this breaking up of the image in the effect such discourse has on both the colonizer and the colonized. Both "identities" are called into question when "the Other" of power mimics power's terms. According to one perspective, however, such speaking is too readily subsumed in the imperialist's project to have real force. Gayatri Spivak, for example, concludes that the subaltern cannot speak.

In some senses this is true (and may be what Larzer Ziff has in mind when he speaks of the ventriloquizing mode). But, in response to Spivak, Rey Chow argues that the agency of the native "needs to be rethought as that which bears witness to its own demolition—in a form that is at once image and gaze, but a gaze that exceeds the moment of colonization" (144).[21] The work of George Copway, for instance, comes into better focus when it is understood in these terms. Among these texts, his work furnishes probably the best example of sustained subjugated discourse.

As we will see in chapter 5, Copway was an Ojibwa from the Rice Lake Band in Canada who migrated to the United States and published a newspaper called *Copway's American Indian*. His autobiography, *The Life History, and Travels of Kah-Ge-Ga-Gah-Bowh* (1847), is his best-known work. Though it was circulated as an "authentic" Indian text, no identity emerges from the autobiography, which is riddled with contradictions. His preface insists that he speaks as an interloper. "It would be presumptious in one, who has but recently been brought out of a wild and savage state; and who has since received but three years' schooling, to undertake, without any assistance, to publish to the world a work of any kind. It is but a few years since I began to speak the English language" (vi).[22] Copway calls attention to his status as the subaltern here and implies that he has sought help but he never tells us precisely who assisted him. Furthermore, he engages in flagrant mimicry by adopting versions of his own experience in which he tells us he was "brought out of a wild and savage state." His use of the English language might be said to be parodic, making Copway one of those whom Homi Bhabha describes as "the parodists of history" because "despite their intentions and invocations they inscribe the colonial text erratically, eccentrically across a body politic that refuses to be representative [i.e., Indians], in a narrative that refuses to be representational" ("Of Mimicry and Man," 128–29). In Copway's text we must struggle with multiple voices that ultimately shatter both the discourse of savagery imposed upon Indians and the discourse of authenticity with which Indian texts were marked and marketed. Copway *presumes* upon his white audience and insists he be granted an ear, while at the same time he *parodies* the compliant nature as mimic.

Subjugated discourse is full of such deconstructive moments in which its author seems to be nowhere, leaving only the contestatory wrangle of mutually incompatible discourses. But force fields are mapped by this form of rhetoric, and thus the trace of the speaker remains. Indeed, Copway breaks into his own narrative at times, in a move counter to his mimicry, to demand justice for his people. Though this move does not "authorize" him, it does trace an ambivalence in which his gaze "exceeds the moment of colonization," in Rey Chow's terms.

In contrast to transpositional discourse, subjugated discourse calls attention to differential power relations. Its mode is metropolitan, particularizing, interventionist, vertical, and strategic. Whereas Black Hawk disliked "politicking," Copway delighted in it and for a time used it to his advantage.

Having identified through these terms some tendencies of Native American writing, let me say by way of caution that these paradigmatic models are too pure to describe the actual experience of reading these texts. I have purposely set them up in complementary terms because such a grid helps to organize features of this minority discourse that would otherwise remain obscure. Most readers of postcolonial literature struggle with the sense that the writers are both constructed by the colonial power and also resistant to the colonial power's assumptions. The models I propose here are meant to address that double sense. Nevertheless, I am aware that there are problems in creating this binary. To take one obvious example, the opposition between utopian and political is unstable. In the final chapter I will address these problems directly, suggesting ways of deconstructing the pure opposition between these two forms, thus allowing for a less rigid understanding of Indian rhetoric.

All the Native American texts discussed here present mixed modes of both transpositional and subjugated discourse. Indeed, the work of William Apess, with which we begin, offers a particularly complicated mesh. Thus I have addressed his writing in both chapters 3 and 8 as a way of framing my discussion. But how is it possible that a writer might occupy both positions—transpositional and subjugated—at the same time? Isn't there a deep contradiction in behaving as though Indians and whites were on equal footing but then also insisting that they were not?

Here it may be useful to bring into the discussion several ideas prevalent in contemporary literary theory, though I will not do so at length because it seems to me that these are now generally familiar. The first concerns the unity of the author. In *Forked Tongues* David Murray considers the complexities of Indian authorship in a chapter on William Apess entitled "Autobiography and Authorship: Identity and Unity." Murray's basic approach, similar to Krupat's insistence on bicultural composition, is to foreground the issue of "translation," examining all Indian "authorship" (even when the Indian writes in English) as a form of translation that relates at least two cultures and several voices. This approach, which I will also partially adopt, follows to some extent the line taken by Roland Barthes, Michel Foucault, and others who celebrate "the death of the author," so called.[23] The notion here is that there is no unified subjective presence "behind" the text, which is itself simply a field of discourses. Therefore, it is not necessary to resolve the seeming contradiction implied by finding two irreconcilable points of view in the same person's work because all writing involves various forms of translation that in themselves may not be compatible, creating gaps and fissures in the text. In addition, human beings are themselves full of contradictions and often unaware of their own hidden motives and beliefs, so in human discourse one has always already "translated" some material—that is, moved it from one psychic space to another—when one is writing, reading, and speaking.

However, Murray cites Krupat (in *The Voice in the Margin*) for his wish to retain some sense of authorial voice as a "willed line of informed approach" (19), thus modifying the strict line of death-of-the-author critics who refer to "voice" as simply another one of the hypostases of "author," an illusory attempt to assert unity and coherence. Murray says, "My own approach is similar [to Krupat's], and tries to build in a recognition of the collaborative, and sometimes resisting, role of reading in the creation of this voice, which in this case means being aware of the impossibility of finally pinning down any historical figure's 'real' voice" (52).

Here enters a second point drawn from poststructuralism. For a number of critics, and for my own approach to these texts, reading rather than writing is the activity in which meanings are constituted. Though, according to the multiple discourse theory of texts, there is no necessity to resolve the contradiction represented by the joint presence of transpositional and subjugated modes, the reader / interpreter (I) may wish to try to find a framework for making sense of this contradiction in order to provide a more satisfying interpretation of these texts. However, by so doing, it should be recognized, one has changed the "subject" from cultural psychobiography (focusing primarily upon the author's intentions) to what Krupat calls ethnocriticism (focusing upon the text and context and letting contradictions emerge whether these lead to complete resolutions or not).

Of course, given the complexity of the cultural situations in which these writers were operating, it is not surprising that their works demonstrate contradictions. Though I will not dwell at length upon the authors' intentions, I would like to think of my own readings as not too distant from those envisioned by these writers.

Having spent some considerable time here setting up the terms of my argument, it may be useful to summarize before proceeding further. Here in brief are the principal points addressed so far. This book will examine Native American texts in order to see how they contribute to the conversation about American national identity which took place in the nineteenth century. It has been assumed that Indians were not involved in this conversation, but we will contest that assumption. The subject of America will be examined here both as reification and as process. The trope of personification, in which an Indian is placed at the center of the nation known as America, will help us to explore the content of Native American interventions in that process. All nationalist rhetoric is dependent upon stories. The stories Native Americans told were of several kinds. As a way of understanding the complexity of Native American literature, we will look at two types of discourse in these textualized stories: transpositional and subjugated. The goal is to revise prior historical understandings but also to demonstrate respect for Native Americans and Native American literature.

The texts we will look at most closely are William Apess's *A Son of the Forest, Indian Nullification,* and "The Eulogy on King Philip"; Black Hawk's autobiography; George Copway's *The Life History, and Travels of Kah-Ge-Ga-Gah-Bowh* and *The Traditional History and Characteristic Sketches of the Ojibway Nation;* John Rollin Ridge's *The Life and Adventures of Joaquín Murieta;* and Sarah Winnemucca (Hopkins)'s *Life among the Piutes: Their Wrongs and Claims.* In an effort to read these texts against the grain of Euro-American national discourse, we will also consider works of varying kinds by Euro-Americans, but beginning with chapter 3, these will not be our central focus.

Chapter 2 represents an exception. In "Writing Indians" I take up three texts which have been unusually influential in the discussion of nineteenth-century Indian-white relations and nationalism. The purpose of considering them (and their offspring) is to situate what I have to say about Native American texts within the ongoing discussion of these matters. In many ways, Roy Harvey Pearce, Richard Slotkin, and Michael Rogin set the terms for that discussion by publishing enormously interesting and provocative examinations of the construction of Native Americans by Euro-Americans. (They were, of course, soon followed by others: Robert Berkhofer, Brian Dippie, Richard Drinnon, and others.) I hope that by a brief but focused discussion of the way this conversation has developed, the nature of my own contribution will become clearer. One is, of course, always building upon the efforts of those who have gone before, even when one's intentions are revisionist and supplementary, as mine are.

2. Writing Indians

Let us begin our exploration of Native Americans and their relation to U.S. nationalism with one of the now favored stories of the way the nation's self-understanding developed. It goes something like this: To the European mind the Indian was from the beginning a sign of America's difference. But for Anglo-Americans, who saw their role as one of conquering the wilderness and establishing civilization on the new frontier, this difference represented both promise and peril. The promise lay in the dream of difference as superiority. The "New World" offered the opportunity for Puritans in John Winthrop's Great Migration of 1630 to "build a city upon a hill, the eyes of all people . . . upon us." Or so he put it in his speech from the *Arbella* before the emigrants reached shore. But in order to claim for the English colonies a moral fiber superior to that of the corrupt Old World, they had to live up to a higher standard, not only in the watery world of speculation but on dry land as well. Puritans believed they had a special mission to "work wonders" in their new environment, which meant, among other things, the control, transformation, and redemption of the indigenous population, people who were, in their minds, "savages." Yet ironically, this process had the effect of reducing, even expunging, the marker that guaranteed difference in the first place.

Preserving European identity in the New World was no easy matter, and, as this account would have it, both ethnocentrism and the temptation to "go native" led to an exaggeration of differences as whites surveyed the Indians around them. In his classic work on "White Indian imagery," Robert Berkhofer claims:

Whether describing physical appearances or character, manners or morality, economy or dress, housing or sexual habits, government or religion, Whites overwhelmingly measured the Indian as a general category against those beliefs, values, or institutions they most cherished in themselves at the time. For this reason, many commentators on the history of White Indian imagery see Europeans and Americans as using counterimages of themselves to describe Indians and counterimages of Indians to describe themselves. Such a negative reference group could be used to define White identity or to prove White superiority over the worst fears of their own depravity. (*White Man's Indian*, 27)

In their "errand into the wilderness," the English colonizers had expected to set up a strong community, to endure hardships, and to win souls for God. There is no evidence that from the start they envisioned massacring the indigenous population, whose conversion to Christianity, after all, was seen as an important feature of their mission. However, within a hundred years of major settlement, Europeans had wiped out not only Indian land claims but large numbers of the Indians themselves.

Nevertheless, in the eighteenth century the need to find a language for American difference drew Euro-Americans back to the figure of the Indian, who now reemerged as a national symbol. Americans dressed as Indians dumped British tea into the Boston harbor, signifying their resistance to tyranny. The Indian Princess, accompanied by her bow and arrow, was used to represent American interests on colonial magazines, congressional and presidential medals, and the insignia of voluntary associations.[1] As the new nation was established, it became clear that a new iconography was needed to construct and reinforce an idea of Americanness in a population not used to conceptualizing the thirteen colonies as a cultural and political unit. Berkhofer even claims that "To be an 'American' therefore was as much an image in the minds of the leading citizens of the United States as it was to be an 'Indian'" (136). Both were the result of historical exigencies, and each conception was in some sense the product of the other.

In the nineteenth century the figure of the Native American became central to national identity in many respects, not least in the creation of an "American" literature. In the search for materials that might distinguish the arts of the New World from those of the Old, "nature" and "nature's people" were among the few assets

Americans could claim. Furthermore, "whether American *littérateurs* looked to the past, to nature, or to exotic peoples in their country, they found the Indian each time. . . . Even when an American author looked to the short history of his [or her] own country, he [or she] found the Indian a prominent participant in the colonial struggle or even the Revolution" (Berkhofer, 87). Thus, at the very moment when America was about to engage in widespread genocidal practices, in another part of the forest, so to speak, it was exalting the image of the Native American as a national treasure.

This is a synthesized version of several stories that have come to dominate conceptions about Indians and nation-building in the New World. But let us pause to ask some questions of this account. What explanation does it offer of the contradiction between aggression and exaltation? What role does it assign to Native Americans themselves? Finally, has this story helped us to reshape the course of American nationalism, and if not, are there other stories we could tell that might do so? These are the questions this chapter will explore.

But first we need to back up a bit to consider the story that preceded this one. Before the story I have just told became hegemonic, American historians—who were the people mainly responsible for looking at relations between Indians and whites—tended to focus primarily on the misunderstandings that had occurred between natives and Europeans. When mutual agreements broke down, so this prior story went, the technological superiority of the settlers, coupled with the effects of disease, alcohol, and displacement on the Indians, inevitably resulted in the triumph of Europeans over the relatively weaker indigenous people.

This story still retains a certain plausibility, but it does not address the positive value of the Indian for the construction of American identity, a value that might well have altered the course of events and prevented the slaughter of the people whose prior occupancy of the land gave them a significant claim to it. In order to explain not just what happened but how what happened was linked to a pattern of exclusionary Americanization repeated in generation after generation, a different form of explanation was needed. Beginning in the 1950s, the new story began to unfold among scholars not trained primarily in history. This story was, in some sense, the product of the new American Studies, which might be said to be "the author" of the now more influential account with which we began. It is important to note that this is a story not just of cultural conflict and colonial oppression (wars and treaties) but of psychic investment and the struggle over representation. How did it come into being?

Most accounts of the formation of American Studies in the 1940s and 1950s agree that it arose out of a holistic desire to address issues in more complex ways than the individual disciplines such as History and English had been able to do thus far. The interdisciplinary thrust of American Studies brought popular culture and "high culture" together, using intellectual history (the history of ideas) as a way of understanding a whole range of cultural phenomena including literary texts, political decisions, dime novels, religious tracts, opinions of the Supreme Court, and nationalist propaganda. Proponents of American Studies were not uncritical of the way Americans had comported themselves in the past, but they were committed to a notion of American exceptionalism just as the Puritans had been three centuries earlier. As Gene Wise notes, the field operated according to certain assumptions.

Reduced to essentials, the assumptions are as follows:

a) There is an 'American Mind.' That mind is more or less homogeneous. Though it may prove to be complex and constructed of many different layers, it is in fact a single entity.

b) What distinguishes the American Mind is its location in the 'New' World. . . .

c) The American Mind can theoretically be found in anyone American. But it comes to most coherent expression in the country's leading thinkers—Williams, Edwards, Franklin, Cooper, Emerson, Thoreau, Hawthorne, Melville, Whitman, Twain, Dewey, Niebuhr, et al. . . .

d) The American Mind is an enduring form in our intellectual history. Its distinctive themes—Puritanism, Individualism, Progress, Pragmatism, Transcendentalism, Liberalism—run through virtually the whole of America's past. (306–7)

It was a heady time for those who were working in this new area because, as Wise notes, what seemed to be at stake was no less than "*the fundamental meaning of America*" (307) itself.

Out of this context and the revision of it that occurred in the 1960s and 1970s came three works that set the terms for subsequent accounts of American nationalism as a product of the encounter between whites and Indians: Roy Harvey Pearce's *Savagism and Civilization* (1953), Richard Slotkin's *Regeneration through Violence* (1973), and Michael Rogin's *Fathers and Children* (1975). These texts and their descendants—such as Berkhofer's *White Man's Indian*, Brian Dippie's *Vanishing American*,[2] Clive Bush's *The Dream of Reason*, and Richard Drinnon's *Facing West*—examined the way nineteenth-(and twentieth-) century conceptions of America have developed out of a certain placement of the "Indian" in white American minds. Furthermore, though there are important differences, Pearce, Slotkin, and Rogin share some common characteristics which deserve to be noted as well. All three read Euro-American history as an exfoliation of Puritan "origins." All see unconscious motives at work in the way Indians become the objects of hostile projection and scapegoating by Euro-Americans. All believe that American national identity is built upon the destruction of Indian claims. And all read Melville as a writer who helps us to comprehend the murderous course of American history.

In some ways, the first book, *Savagism and Civilization*, seems to be an exception to the founding American Studies model because it refutes assumptions about American "innocence." Like Arthur Miller's *The Crucible*, the play about Salem witch-hunting which also first appeared in 1953, Pearce's book expressed profound dismay at the repeated tendency of human beings to project internal anxieties onto expendable "others," a tendency that had all too recently resurfaced in the scapegoating of Jews by the Nazis, in the dropping of the atomic bomb on Japan, and in the rampant anticommunism of the Cold War fifties. It is wrong to assume that people in American Studies ignored these issues, but Pearce was unusual in the prominence he gave to American misconduct.

In other ways, however, *Savagism and Civilization* is a book of its time. It assumes an "American mind." It focuses on intellectual history. It reads Cooper and Melville as principal shapers of the American mind. And it sees American culture as developing out of Puritanism. In each of these aspects of the argument, Pearce presents the

Indian as playing a double role. *Savagism and Civilization* traces the response of Europeans to Indians from an early image of the Native American as "natural man"—embodying the state of Nature both negatively and positively, that is, both as the object of Calvinist opprobrium and as Rousseau's Noble Savage—to its eventual displacement by the figure of the Vanishing American. He records the fact that the New World was originally seen by Europeans as a place where the wilderness and the Indian were regarded as markers differentiating it from Old World "civilization." Though in earlier avatars Indians might be redeemed or redemptive figures, Pearce argues that after 1830 (Dippie makes it 1814) the Native American was mainly seen as a barbarous and vice-ridden holdover from an earlier era, a ghost of the past destined to be eradicated by civilization. An "impassable gulf" was thus seen to separate American culture from its Native American origins.

Pearce explores the way this vision became the basis upon which American histories were devised. In George Bancroft's *History of the United States*, for instance, Indians are presented as essentially inferior. "Nor is this inferiority simply attached to the individual" Bancroft insists; "it is connected with [his] organization and is the characteristic of the race" (162). Francis Parkman, the powerful storyteller who wrote *The Oregon Trail* (1847) and *The Conspiracy of Pontiac* (1851), based his similar conclusions upon his first-hand experience living with a Sioux tribe. Pearce comments: "What was chiefly to be observed, he noted, was the 'impassable gulf' lying between the white man and the red" (164).

Thus, in Pearce's presentation of "the American mind," American civilization becomes the encoding of difference; at first, perhaps, the difference between New World "nature" and Old World metropolitan corruption but ultimately the difference between savagism and enlightenment. Narratives of national identity in histories, ethnographies, and imaginative literature made such differences part of the story of America's past and the projection of America's future. "In Pontiac's career and in the rebellion which he led, Parkman found a subject which would take him to the vital center of American history. He could know enough about that subject—his generation knew enough about that subject—to work from within it. He could make his readers die with Pontiac, as long as they lived with America" (167).

In this seminal account of American myth-making, Roy Harvey Pearce uncovered a history of racism in those who insisted upon "mastering" the Indian symbolically and literally. Though in the nineteenth century, Indian imagery might be used as part of America's sense of itself, "real Indians" were always those who had disappeared in the early days. Thus, those who remained were ripe for extinction: degraded, uncivilized, and irredeemable. Pearce's palpable moral outrage contributes to the eloquence of the book, sometimes rupturing the stylistic balance of his classical prose. And yet it also points to a problem inherent in his argument. The problem is one of allocating responsibility.

Pearce's work emerged in the era when the Myth and Symbol School dominated American Studies. Henry Nash Smith's pioneering book *Virgin Land: The American West as Symbol and Idea* was published in 1950 and articulated the view that the American mind can be known through interrogating its collective representations. For his part, Pearce examines the way Indians are adapted to American mythology, but unlike some practitioners of "top-down" history in the Myth and Symbol School, Pearce was interested in politics as well as imagery. Though he acknowledges that white Americans could only "see" Indians through the theories, myths, and ideological explanations provided to them (for example, by the work of William Robertson, the Scot whose *History of America* published in 1777 introduced to many the principle that social evolution meant the inevitable demise of Indians qua Indians), Pearce nevertheless wishes to hold nineteenth-century white Americans accountable for their "cruel, illogical, and self-indulgent" (232) attitudes.

In "Character and Circumstance: the Idea of Savagism" he suggests a way to call history to account. The passage deserves quoting at length:

This is what the Scots did for American students of the savage: enabled them both to see and to tell what they had seen; furnished a general theoretical frame which allowed them to bring empirical data together and gain an understanding of savagism. Yet, as they always must, the facts gradually modified the frame, then broke it and made for a new frame, a new theory. But then, as I have noted, it was the 1850's. The Indian was virtually dead, a creature on whom only scientific ethnology and anthropology could operate, one whom only philanthropy could bring alive. (90–91)

In addition to accepting the myth of the Vanishing American, this passage conveys the two conflicting sides of Pearce's argument. One: facts require the context of someone's interpretation in order to achieve significance (Robertson and the Scots "furnished a general theoretical frame which allowed them [i.e., Americans] to bring empirical data together and gain an understanding of savagism.") Two: Facts operate independently of ideology and exert a force that is capable of transforming it ("But then, as they always must, the facts gradually modified the frame.") The tension exposed by presenting these two positions so baldly appears again at the end of Pearce's book where he quotes Melville's *The Confidence Man* on the "Metaphysics of Indian-Hating": "And Indian-hating still exists; and, no doubt, will continue to exist, so long as Indians do." Though Pearce could see why this might be the case, he resisted what he saw and in the process fell prey to his own ideological tendencies: "Yet, meditating [on] the nineteenth-century victory of our civilization over savagism, profiting from both victory and meditation, *bearing the burden of facts,* we may hope not and work with the hope" (emphasis added, 251). The hope seems frail indeed, however, when it is positioned against so much evidence of human fallibility and destructiveness.

In Pearce's analysis both psychology and myth-making play a part, but they enter what is basically an example of historical literary criticism (the old historicism) in what we might call their vernacular modes. For example, post-Freudian psychology enters in Pearce's account of "polarities deep in the American character, in all human character" (74) that lead to denigration of what is temptingly different. Myth-making appears in Pearce's account of "the development in the American mind of the Indian as a symbol for all that over which civilization must triumph" (73).

These terms—American character and the American mind—were

at the forefront of American Studies as practiced in the 1950s. But they were soon to come under fire, as top-down theories were challenged in the late 1960s and early 1970s by advocates of "bottom-up" history, and humanities-based American Studies was challenged by the social sciences. In 1973 Robert Berkhofer clarified this conflict in an article entitled "Clio and the Culture Concept: Some Impressions of a Changing Relationship in American Historiography" by teasing out some of the new questions (and the new answers): "From whose view among the actors in the historical drama should the tale of the past be told? Older historians debated this issue in terms of popular versus intellectual thought or of cosmopolitanism versus localism in outlook, but the younger generation tends to consider the question in relation to the role of minorities in general American history or whether to view history from the top-down or the bottom-up" (93).

Also in 1973, Richard Slotkin published his now famous *Regeneration through Violence: The Mythology of the American Frontier 1600–1860*, in which Indian folk culture, tales of the frontier, and canonical works of "high" culture were placed side by side. Though he does not quote Pearce, Slotkin addresses a point that Pearce made in passing, transforming it into the centerpiece of his lengthy analysis. Whereas Pearce had merely suggested, before passing on to another point, that white people might have found Indians both frightening and attractive, Slotkin sees such psychic dissonance as the main incentive to myth, and he develops myth-making as the central activity of national self-understanding. "As American society evolved through years of historical experience, the differentiated literary forms were gradually drawn together by writers who more or less deliberately sought to create a unified and compelling vision of the total American experience—an American myth" (19). Further, Slotkin extends the range of myth-making's destructive force into our own time, using it to call into question America's quest for heroes.

The trophies they [American heroes] are perpetually garnering have no material value; their sanctity derives from their function as visual and concrete proofs of the self-justifying acts of violent self-transcendence and regeneration that produced them. So the Indians (no less "American" than

[Davy] Crockett) garnered trophies as proofs and reminders of their battle valor and as kernels around which to build their names and the myth-tales of the tribe. In Vietnam it was called the body count. (564)

Slotkin's narrative, like Pearce's, emerged in a postwar period when Americans were in a reflexive mood. Both concentrate on myth and image, though Slotkin is more profoundly influenced by psychology and anthropology than Pearce was. In Slotkin's work we can see the effects of Structuralism (and Claude Lévi-Strauss) on American Studies as he searches for the deep structure that defines the American ethos and finds it in the repetition of violent acts as the means of regenerating the community. He is especially compelling when he is analyzing the kinds of historical narratives Euro-Americans have constructed about their experiences, showing how these stories are repeated in generation after generation. Furthermore, he takes into account Native American tales and rituals, suggesting ways in which Puritans might have seen their own rituals mirrored in the creation myths, initiation rites, and dramas performed by Indians.

Yet, ultimately Slotkin's structuralist orientation serves to obscure what is *different* about Native Americans, including the differences among Indian tribes themselves. He frequently refers to Indian cultural practices, such as those surrounding land use and marriage, as though all tribes operated in the same way, which is far from true. And, in his attempt to diagram the similarities between Protestant and Indian behavior, he sometimes loses sight of another point he lays the groundwork for elsewhere, that seemingly similar paradigms turn out to be quite different when they are embedded within divergent cultural matrices. This point calls into question conclusions such as "In point of fact, the Puritan and Indian responses to the life of the wilderness were, at bottom, strikingly similar" (55). Though violence and warfare were present in both societies, and it may be true that both societies (Algonquian and Puritan) used war stories to structure their conceptions of the nation, Puritan and Indian responses to the life of the wilderness were, at some level, strikingly different. Whether this level was the "bottom" or not depends upon how one decides to spatialize the cultural description.

By 1975, the year in which Michael Paul Rogin published *Fathers and Children: Andrew Jackson and the Subjugation of the American Indian,* American Studies had become preoccupied with American iniquity, and the social sciences, which had been highlighting responsibility issues for many years, were enjoying unprecedented influence within the field. Though trained as a political scientist, not a field with a history of American Studies involvement, Rogin carried on the interdisciplinary tradition of American Studies by combining a human-actors form of political science with Marxist political theory, a psychoanalytic approach to human behavior, and extensive historical documentation. Rogin does acknowledge Pearce ("Here and throughout I have relied heavily on Roy Harvey Pearce's seminal *Savagism and Civilization,*" 319), but he does not mention Slotkin. (Presumably he had finished his work by the time Slotkin's came out.) Nevertheless, *Fathers and Children* is far closer to Slotkin than to Pearce, especially in its discussion of the "regenerative wars" fought by the frontier fathers.

Both Slotkin and Rogin use Freudian terminology and post-Freudian readings of history to probe the mentality of Indian fighters. Slotkin discusses the unconscious, projection, displacement, the id, dreams, and the importance of sexual repression in the creation of the hostile personality. However, his orientation is the archetype; Carl Jung's work on symbolization is probably a more direct influence than Freud's. Rogin, on the other hand, looks specifically at the convergence of historical tragedy with Oedipal conflicts and the family romance (*Fathers and Children* begins with a genealogy of Andrew Jackson's family as his next book — on Herman Melville — begins with a genealogy of Melville's family.)

Probably the most telling difference between Slotkin and Rogin, however, is their attitude toward Structuralism. As the following quotation suggests, Rogin was highly suspicious of structuralist poetics. This passage illustrates some of the challenges to Structuralism's ahistoricism that were mounted in the mid-1970s and that led to the increase in interest in social history over the kind of anthropology practiced by Lévi-Straussians. Rogin writes:

It is a peculiarly split view of human existence [not, therefore, Rogin's] in which symbolizations of meaning operate in a closed universe of their own, divorced from the "real" facts of historical causation. Men make history; they develop complex inner worlds because they do not make it in circumstances of their own choosing. These inner worlds, projected outward, become part of the continuing history men do make. Objective forces act only through men; men transform external causes into internal principles of action. (12)

Though one recognizes echoes of Marx here, this passage (with its discussion of "inner worlds") also alerts the reader to Rogin's psychoanalytic framework which he will use to mediate between cultural discourses and political acts. It further prepares us for his concentration on a single significant player, Andrew Jackson, long a figure of interest in American Studies. In a summary of the cultural conditions which impinged upon Andrew Jackson, Rogin writes: "The symbiosis between developed east and virgin west not only fueled American economic development; it also created the psychology and ideology which sanctified capitalist hegemony. Wilderness expansion established a heroic American identity transcending the petty transactions of market self-interest. Indian destruction generated a powerful nationalism." In such a context, "Jackson developed in Indian relations the major formulas of Jacksonian Democracy" (13).

Rogin provides both a sweeping cultural context and an interiorized focus on an individual psyche. Drawing upon psychoanalysis, Rogin puts before us an orphaned Jackson at war with his body, riven by aggressive impulses against an idealized dead father, afflicted with an unresolved and unresolvable Oedipus complex. Indians, as in Slotkin's view, bear the brunt of Jackson's feelings of guilt and rage. In addition, Rogin argues, the treatment of the Indians as "children" and the taking of their lands were directly connected to social disruptions caused by the rise of capitalism. Like Weber he sees the Puritan temperament evolving into the capitalist personality:

The Jacksonian landscape, as the images of Indian policy proclaim, directed attention westward to empire; it did not redirect attention to self or society [the tormented spaces of Jackson and capitalism respectively]. The West thus provided not merely an actual space for capitalist expansion, but also a mythic flight from its significance. Max Weber's demystified acquisitive and bureaucratic spirit was remystified on the frontier. (312)

Pearce, Slotkin, and Rogin are all profoundly dismayed by Euro-American treatment of the Indians. And these three books—which furnished the outlines of the story with which I began—continue to be used by scholars seeking to call America to account. Nevertheless, it remains true that in all three of these "histories," Indians figure mainly as the *objects* of Euro-American needs: psychological, political, economic, and nationalistic. Furthermore, as I noted in the first chapter, more recent scholarship does little to challenge the basic assumption that Indians were mainly on the receiving end of American predatory nationalism. The subtext of much of the scholarship concerning the place of the Indian in national rhetoric is violence. A disturbing question hovers in the background: to what degree is the identity of the nation itself bound up with aggression, injustice, scapegoating, and other forms of destructive activity that replicate themselves in every generation? Must the contradiction between idealizing the Indians and demonizing them lead to genocide then?

If we go back to *Savagism and Civilization,* we can see that Pearce was somewhat optimistic, tentatively offering a way out of compulsive repetition by means of a belief in the power of "facts." The hardness of facts seems to constitute for him a kind of bulwark against the temporary distortions of history. Nations may engage in distortions in their founding moments, but in time these distortions will be rectified.

Slotkin was far less optimistic, however. *Regeneration through Violence* ends with a chilling series of images which Slotkin builds up in order to suggest the momentum of error. Beginning in the seventeenth century, American history seems to be nothing but "A Pyramid of Skulls." Here quoted is but a part of the list of violent national acts that ends *Regeneration through Violence:* "the Indian debased, impoverished and killed in return for his gifts; the land and its people, its 'dark' people especially, economically exploited and wasted; the warfare between man and nature, between race and race, exalted as a kind of heroic ideal; the piles of wrecked and rusted cars, heaped like Tartar pyramids of death-cracked, weather-browned, rain-rotted skulls to signify our passage through the land" (565). Thus, the past lays claim to the present and future and somehow "we" (Slotkin apparently assumes his readers are white) are responsible.

Rogin's work is more bound by the time period he describes and therefore at first it seems less fatalistic. He remains focused on the development of nineteenth-century American nationalism and does not attempt to trace the continuities between Jacksonian Democracy and later developments, except briefly where he links Jackson up with Frederick Jackson Turner, Theodore Roosevelt, and Woodrow Wilson. One may be soothed by the reflection that these are not the heroes of our own time, and thus the connection with later history may not be inevitable.

But even in Rogin's book, one encounters a sense of fatality. Since history there is a function of human actors, and we are always in disturbing ways "strangers to ourselves," aggression against others comes to seem more likely than not. If Andrew Jackson's family situation (his father's early disappearance, his mother's subsequent centrality as a single parent until her death in Jackson's teens) led to the development of a personality structure that needed to control women and find permissible male victims, our own society would seem to be at even greater risk of developing destructive desires on a grand scale for our society is full of such family configurations. A human-actors orientation such as Rogin's here, though it may provide a complex picture of political decision-making, does not necessarily avoid a sense of fatalism.

My point in surveying these arguments about the role of Indians in nineteenth-century conceptions of the nation is that the narrative repeatedly put into play is one that seems to lead directly and inevitably to the pyramid of skulls. Though each of the writers I have quoted acknowledges the central role of interpretation in constructing history, each also tells a story in which "facts" take shape in a realm of fate. Thus, it becomes difficult to imagine cultural collision in the life of the new nation as resulting in anything other than violent "removals." Such removals, we must remember, encompassed not only the physical exile of Indian peoples and the deaths that ensued (at least four thousand on the Trail of Tears alone) but the intellectual amnesia of the conquerors as their role in Native American destruction became transformed through an ideology of progress and inevitability.

So where might we look for a story that does not imagine the nation as founded upon the exclusion and massacre of Native Americans? In *Hard Facts,* Philip Fisher may help to provide a context for challenging the narrative of inevitability from a poststructuralist perspective, where he shows that the interpretations of the dominant culture, often created in important ways by literary texts, are what make certain facts seem primary, causing others to be forgotten. "It is only at a certain moment that the future becomes evident and inevitable and that then, as a result, the past can be sorted into, on the one hand, significant features that contributed to the founding of what can now be seen to be the future and, on the other hand, historical debris, fruitless possibilities that will never be realized" (25).[3] For Fisher, then, though there are "hard facts" in the sense of historical realities, there are no hard facts in the sense of inevitable turns of fate. The cultural work done by literature (as history, ethnography, and above all popular fiction) simply provides the illusion that "the great, central, hard facts" (73) were always there for everyone to see. Thus, Fisher's text (though it too looks only at Euro-American hegemonic narratives because these are seen as doing the most important "cultural work") makes it possible to reopen the question of what counternarratives there might have been in the nineteenth century that did not lead to Indian genocide but instead to a more democratic and pluralistic conception of nation.

Fisher's argument may also help us return to the pressing problem Roy Harvey Pearce's work raises: how is it possible to hold anyone responsible if human beings are simply the "effects" of ideologies (or, as Naturalism suggests, environments) over which they have no control? Fisher himself raises this question in terms of the sleight of hand performed by such historical novels as James Fenimore Cooper's. "The profound analysis built into Cooper's plot is not the feeling of inevitability of the most repulsive historical facts such as massacres. The ethical question of responsibility—who exactly is to blame and what punishment would be just?—is [simply] put aside. It is felt to be irrelevant. But such a Hegelian demonstration, because it is always the self-serving history told by the winners, remains too convenient to be acceptable" (72–73). Indeed, it would seem from Fisher's comments here that we should resist it.

As both Pearce and Fisher demonstrate, cultural hegemonies are by definition very powerful and they do indeed organize people's thoughts so that it becomes difficult to oppose them. However, we must also keep in mind that no hegemony is ever total.[4] It is useful to look at what Indians wrote about America and nationhood in the nineteenth century because by doing so we can see that there were other ideas in play as well as those of the increasingly hegemonic discourse. Not everyone, not even every Euro-American, agreed with the views of a Francis Parkman;[5] Herman Melville did not. Lydia Maria Child did not. Likewise, the nature of nationhood itself was always contested. As long as we preserve the sense of multiple possibilities, we can hold America responsible for its misdeeds because we can see them as in some sense chosen.

From here on we will be mainly concerned with "writing Indians" in the sense not of Euro-Americans who wrote Indians in a specific way into the national narrative but of Native Americans who wrote to an American audience. Their stories advance a different set of possibilities. For we need to do more than show how amorphous views about Native Americans hardened into a commitment among some Euro-Americans to seeing the Indians vanish. The contradiction between admiration of Indian virtue (represented in the national imagery) and condemnation of Indian difference (represented by most of the policies of the American government) could have been resolved differently. It will be the task of this exposition to show how Native American texts contest the notion that the past had to take the shape it did. The stories these texts tell imagine a nation (or multiple nations) committed to a policy of mutual accommodation. Though these imaginings never fully materialized, they cannot, without injury to our sense of America itself, be dismissed as irrelevant. To do so is to write the history of conquest as the history of fate, and so to add our own literary trophies to the ever-mounting pyramid of skulls.

3. The Irony and Mimicry
of William Apess

The earliest example of Native American writing in English to engage the issue of nation at length is William Apess's *A Son of the Forest*, an autobiographical work first published in 1829 and then revised in 1831. Apess's interest in the new nation may be due in part to the fact that he did not grow up in a tribal community but as a marginal member of white society, the son of Pequot parents whose Native American ethnicity was mixed with white blood and who did odd jobs within the white community. At the age of four, William was removed from his family and subsequently raised by whites. Though his education was spotty, with his considerable intelligence he made the most of what he was able to pick up. Indeed, he published several impressive works before his career faltered and alcoholism ended his life in 1839.

The texts I wish to focus on in this part of the discussion are *A Son of the Forest*, "An Indian's Looking Glass for the White Man" (published as part of *The Experiences of Five Christian Indians of the Pequot Tribe* in 1833), and *Indian Nullification of the Unconstitutional Laws of Massachusetts Relative to the Marshpee Tribe* (1835). The "Eulogy on King Philip," which provides the richest example in my discussion of national personification, will be addressed in chapter 8.

William Apess's work, though it comes first in terms of chronology, is one of the most interesting bodies of Native American writing in the nineteenth century. Its most salient quality is irony, and yet, due to the enormous influence of Christianity on him—he converted to Methodism and became an evangelical minister—his work is also heavily laced with phrases that sound as though they have been lifted directly from Euro-American evangelical literature which by and large lacks such irony. Thus, Apess provides us with a good starting point from which to explore the hybrid modes of Native American writing, its combination of irony and earnest imitation, for example.

Furthermore, we can see the effect of this mixture highlighted in Apess's orientation to the issue of nation which, as will become clear, brings to the fore his ambivalence concerning both the relationship between America and its Native American population and that between whites and peoples of color more generally. Due to the recent republication of Apess's major works,[1] we can now explore in far greater detail the way this early Native American writer both taunted and appealed to the America of his day to rethink the implications of its nationalist rhetoric. Finally, given the complexity of Apess's orientation to white culture, it is not surprising that this work would include, among other discursive strategies, both transpositional and subjugated modes of discourse.

As the earliest Native American example of full-length autobiography, *A Son of the Forest* is the starting place for what will remain for many years a principal genre of Indian writing in English.[2] As well as looking forward to subsequent Native American texts, however, *A Son of the Forest* also looks back to an earlier genre, that of the Euro-American conversion narrative. The conversion narrative, it will be remembered, typically tells the story of a sinner's redemption through the grace of God. Since part of the story highlights the undeserving nature of the redeemed person—and thus illustrates the utterly free character of God's choosing (grace is not earned but freely offered to those God singles out to receive it)—the narrative frequently indulges in terms of self-abasement similar to those Apess employs when he describes himself, near the beginning, as "nothing more than a worm of the earth" (4).

However, in this example of conversion narrative, there is a difference, a difference we may see more clearly if we compare the opening of *A Son of the Forest* to Jonathan Edwards's "Personal Narrative," a classic example of the genre. In Edwards's text, he says nothing specific about his family and very little about his social context, preferring to dwell upon his groveling sense of vileness and sin, in order to demonstrate the feeling of perfect joy that arises from a total dependence upon Jesus Christ. "But, in process of time, my convictions and affections wore off; and I entirely lost all those affections and delights, and left off secret prayer, at least as to any constant preference of it;

and returned like a dog to his vomit, and went on in the ways of sin" (82). The timeless, placeless feeling of an individual soul struggling with the demands of faith is appropriate to Edwards's frame of reference, which is the contrast between this world and eternity.

By contrast, Apess's frame of reference seems far more temporal and earth-bound. Contrary to Edwards's abstraction, he begins with an insistence upon family genealogy and context:

William Apess, the author of the following narrative, was born in the town of Colrain, Massachusetts, on the thirty-first of January, in the year of our Lord seventeen hundred and ninety-eight. My grandfather was a white man and married a female attached to the royal family of Philip, king of the Pequot tribe of Indians, so well known in that part of American history which relates to the wars between the whites and the natives. My grandmother was, if I am not misinformed, the King's granddaughter and a fair and beautiful woman. This statement is given not with a view of appearing great in the estimation of others—what, I would ask, is *royal* blood?—the blood of a king is no better than that of the subject. We are in fact but one family; we are all the descendents of one great progenitor—Adam. I would not boast of my extraction, as I consider myself nothing more than a worm of the earth. (3–4)

One is struck at the outset by the number of overlapping discourses in this passage. Though this text purports to be an autobiography, the first sentence has the author speaking of himself in the third person. In addition to depersonalizing the narrative, one effect of this is to make the reader attend to the text as history rather than meditation. Furthermore, history as an account of the nation ("American history") almost immediately intervenes with Apess's reminders about the seventeenth-century wars between the Puritans and the Indians, which were often recalled during this period as the crucible in which the beginnings of American nationhood were forged.

Apess, of course, tells the story from the native rather than the colonizer's perspective, and there are other turnabouts here as well. Apess's association with (an Indian's) "royal blood" is asserted (one thinks of the Puritans' claims to be acting in the name of the king) only to be deconstructed in republican terms: "what . . . is *royal* blood?—the blood of a king is no better than that of the subject." All of which brings Apess to his Christian point: we are all of one family, children of the creation like the "worm of the earth." However, the worm has a different resonance in Apess than it does in Edwards's "Sinners in the Hands of an Angry God," for instance, where it signifies insignificance and vileness. In Apess, as in Native American cultures generally, the creation is sacred throughout, not a vertical ladder like the great chain of being. In short, we can see here the imbrication of several overlapping forms of narrative: Native American, republican, nationalist, and Christian at the very least.

Are there moments in which William Apess, like other writers of conversion narratives, humbles himself in a specifically Christian manner and engages in self-abasement? Absolutely. Yet Arnold Krupat's contention—that this text is principally an example of "salvationist" rhetoric—seems to me to overprivilege this mode at the expense of the others. Though I agree with Krupat that the Indian narrator seeks a "principled community" (a new nation?) rather than simply individual redemption, I do not see this text as quite the example of (even revised) salvationist rhetoric Krupat does.[3] This autobiography is as much a discourse upon the various conceptions of nation to which Apess had been exposed as it is a tale of redemption.

Part of the story Apess tells here concerns his belief (shared by many others in his day, both Indian and white) that the Indians were one of the ten lost tribes of Israel. To this effect he inserts a rather lengthy series of quotations from Elias Boudinot (the white journalist and ethnographer whose name the Cherokee "Elias Boudinot" adopted) about "the general character, manners, habits, and customs of the Indians" (87). That he quotes these passages is interesting in itself because it makes clear that Indian nationhood is available to him mostly through written narration rather than through direct inheritance or even oral tradition. Like the conversion narrative, these references also "textualize" the account of Apess's life and remove it from the realm of simple personal reminiscence. We see that this Indian self is a construction made up from several sources both native and not. (Twenty years later John Rollin Ridge, known as Yellow Bird, would also quote extensively from whites—e.g., H. W. Longfellow and H. R. Schoolcraft—in his account of Indian customs.)

Much of Apess's discussion here has to do with the nature of Indian nations and their similarity to Hebrew tribes, as in the following: "If you go from [Indian] nation to nation, you will not find one who does not lineally distinguish himself by his respective family" (92), just as the Hebrews did. Family, of course, is not nuclear family here but familial group or clan.

Thus, Apess's opening with his family connections in *A Son of the Forest* is itself a statement about the importance of nation. Throughout Apess's work, his nation appears by turns as "America," the Pequot tribe, and Indians in general. By contrast, "family"—understood as his close relations—seems a more problematic issue, one that he might well wish to dissolve into a larger organizational unit, since Apess's early childhood was not very happy. Indeed, he is only "a son of the forest" in an ironic sense, since his youth was not spent in a tribal community, as the common usage of "sons of the forest" implied, but in a variety of semirural settings among both Indians and whites, where he was perhaps more closely connected to the geographical setting (the forest) than to the individuals with whom he lived. For three years he abided, he says, "in comparative comfort" in a hut in the woods with his parents and uncle. Liquor was a disruptive element in this setting, however. His parents often quarreled, finally split up, and left the children with their maternal (Pequot) grandparents. But this was no improvement. In a drunken rage, his grandmother so severely beat him that he had to be rescued by his uncle. From then on, he was raised by whites, meeting his father only occasionally when he periodically ran away from his foster homes.

In his white context, William is frightened by stories of sinister Indians and runs away in terror when he meets some Indians in the woods. "It may be proper for me here to remark that the great fear I entertained of my brethren was occasioned by the many stories I had heard of their cruelty toward the whites—how they were in the habit of killing and scalping men, women, and children. . . . If the whites had told me how cruel they had been to the 'poor Indian,' I should have apprehended as much harm from them" (11).

Caught between two cultures, William Apess emerges in the autobiography as a man in search of both an identity and a community, two elements of human experience frequently furnished, according to Benedict Anderson, by the idea of "nation." Eventually, as we see in this narrative, the young William enlists in the American army as a drummer boy and is then pressed into service in the War of 1812. Here both transpositional and subjugated forms of discourse come into play as the young soldier, on the one hand, identifies with the American cause and, on the other, regards the British with a highly un-American equanimity. In the Battle of Plattsburgh on Lake Champlain, the British troops, numbering some fourteen thousand, fall before "a handful of militia." Apess exults over the victory. "This was indeed a proud day for our country. We had met a superior force on the lake, and 'they were ours' " (30). His attitude to the British, however, is not consistently negative. As their ships appear on the lake, he pauses to admire their visual splendor. "It was a fine thing to see their noble vessels moving like things of life upon this mimic sea, with their streamers floating in the wind" (29). The very lyricism of these sentiments calls into question the authenticity of Apess's nationalistic fervor. And what does he mean by "this mimic sea"? The water of Lake Champlain was real enough, though it might not be a "sea" in the strictest sense. Perhaps he means to imply here that his whole involvement with the army had an air of unreality about it, or perhaps he wishes us to understand that this phase of his life—and he does show this—forced him to adopt a pattern of mimicry in order to get along with his white mates. A man who can exult in the beauty of his enemy's warships occupies a somewhat indeterminate ideological space, to say the least, just as the phrases quoted above imply both patriotism and alienation.

In fact, though Apess fought on the American side and identifies himself with the interests of the "Green Mountain Boys," he grumbles about his treatment by the government. The soldiers were never paid. Furthermore, he takes the opportunity to identify the mistreatment of the Indians as a special example of bad faith. Though the white soldiers were also denied their bounty money and arrearages, Apess comments: "I could never think that the government acted right toward the 'Natives,' not merely in refusing to pay us but in claiming our services in cases of perilous emergency, and still deny[ing] us the right of citizenship; and as long as *our nation* is debarred the privilege of voting for civil officers, I shall believe that the government has no claim on our services" (emphasis added, 31). The word "nation" in Apess's work usually refers to ethnicity—the Indian nation(s), for instance—but he consistently speaks of his "country" as the United States of America.

Though he does raise questions about the appropriateness of native loyalty to the United States here, he has more to say on the subject in the next chapter where he goes on to challenge the rhetoric of liberty, used as a rallying cry for the Americans against the British, by juxtaposing the case of Indian liberties transgressed by these same Americans.

Let the poor Indian attempt to resist the encroachments of his white neighbours, what a hue and cry is instantly raised against him. It has been considered as a trifling thing for the whites to make war on the Indians for the purpose of driving them from their country and taking possession thereof. But let the thing be changed. Suppose an overwhelming army should march into the United States for the purpose of subduing it and enslaving the citizens; how quick would they fly to arms, gather in multitudes around the tree of liberty, and contend for their rights with the last drop of their blood. And should the enemy succeed, would they not eventually rise and endeavor to regain their liberty? And who would blame them for it? (31)

The strategy of mirroring is used here to excellent effect as Apess turns the tables on his white readers, asking them to imagine themselves transpositionally in the position of the Indian. The use of specific words and images drawn from American nationalist rhetoric— "fly to arms" and "tree of liberty," for example—help to drive home Apess's point that American policy has been deeply hypocritical in its treatment of the Indians.

The kind of irony Apess employs in such passages may seem surprising. Yet other examples of Native American rhetoric from the period support the belief that Indians were well aware of the way comparisons between American relations with Britain and Native American relations with America undermined the doctrines of American exceptionalism and moral superiority. Take, for example, the memoirs of the Seneca known as Chainbreaker (Governor Blacksnake). Blacksnake died in 1859 when it was estimated he was about 106 years old. Thomas Abler has recently brought to light a manuscript dictated by Blacksnake "in his ninth or tenth decade" (3) to a young Seneca who spoke and wrote some English, Benjamin Williams. This manuscript is far from the literate and witty writing of William Apess, but it remains a fascinating, if often frustrating, account of Blacksnake's memories of the Revolutionary War, in which he fought on the British side with a substantial force of other Indians. Abler says that though Blacksnake was remembering events and speeches made more than seventy years earlier, the substance and even many of the words he recalled have been authenticated.[4] After the Revolutionary War, the Americans made treaties with the Iroquois Confederacy, bringing together Red Jacket, Blacksnake, and his uncle Cornplanter with George Washington. According to Williams's rendering of Blacksnake's words, Washington and Red Jacket used to spend hours together telling stories about "human nature" and discussing the character of different nations. "Both understood the Business Well" (179). But the treaties Washington made with the Indians to keep their lands ("in your hands forever as long as the Sun Rises and Water Runs and the Grass grew on Earth this is the bargain," 179) were no more reliable than the treaties the British had made, which caused Cornplanter to call the English "deceivers."

Even before the Revolution, the Senecas had had trouble with both the Americans and the representatives of the Crown. Blacksnake's group of western Senecas fought in the uprising led by Pontiac (1763–66) and were subsequently punished by the British. For their part, the Americans were constantly impinging on Indian lands and did not have the financial backing of the British and French to soothe feelings with presents. When British-American hostilities broke out in the 1770s, the Americans at first tried to prevent the Indians from joining either side. Conferences were held in several places including Pittsburgh to advise neutrality. At one of these, we can see Red Jacket turning American rhetoric back on the Americans in a way that suggests a strategy of mirroring similar to that used later by William Apess. The substance seems to be that the Americans found themselves in a situation quite similar to that of the Indians, who were also given "a covenant chain of peace" that eventually proved unreliable. Blacksnake (through the semiliterate Williams) recalls Red Jacket's speech as follows:

> Brothers Now attest—when your fathers Crossed the great waters and came over to this land, the King of England gave them a talk, assuring them that they and their children Should be his children, and that if they wanted [to] leave their Native Country and make Settlements, and live here, and buy and Sell and trade with their Brethren beyond the water, they should Still Keep hold of the Same covenant chain and enjoy peace &c

> But where is the covenant chain of Peace, and it Seem that chain got Rusted and little poling [puny?] Broken one, is not good for nothing, when, shall you go to be mented and seeking for the pinsers and Shop But you cannot fined it and Now you got to Built it your own, the King of England interfere you Builting you a Shop he says come to me, But you Determent that you shall Built one for your own and the King also Determent that you shall go to him, that created quarrel

> it is true that all the Indians Nations has nothing to Do with your father children quarrels we are therefore take upon the consideration with your opinion and with ours agreeable and we take your advise and we shall stand Notual [neutral]. (55–56)

Abler comments, "The reply Red Jacket is reported to have made the next day is garbled and open to at least two interpretations. It makes reference to a 'covenant chain,' which usually is a metaphor for the alliance between the Iroquois and the Crown" (44), not that between the British and Americans. Though Abler comes to feel that Blacksnake's rendering of this speech is confused, one is tempted to see not confusion but sarcasm in Red Jacket's comments here. If these were not Red Jacket's actual words, perhaps Blacksnake wasn't so much confused about the facts as influenced by subsequent events in Indian relations with the Americans to report this speech later, in 1845, as one which might resonate in two directions. We can identify here a number of themes of Indian-white relations: "fathers" promising "children"[5] protection and refusing them independence, the dawning realization that the nation must consider its own welfare and reject such dependence since the covenant chain has been broken. Red

Jacket's irony draws attention to these transpositional parallels before succumbing to the American arguments and committing himself and his people to neutrality.

Other speeches in Williams's text also carry a strong undertone of such irony. When, after the Revolutionary War, Washington was sent to negotiate with the Six Nations, to make them cede lands to the government and accept the boundaries of an eastern reservation, Blacksnake's uncle Cornplanter responded to Washington's request with words that echo with understandable bitterness.

> Cornplanter, J. Obail [O'Bail was his father's name] than got up and Said unto them, you white man come from on the other Side of the big waters, where your Brother Great Britain live, and you have Fought withe him, for you to again Liberty and you gain a Day, and it is Right for he is Deciver, as he has Decive the Six Nation of Indians as you called the Red men. *But we are tru american* we live here this continent, our God created us here the lord gaven us all this lands have I had a Right to make Reserve now for my people to live on while the land is belonging to the Indians if I had I shall make Reserve land for my people, and to our Satisfaction. (emphasis added, 178)

Cornplanter claims that the Indians are the "true Americans" and presents a geographic and sacral view of nation as given by God, rather than the modern political one assumed by the United States. Furthermore, these speeches suggest that the ironies of American republican rhetoric about liberty and justice were not lost on Native Americans. Well before William Apess developed the foregrounding of these ironies into an art, other natives were already holding up an "Indian's Looking-Glass" in the white man's face.

However, unlike Cornplanter and Blacksnake, Apess was a literate Indian, after his "six winters" of schooling mostly self-educated but nonetheless knowledgeable about literary texts and print culture. Therefore, his work invites us to see mimicry as well as irony in his interventions which are not limited to undermining the white man's claims. For example, in *A Son of the Forest* Apess frequently falls into the typical style of the repentant Christian that Krupat has called "salvationist." He moans: "The waters of affliction had well-nigh overwhelmed me—my hopes were drowned, and having been ex-

cluded from the pales of the church [for preaching without a license],
I viewed myself as an *outcast from society*. Now the enemy sought to
prevail against me, and for a season overcome me; I gave way for a
little while but soon returned to my *first love* [the Church]" (emphasis
in original, 46). If there is irony here, it is that second level of irony
Homi Bhabha describes where the colonized seems to emerge as "different" at the very moment and in the very language he has adopted
to appear authentically "the same." As we have seen above, Apess is
more than capable of intentional irony, but this passage sounds like an
earnest appeal to the reader to take seriously Apess's struggles with
temptation and backsliding, to take him, therefore, as an authentic
Christian whose life may be represented according to the conventional white Christian pattern of the conversion narrative which almost always involves periods of backsliding followed by a return to
faith. A level of dramatic irony comes into focus, however, when we
realize that one of the forms temptation takes for Apess is the rejection of white culture because the community has rejected him. (Upon
his excommunication, he goes immediately to his people: "I went
then to my native tribe.") Nevertheless, the terms Apess appropriates
to tell this story must be the terms of the rejecting culture itself; they
come from the same church society which Apess tells us is deserving
of his "love."

When Apess employs these agonistic tropes of salvationist rhetoric—"the enemy sought to prevail against me, and for a season
overcome me"—he is engaging in what I have called "subjugated
discourse." Implicit in this mode are hierarchies of power and privilege which generate, according to the logic of *ressentiment*, both
obedient submission and angry denunciations. This is not to say, of
course, that Christianity itself necessarily implies the subjugation
of Native Americans. Christian principles may be asserted in the interests of revolution as well as submission, as many examples of African American and Latin American rhetoric attest. However, as used
here, salvationist rhetoric demands that Apess occupy the role of the
mimic, who must *seem* to be aspiring to assimilate even if that desire is
complicated by other factors. The persona of the "poor Indian"—
words that echo in various passages in Apess's work—is not pre-

sented purely ironically, I would argue. To some degree, Apess must present himself as a "poor Indian," if he is to be heard at all.

However, if we turn now to "An Indian's Looking-Glass for the White Man," we find William Apess taking white Americans to task for their racism and lack of Christian charity. Apess demands: "Now, if the Lord Jesus Christ, who is counted by all to be a Jew—and it is well known that the Jews are a colored people, especially those living in the East, where Christ was born—and if he should appear among us, would he not be shut out of doors by many, very quickly? And by those too who profess religion?" (160).

"An Indian's Looking-Glass" gives us an example of another type of subjugated discourse, one that rejects mimicry as its primary strategy while retaining a focus upon differential power relations and the theme of oppression. The subject of this passage, after all, is the subjugation of blacks and Indians. That makes it different from the transpositional moments in which "we are all the descendents of one great progenitor" or those where Apess (and others) imply we may change places with one another since we are all fundamentally the same. Here Apess says: "Let me for a few moments turn your attention to the reservations in the different states of New England, and, with but few exceptions, we shall find them as follows: the most mean, abject, miserable race of beings in the world—a complete place of prodigality and prostitution" (155). In such passages, his view of Indians as "mean, abject, miserable" does not differ materially from that of the dominant culture. Apess's aim, of course, is to induce white Americans to treat Indians differently. "Now I will ask if the Indians are not called the most ingenious people among us. And are they not said to be men of talents? And I would ask: Could there be a more efficient way to distress and murder them by inches than the way they [the whites] have taken?"

The one transpositional touch here is where he adds: "And there is no people in the world but who may be destroyed in the same way" (156). Yet Apess's main thrust is not universalizing but particular and political: America must allow Indians (and other peoples of color)[6] to participate fully in the life of the nation. He asks: "Why are we not protected in our persons and property throughout the Union?"

(156). And again: "Let me ask why the men of a different skin are so despised. Why are they not educated and placed in your pulpits?" (159). Obviously transpositional rhetoric alone will not do, because Indians *cannot* change places with whites: difference (including differences of power and interest) obstructs this.

When whites are imagined by Apess as a nation, sitting in the minority among the other, much more numerous, colored nations of the earth, he sees them as eminent only in their iniquity. "Now suppose these skins were put together, and each skin had its national crimes written upon it—which skin do you think would have the greatest?" (157). The vertical image Apess implies here, the language of greatest and least, is characteristic of subjugated discourse. It reminds us of the Old Testament prophets, even as the New Testament's "the last shall be first, and the first last" (Matt. 20:16) resonates in the background, reversing earthly hierarchies of power.

Many examples of subjugated discourse are not as polemical as these. But they all share a common thrust. The implication of subjugated discourse is that one cannot imagine America as an egalitarian society until major changes are made in economic, social, and spiritual realms. Transpositional discourse, because it seems to ignore this fact, may appear by contrast naively utopian. Subjugated discourse, even when—as in the cases of George Copway and John Rollin Ridge—it seems to buy into problematic assumptions about the superiority of white culture, calls attention to inequities and shows the need for political change. It must be said, of course, that sometimes this appears as the intention of the writer and sometimes it seems merely an "effect" of the writing.

If Apess can speak the white man's language but is denied the white man's privileges, his difference must be weighed against his (potential) similarity. This is why it may be said (by Homi Bhabha, for instance) that mimicry breaks up the integrity of the human image on both sides, destabilizing not only identity but the concept of nation which usually depends upon fictional beliefs about "natural" insiders and outsiders, native speakers and "naturalized" citizens. Indians are seen as outsiders, but, like mimicry, political action often removes them from their "original" tribal space as well. Thus, certain questions come into view. Is one's national identity given, or merely strategic, a product of historical forces, a costume?

Black Hawk's meeting with Andrew Jackson was not a "political" occasion. Even in defeat, he remained essentially a Sauk, unwilling to engage in either mimicry or the politics of self-presentation. For their part, Apess, Copway, and Ridge sought a new role for the Indians, one in which they could benefit from the political arrangements of a reconstructed America. To achieve this, they all engaged at moments in subjugated discourse, mimicking, pleading, denouncing, as it served their purposes.

One can see this even more clearly in the document about the Mashpee (or Marshpee) rebellion, which I will call, for convenience's sake, *Nullification* though its longer title—"Indian Nullification of the Unconstitutional Laws of Massachusetts Relative to the Marshpee Tribe; or, The Pretended Riot Explained"—is more useful in drawing attention to the discourse on nation. This section of Apess's collected works is the longest and in many ways the most ambitious.[7] In it Apess recounts the problems encountered by the Mashpee tribe who sought to replace the white missionary imposed upon them by their Massachusetts "trustees." This missionary had done little for the tribe and seems to have been completely ineffectual both in bringing about conversions and in educating the Indians.

What Apess and others wanted was his removal from the Indian community and the redirection of the funds for his salary to another minister, Apess himself. Furthermore, they wanted control over the land and its timber which was being cut down and carted away by whites living adjacent to the colony. In sum, they wanted what the Americans wanted at the time of the Revolutionary War: recognition of their semi-independent status and redress of their grievances. But the symmetry of the two positions was lost on the leaders of the Commonwealth who threatened to call out the militia, after Indians had prevented white settlers from taking more timber. Indeed, William Apess was imprisoned for a time over just this issue, an act that created a good deal of local controversy.

Nullification includes many documents not written by Apess himself: columns from the local papers about the incident, letters, testi-

mony, and so on. It is a deeply political work in which Apess (and
others who wrote in defense of the Mashpees) used republican and
Puritan rhetoric to establish the injustice of the treatment they received. In this it is an extremely witty work as well. For instance,
Apess tells us that when he arrived in the community, he went to the
little church to meet in fellowship with his Indian brethren, the missionary's converts. In his account of this event, he says he held out
the hand of friendship, only to find the other converts all had "pale
faces, and, in my disappointment, it seemed to me that the hue of
death sat on their countenances" (170). It turns out, of course, that
most of the people who attend the missionary's services really are
"pale faces," that is, white. Apess goes on: "Recovering a little from
my astonishment, I entered the house with the missionary. It had
the appearance of some eminent monument set upon a hilltop, for a
landmark to generations to come." We cannot know, of course,
whether Apess was familiar with Winthrop's "city on a hill" speech
or whether he like Winthrop was mainly echoing the biblical passage
"You are the light of the world. A city set on a hill cannot be hid"
(Matt. 5:14). If we compare Apess with Winthrop, he seems to be
suggesting the beginning of a new order in which Winthrop's original idea of knitting all the members of the community together
through the bonds of love and faith would for the first time allow
Indians to be included with whites. Such a reading of this passage
would certainly be consistent with views Apess expresses elsewhere.

The officers of Massachusetts had other ideas, however. After
the incident with the wood, ex-governor Lincoln wrote a letter to
the *Boston Courier* insisting that the Indians were incapable of self-
government and needed the supervision of a parental authority. To
this letter Apess responds in the text:

Does it appear from this, and from his message, that the ex-governor is a
man of pure republican principles? He seems to consider the Marshpees as
strangers and thinks they ought to be driven to the wilds of the Far West, in
humble imitation of that wise, learned, and humane politician, Andrew
Jackson, L.L.D.

I do consider that neither I nor any of my brethren enjoy any political rights; and I desire that I and they may be treated like men, and not like children. If any among us are capable of discharging the duties of office, I wish them to be made eligible, and I wish for the right of suffrage which other men exercise, though not for the purpose of pleasing any party by our votes. I never did so, and I never will. Oh, that all men of color thought and felt as I do on this subject. (225)

Again, there are a number of rhetorical moves to be noted in this passage. Apess accuses the ex-governor of departing from the "pure republican principles" that are supposed to guide American policy. Furthermore, he puns on the word "strangers" which in Puritan rhetoric means not just those who are from elsewhere, thus not "natives," but also those who are outside the protection of the church, the polity. Apess makes clear that the Indians are treated as strangers in both senses since they are made to feel like outsiders even in the church and are denied political rights. As this extract also shows, his view of Andrew Jackson in 1835 was quite different from Black Hawk's. It will be remembered that Black Hawk thought Jackson "a good man" and "a great brave." Apess, by contrast, speaks sarcastically of Jackson's wisdom, learning, and humanity, highlighting his law degree as evidence of the fact that America is deeply hypocritical when it claims to be governed impartially by the rule of law.

One final word about Apess's rejection of the word "children" to describe the Indians. He is not alone in his discomfort with this terminology as we will see in the chapter on George Copway. Furthermore, *Nullification*'s publication in 1835 makes it concurrent with President Jackson's insistence on Cherokee removal from Georgia. There the term "children" was not merely derogatory but political, as Michael Rogin makes clear:

Rendering the Indians children did not simply free the government from responsibility, but also freed it to act as it wished. If Indians were driven by white pressure to "childish" squabbling among themselves, Jackson could recognize some chiefs rather than others. If a tribe was disorganized by state policies and white intruders, Jackson could treat its members as "children," ignore tribal preferences, and act in the Indians' "best interests." Georgia Governor Wilson Lumpkin, urging forcible Cherokee removal without benefit of treaty, wrote Jackson, "Have not these Indians lost all claim to national character? Ought not these Indians to be considered and treated as helpless wards of the federal government?" (232–33)

No wonder Apess, who was aware of the Cherokee situation, bridled at the use of the term "children" to describe the Indians. No wonder he opted for political efforts and pressed for Indian citizenship in an effort not to fall victim to such policies.

As the many examples of William Apess's wit illustrate, he was fully capable of using the techniques of mirroring to make his case that, on the one hand, Indians were not hampered by any basic racial inferiority (and therefore could handle the duties of both self-government and citizenship perfectly well) but that, on the other, they were severely disadvantaged and debased by the unequal power relations through which they had been subjugated. In one of the most poignant moments of the document, he bemoans the lack of unanimity among "men of color" on these political issues.

Like David Murray[8] I am struck by the contradiction implied by the fact that Apess is ready to indict white society as thoroughly corrupt and yet clearly also wants to join it, asking not for complete independence from the American government but instead for "the right of suffrage which other men exercise." Of course, given the nearly complete disestablishment of Native American culture in many parts of America at this time, and given Apess's particular position as a literate Christian Indian, one has to ask, what were his alternatives?

What Apess's work illustrates, among other things, is the general truth that one's perspective varies depending upon one's position within the system. For Indians such as Apess and the Mashpees, their subjugated status called into question the very terms (its commitments to human rights) upon which America sought to claim a special identity. For the ex-governor and others, American paternalism toward the Indians reinforced that identity.

Apess himself makes this point in *Nullification* where he tells the story of the huntsman and the lion.

Let me remind you also, of the fable of the Huntsman and the Lion, when the former boasted of the superiority of man, and to prove it pointed to a statue of one of the old heroes, standing upon a prostrate lion. The reply of the noble beast was, "there are no *carvers* among the lions; if there were, for one man standing upon a lion, you would have twenty men torn to pieces by lions." Gentlemen, by depressing the Indians, our laws [!] have taken care that they should have no *carvers*. The whites have done all the *carving* for them, and have always placed them *undermost*. (emphasis in original, 235)[9]

By seizing the terms of the dominant discourse, Apess sought to become one of the carvers, that is, one of those whose control of the language of signs would shape a nation's understanding of itself and its possibilities.

There are some odd things about this passage, though, which, again, can be treated as an example of both transpositional and subjugated discourses. One is struck by two implications: on the one hand, Indians are like lions, savage beasts. On the other hand, should the laws be changed, they could, in the wink of a rhetorical eye, become "carvers" too, able to change places with "humans," who are here the whites. The first implication reinforces our sense of the passage as subjugated discourse, mimicking white views of Indians as savages (he refers to natives as "them" not "us") and calling attention to the vertical structure of the power hierarchy in which Indians are placed "undermost." The second implication of the text, however, is transpositional. Change the teller, change the tale. Both Indians and whites might occupy the role of storyteller here, and, though the story would be materially different if told from the lions' point of view, there is an unmistakable symmetry in the ethnocentricity in each of the two versions.

Since Apess is intent to point out that the laws of Massachusetts are not simply unjust but *unconstitutional*, he allows for a reading of this document as a critique of national rhetoric. The word "carvers" might be an allusion to the word "framers." Those who frame, or carve, inscribe in the national text the meanings of history, constraining those who come after to operate within certain limits. But the boundaries of the framing discourse are unstable because language may always be reused to generate new meanings. As Apess knows well, subjugated groups may appropriate the oppressor's language for their own purposes, by reversing the original intent or carving a space for themselves within the territory of republican structures, both of which strategies Apess adopts in this passage.

The Mashpee Council, upon which Apess served with other Indians from the tribe, was established in order to provide "the form of a government, suited to the spirit and capacity of freeborn sons of the forest, after the pattern set us by our white brethren" (179). In their public notice, they proclaimed: "we acted in accordance with the spirit of the Constitution, unless that instrument be a device of utter deception" (180). Thus, like the Cherokee who also used the American Constitution as a model for their government, they utilized the terms of American national rhetoric hoping to establish their own claims on a similar basis. This act was clearly strategic, but it may be seen as even more deeply subversive than they intended, for by opening up the possibility that the Constitution's meanings are not fixed but are instead a matter of interpretation (they speak of the "spirit" of the document), they opened the door not merely to their own claims but to all those who in the 1830s and after would use similar republican strategies to lay claim to an American identity.[10] As we can see through a consideration of the work of William Apess, since nations are created in language and through narrative, those who are subjected to the oppressive will of the state may also, by revising and redeploying the national narrative, become subjects in their own right.

4. Black Hawk and the Moral Force
of Transposition

In the previous chapter we looked at William Apess's combinations of transpositional and subjugated discourse in his presentations of and appeals to an idea of nation. In that discussion, it was said that transpositional rhetoric, because it insists upon the interchangeability of rival entities, can seem naively utopian. Apess's political edge is part of what makes his work interesting, and in light of that we see that Apess is by no means content to depend entirely upon transpositional arguments, though his work may be described as transpositional in part.

In this chapter we will look at the *Life of Ma-Ka-Tai-Me-She-Kia-Kiak, or Black Hawk* (1833), which provides an example of Native American writing as close to pure transpositional narrative as one can find in the nineteenth century, and here it will be argued that there is a certain power in transposition, a moral force that cannot be gainsaid. But first it will be useful to recount some basic facts surrounding the creation of this document.

Black Hawk was a Sauk war chief. As he tells us, the Sauk, prior to the events of the autobiography, merged with the Fox to becomes the Sauk and Fox Tribe. This group inhabited a wide area, including parts of what is now Wisconsin, Michigan, Illinois, Missouri, and Indiana, but they mostly lived on the eastern side of the Mississippi River in what is now Illinois. In 1804 a dubious treaty was signed by some minor representatives of the tribe (who were drunk at the time) agreeing to cede vast tracts of land to the government and accept an annuity in their stead. For some years after, this treaty was not enforced, but in the 1830s, during the period when Andrew Jackson was putting in place his plan to remove the Indians west of the Mississippi River beyond what was then the boundary of the incorporated states, pressure was brought on Black Hawk and his tribe to live up to the provisions of the treaty. Outraged at the idea that his people must abandon their village and the graves of their ancestors, Black Hawk went on the warpath in 1832. Though the Indians were successful in a few skirmishes and for a time evaded the soldiers, in the end—according to a pattern often repeated in American history—a great many members of the tribe were massacred, including women and children; Black Hawk was taken prisoner. He spent many months in prison both in the midwest where he surrendered and then at Fortress Monroe in Virginia. Subsequently he was allowed to return to his people but only after a required tour of American cities and technological achievements designed to impress the Indian with the futility of further resistance to American expansion. Black Hawk returned home in defeat but decided, as his last public act of any consequence, to dictate his autobiography in order to communicate his view of the events leading up to and including the Black Hawk War.

The result is an account both simple and eloquent, and for a twentieth-century Euro-American reader, it is especially interesting because it provides an extended example of the similarities and differences between Native American and Euro-American cultural expectations in the early part of the nineteenth century. What I have described as its "transpositional" emphasis may be seen in Black Hawk's juxtapositions of his Indian nation with the American nation he encounters. This text is also unusual in American letters, because it does not desire to unite the two; indeed it offers the most salient argument we have in this literature in favor of an Indian nation entirely separate from the United States. But certain questions arise concerning its authenticity. Can we assume that this is a reliable account of Black Hawk's views, or, because it was translated and edited, must we see it in Larzer Ziff's terms as a text in which "the Indian's voice is supplied by the ventriloquizing culture of the white" (173)?[1]

In 1955 Donald Jackson reedited the autobiography with an extensive introduction discussing a number of issues surrounding it, including the reliability of the text. Jackson rehearses the facts of composition: that Black Hawk dictated the story of his life to a mixed-blood interpreter, Antoine LeClaire, in 1833, and that J. B. Patterson, an ambitious young Anglo-American printer, edited the manuscript and put it into the final form in which it was published that same year.

In 1882 the work was reedited by Patterson and republished with new material added about which there is considerable doubt; some of the original wording was also changed. Jackson spells out the changes but concludes: "If Patterson altered Black Hawk's story in the 1882 edition, must we assume that he did so forty-nine years earlier in the 1833 edition? Not necessarily. . . . If we are to evaluate Black Hawk's story properly, we must disregard the 1882 edition and stick with the 1833 edition, which, despite the intrusive hands of interpreter and editor, is basically a tale told by an Indian from an Indian point of view" (30).

More recently, a number of critics have called into question the idea that even the 1833 edition of Black Hawk's autobiography is "a tale told by an Indian from an Indian point of view." Arnold Krupat, in *The Voice in the Margin*, argues: "*Who* Black Hawk was, that is to say, is not a question that can be answered by some estimate as to whether we do or do not get the 'authentic' or 'real' historical person. 'Black Hawk' is—must be—only the subject who emerges from this text, a collective subject that includes the subjectivity of John Patterson (he, of course, is nowhere mentioned or referred to in the text) foremost among other participants in the making of this Indian self" (149).

Furthermore, Krupat suggests that whatever Black Hawk's "authentic" voice might have been, it was translated in the text into a version of hegemonic discourse that creates "a kind of blanketing effect," because of its insistence "upon the minimalization of difference as a primary condition for coherence and comprehensibility" (188). Mark Wallace goes even further, insisting that an Anglo-Indianized voice was "forced on Black Hawk" (485) and that "not only was [the text's] voice mediated, but it was restrained by whites before it was even conceived" (481).

Though one must agree with Krupat (and Wallace) that the writing itself necessarily produces a version of the Indian that will be comprehensible to a white audience, this need not mean, of course, that Black Hawk inevitably emerges here either as wholly the same as his white readers or as wholly different (other).[2] Furthermore, as both Krupat and David Murray acknowledge, Black Hawk's autobiography is distinctive for its lack of the kind of ambivalence that characterizes other Native American texts originally composed in English; whether or not it is true, as one reviewer wrote in 1835, that "No white man, however great his ability may be, could have executed a work so thoroughly and truly Indian" (quoted in Jackson ed., 25),[3] Black Hawk's autobiography seems far less dialogic than other Native American texts from the same period. If hegemony is at work to reduce the sense of oppositional difference in Black Hawk's discourse, it yet remains true that the views represented here are considerably more *unlike* standard Euro-American views than what one finds in Apess or George Copway. Not that Copway and Apess are uncritical of white people. This is far from true, as we have already seen. But Black Hawk delights in cultural practices, such as scalping, that are never praised by converted Indians. One might argue, with Krupat and Wallace, that this is precisely the effect of Euro-American influence since it encases Black Hawk in the mold of unregenerate Other.[4]

In my reading of the autobiography, however, Black Hawk appears at times significantly different from his white, middle-class readers (as where he delights in the scalp dance) and at other times surprisingly similar, as where he says: "For my part, I am of the opinion that so far as we have *reason*, we have a right to use it, in determining what is right or wrong; and should pursue that path which we believe to be right—believing, that 'whatever is, is right'" (93). This is, in fact, an interesting passage to ponder because it sounds so European, and not only in the quotation, "whatever is, is right," but even in the use of the Enlightenment term "reason." The quotation, of course, is hardly likely to be Black Hawk's since he did not read European languages (or any but sign language) and was presumably unfamiliar with both European philosophy and Alexander Pope's poetry, from which the quotation undoubtedly comes.

On the other hand, should we simply dismiss this passage as one obviously constructed by the editor and therefore not Black Hawk's view at all? The sentiments expressed, the idea that we can depend upon our own judgment for guidance and that ultimately the Great Spirit shows us the right path to pursue, are consistent with many other sections of the autobiography. In this part, the translation goes on to say, "If the Great and Good Spirit wished us to believe and do as the whites, he could easily change our opinions, so that we would see, and think, and act as they do" (93). This is the same stubborn Black Hawk we meet elsewhere in the text who believes in himself and his culture, believes it to be different from white culture, and has no wish to assimilate.

I would like, therefore, to return to the understanding of "voice," described in chapter one as "a willed line of informed approach." Though I certainly acknowledge that the text is the product, as Arnold Krupat says, of bicultural composite composition and I agree that we cannot ever know the "real" Black Hawk, I will for the remainder of this discussion adopt the strategy of referring to that voice in the text as "Black Hawk." A great deal depends upon how we hear this voice. Mark Wallace hears it as a "production" of white hegemony, held hostage to the power relations that governed Black Hawk's position as a defeated warrior. Neil Schmitz, however, insists upon a very different reading, asserting that "Black Hawk's text is everywhere barbed, reproachful, scathing in its irony" (3). His representation of what he calls "captive utterance" is deconstructive, emphasizing the way Black Hawk subverts the assumptions of even its twentieth-century editors who claim that Black Hawk died bitterly regretting his decision to go to war. Schmitz comments: "In captive utterance, through the writing of LeClaire and the rewriting of Patterson, Black Hawk's text attacks that position, its grounding, denies the cultural and martial superiority of the Americans, declares the cultural and martial superiority of the Sauk, gives proper value to what was the last sovereign act of the Algonquin people in the Eastern Woodlands of North America" (5).

Though agreeing in large part with Schmitz's conclusions, I interpret Black Hawk's voice as somewhat less heroically intransigent and more ambivalent and thoughtful. In my analysis of its transpositional and subjugated elements, I will attempt to weigh the effects of both forms of discourse, suggesting that the text is complex and fissured rather than "defiant, litigious, and maledictory" (2) throughout. Therefore, this chapter will examine (1) Black Hawk's perspective on his own "nation," the Sauk, (2) his use of transpositional discourse

and its moral effect, (3) the places in the text where he departs from
a transpositional mode, and (4) the consequences of Black Hawk's
challenge to white hegemony in the rather bizarre co-optation by
Euro-Americans of Black Hawk and his son as personifications of
American virtue.

The meta-narrative about nation in Black Hawk's autobiography
is certainly ethnocentric in the sense that Black Hawk continually
asserts his own Indian context as his frame of reference. But what is
this self that emerges in the text? Black Hawk speaks sometimes as a
historically distinct individual with private feelings and a personal
history. More often, however, he presents himself as a representative
of the Sauk nation, personifying in himself a noble culture fundamentally equal to that represented by his oppressors. A significant example of this tendency is Black Hawk's response to General Gaines
during the period of increasing conflict between Indians and whites
that led up to the Black Hawk War. In 1830 General Gaines made a
trip to the nearby Indian agency with a contingent of soldiers in order
to provide a show of force sufficient to make the tribal leaders agree
to leave their village and retire to an area west of the Mississippi.
Black Hawk was deeply resistant to the idea of leaving Saukenuk, his
village, though at times he apparently appeared to be ready to negotiate a deal.[5] On this particular occasion, he arrived for the tribal council with a band of followers armed to the teeth and singing a war
song. General Gaines made a speech invoking the controversial
Treaty of 1804[6] and insisting that the tribal lands had already been
ceded to the United States. Through an interpreter Black Hawk coun-
tered that he and his followers had never agreed to this treaty. Black
Hawk gives this version of the stand-off:

> The war chief, apparently angry, rose and said: — 'Who is *Black Hawk?*
> Who is *Black Hawk?*'
> I responded:
> 'I am a *Sac*. my forefather was a Sac! and all the nations call me a SAC!!'
> (111)

Black Hawk presents himself here as a personification of the Sauk
(also spelled Sac) tribe. Against General Gaines who appears to represent the United States, he forcibly asserts his own national status.

What do we learn about this nation in Black Hawk's autobiography? What follows is a sampling of his comments about the Sauk.

Like William Apess's *A Son of the Forest*, the autobiography begins not with personal reminiscence but with family genealogy. Black Hawk claims to be a direct descendent of Na-na-ma-kee, founding father of the American Sauk group. He tells the story of the tribe's first meeting with white men and of their migration from Canada to the area they later settled on the Rock River. His own emergence into the narrative occurs when he is fourteen and takes his first scalp. As we soon come to see, Sauk and Fox culture trained warriors because the people often engaged in armed conflicts with other tribes such as the Menominee, the Sioux, and the western Cherokee, who killed Black Hawk's father.

For those not out on scalp hunts, the year was divided between agricultural planting and harvest and work in the lead mines. On the domestic front, Black Hawk describes relations between the sexes and in the family as practical and reciprocal. Men did the hunting, women did the planting. Women were certainly respected for their contributions to the ongoing life of the tribe, but for Black Hawk what men did was more *significant*. That is, counting coups is for him a sign of distinction that elevates warfare above the repetitive tasks performed by the women: agricultural work, work in the lead mines, child care, cooking. These are important to life but not to male honor, and without honor Black Hawk feels that life loses its meaning. The war chief comments in the autobiography, "It is not customary for us to say much about our women, as they generally perform their part cheerfully, and *never interfere with business belonging to the men!*" (emphasis in original, 73).

A common form of contempt among Indian braves was to say that someone acted like a woman, which usually means in a cowardly way. Yet Black Hawk himself never has recourse to this form of derogatory comment, preferring to dismiss someone by saying that he spoke like a child. In his autobiography women *do* participate in politics, giving their opinions about important decisions facing the tribe. At one point, when Black Hawk has organized a group to resist the whites who are encroaching on his village and destroying Indian plantings, he is opposed by Keokuk. Black Hawk recalls: "Ke-o-kuck, who has a smooth tongue, and is a great speaker, was busy in persuading my band that I was wrong—and thereby making many of them dissatisfied with me. I had one consolation—for all the women were on my side, on account of their corn-fields" (107–8). Women have a voice in the decision making, but the men decide which counsels are most compelling.

Black Hawk himself may have been unusual in the degree to which he took women seriously, however. In the passage quoted above, where Black Hawk says the women do not interfere in the business of men, he goes on to say: "This is the only wife I ever had, or ever will have. She is a good woman, and teaches my boys to be *brave*" (73). Black Hawk was known to be deeply devoted to his wife, Singing Bird, with whom he seems to have had a reciprocal relationship, each working for the other to promote the ends of both.[7]

To place Black Hawk's statement about his wife in perspective (and to underscore his loyalty to her), Jackson's note tells us that a Sauk might have several wives. Black Hawk did not. James D. Riskell, in the 1912 edition of the autobiography, went much further, giving a suspiciously sanguine view of women's lot in the tribe in *his* note.

The position of the women among these Indians was not one of slavery, nor was their lot a particularly hard one. Housekeeping was not a very laborious task with them. If, for any cause, the work of the women became burdensome, the husband solved the servant-girl problem by taking a new wife. The women seem to have made no objection to this arrangement, but in all reported cases appear to have welcomed the newcomer as a valuable addition to the household. (153)

Black Hawk's own account of marriage customs is equally upbeat. He shows the way courting rituals allowed a girl to choose the man she wished to marry. They lived together for one year, during which time they could break up if either side were dissatisfied and seek other partners: "If we were to live together and disagree, we should be as foolish as the whites. No indiscretion can banish a woman from her parental lodge—no difference how many children she may bring home, she is always welcome—the kettle is over the fire to feed them" (91).

However, it is clear that Black Hawk indulges in some romanticizing when he reflects back on the way life in the nation was organized. Perhaps family life always went as smoothly as Black Hawk suggests, but other documents cast doubt on this. In John Tanner's account of life among the Ojibwa, published as *The Falcon*, he casually reveals the presence of domestic violence, lack of support, and betrayal within Indian family life, though admittedly alcohol had already unraveled much of the traditional cultural fabric by this time. Were the Sauk so different? One should not be too ready to assume that no conflicts divided males and females, or parents and errant children, in the tribe. Even if, as Riskell admits, polygamy was rare, it is hard to imagine that when it did occur, it caused no friction, especially since we have recently begun hearing from women in other polygamous societies (for instance, in Africa and in American Black Muslim communities) who have told a different tale after years of being represented as content with this system. In *Cheyenne Autumn* Mari Sandoz recounts a story of an Indian woman who kills herself when her husband takes a second wife.

Another place where Black Hawk seems to present an idealized portrait of the Sauk nation is in his reflections on the way the past differed from the present.

We always had plenty—our children never cried from hunger, nor our people were never in want. Here our village had stood for more than a hundred years, during all which time we were the undisputed possessors of the valley of the Mississippi. . . . At this time we had very little intercourse with the whites, except our traders. Our village was healthy, and there was no place in the country possessing such advantages, nor no hunting grounds better than those we had in possession. If another prophet had come to our village in those days, and told us what has since taken place, none of our people would have believed him. (89)

Perhaps it is only the misery of the present that inspires such an Edenic vision of the tribal past.

Nonetheless, it is hard to disagree with Black Hawk's historical assessment that the life of the tribe became steadily worse as the white settlements moved closer to Indian lands, especially, as Black Hawk notes, because of the introduction of alcohol. One index of Black Hawk's virtual exile from that past is his decision to use an interpreter to convey his story *in writing* to a white audience. Only thus, he now seems to feel, can the past be made present once again. Exile is often the nursery of nationalism, and Black Hawk was a man living in exile from the end of the Black Hawk War in 1832 to his death in 1838.

First he was imprisoned, enchained, and sent East for many months. When he returned, his power in tribal councils had been removed by Keokuk. He relocated with his family to a lodge of peeled bark by the Iowa River, exiled from his beloved village and the graves of his ancestors. His nation had lost its center, and with that loss went Black Hawk's own sense of identity. As Timothy Sweet puts it, "In the face of white military and political efforts to emasculate the tribal warrior, the *Life of Black Hawk* emerges as an attempt to preserve his traditions" (477).

The elderly Sauk ex-chief had no hope of winning back his lost territory or returning his people to the proud position they once occupied, so perhaps the risky business of dictating his autobiography to be circulated in the world of the whites was the best option he could devise. That it represented a turnabout from Black Hawk's earlier attitude to writing, however, cannot be doubted. Black Hawk was, first and foremost, a warrior, and a Sauk warrior at that.

In the autobiography, he pours scorn on European modes of fighting. Taking up the criticism leveled at Indian warriors—that they attacked without warning, often at night, and retreated when they saw that they were outnumbered—Black Hawk asserts what he thinks of as a superior principle of warfare: fight to win without fear of death but preserve as many warriors as possible. It seems incomprehensible to him that the British and Americans do otherwise. "Instead of stealing upon one another, and taking every advantage to *kill the enemy* and *save their own people,* as we do (which with us is considered good policy in a war chief), they march out, in open daylight, and *fight,* regardless of the number of warriors they may lose! After the battle is over, they retire to feast, and drink wine, as if nothing had happened; after which they make a *statement in writing,* of what they have done— *each party claiming the victory!*" (emphasis in original, 71).

The contempt Black Hawk expresses for writing is significant, for it reflects his belief that courageous acts, storytelling, and ritual dances are the most vital national practices. Writing is associated here with dishonesty. Only in defeat does Black Hawk decide to "publish" his autobiography in a form of writing directed to a white audience.

What was his motive in undertaking this project? In his 1992 book *Black Hawk and the Warrior's Path*, Roger L. Nichols interprets Black Hawk's aggressive behavior as directly contributing to the destruction of the Saukenuk people. Characterizing Black Hawk as an ultra-traditionalist who was unflaggingly antiwhite, Nichols insists that resistance was counterproductive because the Americans were destined to win out in the end. Therefore, Nichols argues that Black Hawk should have resorted to negotiation rather than taking up arms. (He admits, however, that Keokuk—Black Hawk's principal rival among the Sauk and a proponent of accommodation—was no more successful at achieving long-term stability for the tribe.) Nichols claims that Black Hawk rewrote history when he insisted that the Sauk had never understood the treaties that ceded their land to the whites, pointing out that they accepted annuities based upon the 1804 treaty at least up until 1818, and that Black Hawk himself had signed a second treaty confirming the provisions of 1804 in 1816.[8] In Nichols's view Black Hawk could never see beyond his role as a warrior to participate in true negotiations. When his modes of resistance were rendered obsolete, he had no choice but to lie about the past.

In my reading, however, Black Hawk dictates his memoirs because he has an ardent belief in the truth. As Neil Schmitz suggests: "Often [the narrative] seems not to address us, Patterson's Jacksonian public, but some transcultural Justice, some future multiracial United Nations, or sovereign Algonquin nation" (3). He seems less concerned about salvaging his own reputation (his motive, according to Nichols, for lying about the past) than he is about refusing charges of double-dealing directed against the tribe. And here is where we must turn our attention to the way Black Hawk's use of transpositional discourse becomes a rhetorically effective mode for the reader. It might be argued that his insistence upon the fundamental parity of native and white cultures, though it ignored certain obvious disparities, was the only form of resistance open to him after his defeat. It is certainly one which raises the moral problems of Manifest Destiny in the clearest possible way. For him the superiority of white culture never goes beyond that of numbers, weapons, and technology. That is, in Black Hawk's view, white power has no moral, spiritual, or historical justification that puts it in charge of the future. The autobiography, then, remains a document of fierce moral (rather than merely personal) outrage, certainly utopian in its assumptions but a challenge to the idea that history unfolds as it must and should which remains unanswered to this day. "So he speaks to a History that is not American History" (4), notes Neil Schmitz.

If it is not true that Black Hawk set out to cover up the truth, Nichols's belief that Black Hawk was unstintingly "antiwhite" is not borne out by the autobiography either. Though Black Hawk found much white behavior surprising, the text suggests that he was constantly gathering information and revising his previous judgments, as where he discusses the Indian war dance and then adds: "This national dance makes our warriors. When I was travelling last summer, on a steam boat, on a large river, going from New York to Albany, I was shown the place where the Americans dance their national dance [West Point]; where the old warriors recount to their young men, what they have done, to stimulate them to go and do likewise. This surprised me, as I did not think the whites understood our way of making braves" (92). Again and again Black Hawk comes to fresh conclusions and revises his previous views. After commenting negatively on American military prowess in the early parts of the autobiography, he shows why he later decided that the Americans could be good warriors after all.

We can also see a resistance to purely racialist thinking in the sharp distinctions he draws between the English and the Americans, as where he says that the Sauk were not disposed to join the Americans in the War of 1812 (during which they were eventually drawn in to fight on the side of the British) because "I had not discovered yet one good trait in the character of the Americans who had come to the country. They made fair promises but never fulfilled them, while the British made but few, and we could always rely implicitly on their word" (60).[9] The words "I had not discovered yet" illustrate Black Hawk's emphasis on experience and data gathering as the basis for his thinking. Instead of judging him a racist (as Nichols does), it would be fairer to say that Black Hawk was fiercely *nationalistic* in his understanding of life.

It is certainly true that he has moments of bitterness against whites, as where he breaks out in denunciations of white interference in Indian culture, usurpation of Indian lands, and dispensing of alcohol. "Here I was again puzzled to find out how the white people reasoned; and began to doubt whether they had any standard of right and wrong!" (106). But throughout the autobiography one can see his attempts to be fair-minded. When Black Hawk visits the East as a prisoner and is shown the great cities and the railroad, he comments: "They certainly deserve great praise for their industry" (145). Similarly, he both praises and blames the American soldiers he and his warriors encounter in battle. When the Indians are tricked by one war chief (Lt. John Campbell) into an attack in which they (the Indians) sustain casualties, he adds: "Some of their men jumped out and pushed off the boat, and thus got away without losing a man! I had a good opinion of this war chief—he managed so much better than the others. It would give me pleasure to shake him by the hand" (79). Of Zebulon Pike he comments approvingly, "He was a good man, and a great brave—and died in his country's service" (53).

Even the dedication of Black Hawk's autobiography, written in defeat, carries a transpositional subtext. The 1833 edition is dedicated to Brigadier General Atkinson (called White Beaver) who was victorious over Black Hawk in the Black Hawk War. It concludes with the following words:

I am now an obscure member of a nation that formerly honored and respected my opinions. The path to glory is rough, and many gloomy hours obscure it. May the Great Spirit shed light on your's [*sic*]—and that you may never experience the humility that the power of the American government has reduced me to, is the wish of him, who, in his native forests, was once as proud and bold as yourself. (unpaged)

Individually, personally, Black Hawk is capable of being subjugated, capable of being reduced in stature by American military power. Yet the "nation that formerly honored and respected" his opinions is still presented as his locus of value and appears here untarnished. Furthermore, in his address to General Atkinson, he draws a parallel between his role in the Sauk nation and the general's role in the American nation. Even in dishonor the Black Hawk of this text insists that he "was once as proud and bold as yourself." The dedication thus seems to support the point made earlier that, despite its composite composition and adoption of non-native formal devices (such as the dedication itself), this text is no pure product of Euro-American assumptions about Indians, either positive or negative.

Addressing General Atkinson, Black Hawk still seems to be measuring by his own yardstick. It is important to underscore that transpositional discourse, in its horizontal referentiality moving between self and other, need not be seen as implying that cultures are basically the *same* or that one cannot be disadvantageously compared to the other on particular grounds. What it resists is savagism's racialist assumption of hierarchical unities: the Red Man as inferior to the White Man, for instance, or vice versa. Black Hawk criticizes the Sioux along with the whites because both kill women and children. Conversely he praises the white people who live in the Eastern mountain regions (as against the roaming Sioux) because they seem content with what the Great Spirit has given them and "prefer living in their *own* country, to coming out to *ours*, and driving us from it" (144).

There *is* a principle of sameness invoked by Black Hawk, not a cultural sameness but a metaphysical principle of equality. Here he goes on to say, "In my intercourse with the whites, I have learned that one great principle of *their religion* is, 'to do unto others as you wish them to do unto you!' These people in the mountains seem to act upon this principle; but the settlers on our frontiers and on our lands, seem never to think of it, if we are to judge by their actions" (145). Black Hawk is always willing to give credit where he feels credit is due, and this, as much as anything, makes reading the autobiography feel like an experience of engaging with the mind of a just man.

It would be a mistake, however, to allegorize Black Hawk as some kind of Indian saint. He was certainly capable of jealousy as one can see by his contemptuous assessment of Keokuk, his pacifist rival, a man much admired by Americans, including his editor J. B. Patterson and George Catlin, the ethnographic writer and painter. After the war, when Major John Garland made a speech at Fort Armstrong in Sauk territory enjoining the warrior to be ruled henceforth by Keo-kuk, Black Hawk was overcome by rage. "In this speech he said much that was mortifying to my feelings, and I made an *indignant reply*" (150), says Black Hawk. Later he recanted, but at an Independence Day celebration shortly before his death, he apparently attributed all his woes to Keokuk: "I was once a great warrior," he said. "I am now poor. Keokuk has been the cause of my present situation" (156). Though Keokuk certainly represented the internal opposition to Black Hawk's intransigence (and grew rich, fat, and alcoholic with white support), he can hardly be saddled with responsibility for caus-ing all Black Hawk's miseries. It is consistent with Black Hawk's tendency toward personification, however, that he came to see his rival as the epitome of those practices (such as cowardice and deser-tion) that he so deeply despised.

In another instance, too, his judgment must be challenged, and challenged precisely because here again he fails to apply his usual transpositional code to a human situation. Near the end of the auto-biography, Black Hawk mentions that his views on a number of social issues facing the Americans had been solicited during his travels throughout the East. Black Hawk and his entourage were celebrities in places like Albany and New York where he was greeted by crowds of thousands. Here he claims his views were sought on "the subject of colonizing the *negroes.*" Though Black Hawk says he did not answer many of these inquiries at the time, due to the lack of a proper inter-preter, he now feels ready to present his plan "as to the best method of getting clear of these people." His answer to the problem, which he says he hopes will be adopted, is the following:

Let the free states remove all the *male* negroes within their limits, to the slave states—then let our Great Father [the President] buy all the *female* negroes in the slave states, between the ages of twelve and twenty, and sell them to the people of the free states, for a term of years—say, those under fifteen, until they are twenty-one—and those of, and over fifteen, for five years—and continue to buy all the females in the slave states, as soon as they arrive at the age of twelve, and take them to the free states, and dispose of them in the same way as the first—and it will not be long before the country is clear of the *black skins,* about which, I am told, they have been talking, for a long time; and for which they have expended a large amount of money.

I have no doubt but our Great Father would willingly do his part in accomplishing this object for his children—as he could not lose much by it, and would make them all happy. If the free states did not want them all for servants, we would take the balance in our nation to help our women make corn! (152–53)

He claims that his plan is the product of "many inquiries on the subject," and it clearly reflects the influence of white racism on his thinking. But this passage is hard to decipher, raising so many questions that it has been virtually ignored by later commentators, including Arnold Krupat, David Murray, and Donald Jackson (who elsewhere provides extensive and illuminating footnotes on puzzling material in the text).

What does this passage contribute to the discourse about nation and what is a contemporary reader to make of it? Typical of his nationalistic thinking, Black Hawk approaches the issue of "unwanted peoples" as a challenge to the nation, and he advises intervention at the federal level. He seems to understand the difference between "slave states" and "free states," suggesting that his view of the United States has become more precise. As usual, he presents his own "nation" as a distinct (and parallel) entity, where he suggests the Sauk might take any black servants the Americans don't want and use them to help the Indian women make corn.

The distressing aspect of this passage is that Black Hawk ignores the obvious parallels between "negroes" (as outsiders inside) and Indians. The geographical displacement he advocates is eerily reminiscent of Indian removals. A very suggestive piece of information is given by Nichols who claims that rumors were circulating in 1831 and 1832 (just prior to the Black Hawk War); these rumors asserted that the whites planned to castrate all the Indian males and then bring in "a horde of Negro men" (106) to breed with the Sauk women to produce a new stock of slaves, in the process also diluting the Sauk people. According to Nichols, not everyone believed these rumors, but it certainly seems likely that Black Hawk (and I suspect this is Black Hawk more than either Patterson or LeClaire here) is somehow recalling this rumor a year later when he dictates the autobiography. The structural similarity between the two stories is too close to be accidental.

But how serious *is* Black Hawk in this passage? The autobiography is full of Black Hawk's sarcasm and bleak humor.[10] Keith Basso's *Portraits of "The Whiteman"* offers wonderful examples of the way Apaches make fun of white people by imitating and parodying their actions. It may well be that Black Hawk's "modest proposal" about how to deal with the "black skins" is an example of such a parody. Certainly when one learns that the Sauk had thought themselves threatened with a similar experiment in racial engineering, it makes sense to entertain the possibility that he is mocking whites more than dehumanizing blacks.

Alternately, Black Hawk might not be calling attention to the inhumanity of white behavior so much as suggesting that such a crisis within the Indian nation would be handled expediently without so much anguish. Perhaps he is indulging in a moment of amused superiority, as though he were saying: we Indians could take care of this problem with no trouble. Indians had always had "slaves," in the sense of people kidnapped in war situations and forced to do manual labor, but they were usually either traded at some point or adopted into the tribe. There was no permanent class of slaves. The Cherokee, of course, had become so acculturated in Georgia that the wealthier members of the tribe had plantations and used black slaves for labor. But, according to Theda Perdue, most Cherokee in the early 1830s opposed the slave trade and advocated "colonization," that is, sending blacks back to Africa where they could live in a nation of their own.

Ultimately, this passage remains opaque to a modern reader. It provides a salient example of a place where Black Hawk seems to depart from his usual transpositional practice in the sense that he denies the parallel humanity of blacks and Indians. On the other hand, if he is imaginatively assuming the role of the Americans—whom he strangely assumes to be *afflicted* by the problem of what to do with the Africans within their borders—perhaps he is still operating in some sense transpositionally. It must be said that the advice he gives seems completely impractical, a factor which in my mind tips the balance toward interpreting this as an example of Black Hawk's sarcasm. I am further persuaded to this view by the rather sardonic sentence: "I have no doubt but our Great Father would willingly do his part in accomplishing this object for his children—as he could not lose much by it, and would make them all happy."

Whatever Black Hawk really thought of the old Indian fighter Andrew Jackson, however, he did tend to see him as a personification of the American nation, and thus he might well assume that Jackson would do what was best for the people just as Black Hawk himself would. At several points in Black Hawk's circuitous travels, the two leaders were both present in the same city. Of one such occasion, in Baltimore, Black Hawk comments: "Our Great Father was there at the same time, and seemed to be much liked by his white children, who flocked around him (as they had done us), to shake him by the hand" (146–47).

The final irony is that, precisely because he at first refused the terms of subjugation issued by Jackson and fought against the United States, Black Hawk became for some a personification of (native) American, not just Indian, virtue. His son, Whirling Thunder, was also enormously popular, and many saw him as an embodiment of the beautiful savage. As one journal described him: "Had his countenance not been wanting in that peculiar expression which emanates from a cultivated intellect and which education alone can give, we could have looked upon him as the living personification of our *beau ideal* of manly beauty" (quoted in Jackson ed., 13).

It is relatively easy to comprehend how Black Hawk in his own text becomes a personification of the Sauk; more surprising is the fact that in the aftermath of the Black Hawk War his image was incorporated into the iconography of American national identity as well. One principal way this was accomplished was through portraiture. George Catlin, known for his precise and unromantic drawings of

Native Americans, sketched Black Hawk when he was in chains at Jefferson Barracks, and his portrait, probably the one most frequently reproduced, is now in the Smithsonian, a sign that Black Hawk has become an American monument.

Other portrait painters, such as Samuel M. Brookes, also took advantage of the opportunity to use the captives as models. Robert M. Sully spent six weeks with them at Fortress Monroe, painting not only Black Hawk but also his son and the Indian known as the Prophet, who had disastrously misinformed Black Hawk about British support for his rebellion. John Wesley Jarvis's stunning portrait of Black Hawk side by side with Whirling Thunder, now in the Thomas Gilcrease Institute of American History and Art in Tulsa, Oklahoma, graces the cover of *After Columbus: The Smithsonian Chronicle of the North American Indians*. Later Charles Bird King did a solemn and intelligent-looking likeness which hangs in Newport, Rhode Island, probably the least known (according to Jackson) of all the Black Hawk portraits. From Washington to Tulsa to Newport, Black Hawk has become a symbol of America's past, inextricably part of our national identity.

What do these portraits convey? Some present the old warrior as a savage, imprisoned in his otherness, with his partially shaved head, pierced ears and native dress. He almost always has a firm, intransigent expression and is seen looking off to right or to left, as though unable to confront the present moment. He appears to be looking back to the past or stoically surveying his people's dismal future. Several of the portraits show him dressed in Western costume, however. According to Cyrenus Cole, Robert M. Sully portrayed the Sauk leader as though he were a senior southern statesman.

The Jarvis portrait is particularly interesting to contemplate for in it Black Hawk wears a high-collared white shirt and frock coat, while Whirling Thunder, his son, standing to his right, is given the naked throat and shoulder more typically associated with Native Americans.[11] Both faces are bronzed and the similarity between them is striking, but reading from left to right, it seems that the younger man, rather than being Black Hawk's son, is Black Hawk himself at a younger age, epitomizing his Indian past. The older Black Hawk, then, dressed in Western clothing (indeed locked into a garment whose neck band might almost be mistaken for an iron fetter) represents a future of enforced acculturation.

Unlike Sully's and Jarvis's, Catlin's work in its ethnographic emphasis reduces the romantic heroism of the Indians he painted. Most of the others, however, make their subjects heroic in a sense, heroes of a narrative already framed by circumstances beyond their control, by a known future in which "American" values will absorb the native past and reprocess it as part of an American identity. Black Hawk's bald head and sickle nose might even suggest a comparison with Hawthorne's version of the American eagle holding its barbed arrows. These effects are due in part to the medium and context in which Black Hawk was painted, in part to the mind-set of the painters, and thus they may be compared to the translation of the Indian into an Anglo-American text and the redeployment of that text in numerous subsequent treatments of "native" American character.

Indeed, in 1938 Cyrenus Cole made precisely this point in his bitter work commemorating the anniversary of Black Hawk's death. After describing Loredo Taft's forty-two foot statue of the old Indian warrior, he added: "Today Black Hawk has been completely incorporated into the American Pantheon.[12] Even the postage machine at the local courthouse automatically stamps its outgoing mail 'Blackhawk — Ogle County.' Illinois has much veneration for the Sauk now that they are gone and with them their claim. Taft's statue, floodlit and a ghostly white after sundown, looms larger than any other monument commemorating that dirty little war" (295).

The process of incorporating Black Hawk as an Indian into a particular view of national identity did not take long to get underway. Almost immediately after the end of hostilities, there was an outpouring of literature about Black Hawk and the Black Hawk War. In 1838 Benjamin Drake wrote *The Life and Adventures of Black Hawk*. Drake did not see Black Hawk himself as a hero but wrote the book, so he tells us, to gratify the curiosity of the many Americans who did. Drake preferred to see the Sauk leader as a product of American history, the "common man" lifted to heroic heights by virtue of events he could not himself have determined.

One of the most curious and resonant examples of the appropriation of Black Hawk for national purposes is Elbert H. Smith's epic, *Ma-Ka-Tai-She-Kia-Kiak; or Black Hawk and Scenes in the West, A National Poem* (1848). Though published in New York, this three-hundred-page text frames the story of Black Hawk with Smith's travels to the Midwest and his residence there. Much of it, like Patterson's 1882 edition of the autobiography, dwells on particular places in the Midwest that are dealt with in glowing detail, whether or not they have much to do with Black Hawk himself. (Patterson's appendices on midwestern cities are basically promotional settlement literature.) But the central focus of Smith's epic is the Indian as a personification of American values and identity. It begins:

> Americans! magnanimous of soul!
> With hearts as warm, as generous and as free
> As that pure atmosphere in which ye breathe;
> Come, listen, while I sing of one poor man,
> The self-taught hero, aboriginal,
> Of the Indian race his genealogy—
> *Illustrious,* so deserving of renown,
> And causes which impelled him to the war.
> (*emphasis added*)

In this Virgilian opening Smith invites his readers to see themselves as bound to the story of the Indian by two themes: magnanimity or greatness of soul, which, as will develop, is a quality he also associates with Black Hawk, and the free, pure "atmosphere" of the American landscape. As in Drake's account, Black Hawk is an image of the common man, "the self-taught hero, aboriginal," but for Smith he is at the same time heroic, illustrious, deserving of renown. All these are qualities that make "Americans." Like the *Aeneid,* which Smith's poem consciously invokes, this poem is about the founding of a nation.

Smith does not go directly to Black Hawk and the Black Hawk War but surrounds that story with a national narrative in which other Indians are also provided with a place in the epic development of American identity. A particularly clear example of the way America is seen to absorb its aborigines into its "imagined community" is the story he tells of Pontiac, a precursor to Black Hawk. Pontiac was an Ottawa warrior who led an attack on the British in 1763, beginning with a surprise move against Detroit. The Indian tribes were facing increasing encroachment by white settlement; the British under Lord Jeffrey Amherst had undertaken a policy of retrenchment in terms of gifts and were instead insisting upon a harsh program of Indian control. The British were not prepared for organized military action on the part of the Indians and lost a great many forts before reasserting their control. Philip Fisher sees this as the last moment of real possibility for Indian resistance to acculturation, calling the uprising "the moment of a counter-attempt at genuine national Indian identity under the leadership of Pontiac who is, in effect, a failed George Washington for a possible, but now canceled Indian nation" (31).

Elbert Smith, however, gives a different picture of Pontiac's Rebellion, seeing in him the beginning of the end of one identity but celebrating his part in the creation of another.

> Live on, O mighty prince of Ottawa!
> Live in thy people's hearts, while they remain—
> Until they fall, and dwindle out of sight!
> Thy memory, Chief! thy country has embalmed!
> They call their children for thee, Pontiac!
> (37)

Nothing could be clearer than Smith's sense of Indians here as "vanishing Americans" whose national identities will be, indeed already have been, incorporated into a new American identity. "Thy country" is no longer an Indian nation but the United States which will "embalm" and carry forward the memory of its native past while Indians themselves "fall, and dwindle out of sight!" The future belongs to the children of the whites who are here (rather surprisingly) named after Pontiac, a personification not of treachery but of the glories of republican resistance.

In canto IV, xix, where Smith has finally moved into his discussion of Black Hawk himself, he similarly presents the Sauk warrior as a personification of 'native' American virtue. He calls Black Hawk

"Nature's own child, and own primeval offspring, / For liberty and equal rights contending, / On the broad base of true republicanism" (185). Strangely, Smith seems to see no contradiction in connecting Native Americans who fought against whites with the Euro-American project of creating a white national allegory. Though I have some trouble accepting Arnold Krupat's decision to call Black Hawk's autobiography "comic" (in spite of his insistence that comedy here is not meant to imply humor but to describe this text's reinforcing effect on white readers), I can certainly see the appropriateness of calling Elbert Smith's epic poem prevailingly "comic." The constant use of exclamation points (which, as far as one can tell, is in no way meant to suggest irony) gives one the impression that Smith is simply delighted by all that he recounts, just as he is delighted by the Midwest itself, its fresh lakes and green countryside teeming with fish and game.

Smith is convinced that Black Hawk was unjustly treated but in some form justice, he believes, is nevertheless served. The "magnanimity" mentioned in the first canto as characteristic of true Americans will somehow triumph as we learn to revere our Native American past. Perhaps only in the final lines of the poem does Smith suggest genuine uncertainty about his progressive vision where he says:

> Sleep thou in glory's bed,
> In quiet, mighty chief of nation red!
> Alone had wisdom in thyself to know,
> And *magnanimity* to vindicate just claims,
> Thy people's rights; appealing to the sword
> The last resort, when efforts else had failed;
> Ill-fated hour, and desperate cause, though just;
> Hurling defiance 'gainst gigantic power;
> Who tyranny in every shape condemned;
> While Dodge and Doty, Tallmadge, prudent men,
> Far in the north, and Renolds [*sic*], Duncan, Ford,
> Govern successively this land of thine,
> Of Nit-o-me-na and Omaint-si-ar-nah!
> (*emphasis added*, 298–99)

The "prudent men" Smith mentions—Thomas Ford, Joseph Duncan, Colonel Henry Dodge, John Reynolds—were all political figures in the Midwest, several of them regional governors who had fought in the Black Hawk War. Yet when Smith introduces them here at the end, they fail to evoke the awe we might expect. They are merely "prudent men," whereas Black Hawk in his imprudence seems a Miltonic or, perhaps more appropriately, Romantic figure "hurling defiance 'gainst gigantic power." By ending the poem with Indian names for Black Hawk's territory and by calling it "this land of thine," Smith leaves his readers with a sombre message, rather discordant with the triumphal march of the rest of the poem.

As we look at the qualities Elbert Smith associates with Black Hawk—true republicanism, egalitarianism, self-dependence, wisdom, magnanimity, forbearance, resistance to tyranny—it is easy to see the connection with themes of national identity given an Indian face on national medals, coins, magazines, warships, and other signifiers of nineteenth-century American culture. And perhaps Smith's poem should be taken no more seriously than these. But upon reflection we might also say that many of these qualities *are* present in the voice of Black Hawk we hear in the autobiography, which is usually the voice of a man who does try "to vindicate just claims" whether they be the claims of his people or the claims of others.

In many ways, the transpositional discourse of the autobiography, rather than being simply naively ethnocentric, is exocentric: a sending out of the center into an imaginary space from which Black Hawk himself, since he cannot read the text, is exiled. The text constructs a nation and with it a national identity, a synecdochic self. In this textual space two nations—America and the Sauk—meet on comparatively equal footing, which, for all Elbert Smith's Indian hero worship, is not the case in *Ma-Ka-Tai-She-Kia-Kiak; or Black Hawk and Scenes in the West, A National Poem.* The moral force of Black Hawk's transpositional argument, which refuses to accept politics as the art of the possible, reveals that national narrative is often simply a tale told by the winners, not in itself a justification for the displacement and murder of vast numbers of indigenous people over three centuries.

5. The Terms of George Copway's Surrender

The Life History, and Travels of Kah-Ge-Ga-Gah-Bowh (1847), by George Copway (Ojibwa), is at the other extreme from *The Life of Black Hawk*, presenting an almost textbook case of subjugated discourse both in its evidence of political longing and in its disturbing implications of self-division and even despair. The text itself is far more overtly problematic in terms of its "authorship" than the multiply composed Black Hawk text, despite the fact that Kah-Ge-Ga-Gah-Bowh (Copway) was literate and did not need to rely upon the services of a translator. Here again, however, we must think seriously about how to apply the notion of "monologism" if it is to be understood as an alien discourse imposed upon "the mind of an Indian," for these two hypostases—monologism and the mind of an Indian—are everywhere entangled in Copway's work.

Like Black Hawk, Copway was born into an Indian tribe, the Rice Lake Band of Canada West, and grew up learning the lore of his people. Interestingly, both tribes claimed identity through the Crane Totem, and both Copway and Black Hawk narrate the story of the migration of the Sauk, who were part of the larger Chippewa group, from a location in Canada to one much farther south. As Black Hawk recounts his entry into full manhood with a killing and a scalp, Copway marks his by telling a story of hunting and the killing of a bear. But there almost all similarity ends, for Copway looks back upon his days as a hunter with seeming disdain. "I loved to hunt the bear, the beaver, and the deer; but now, the occupation has no charms for me. I will now take the goose quill for my *bow,* and its point for my *arrow*" (32). Whereas Black Hawk distrusts writing, and is driven only in extremity to preserve his Indian identity through the medium of a written text, Copway urges his reader to see him as a text, a personification of Indian progress toward acculturation. The very premise of the book, then, asserts the superiority of that monologism, that form of western progressive discourse, which the texture of the text will confound.

Unlike Black Hawk, Copway doesn't seem to know quite who he is, and thus he represents what David Murray calls "a certain stage in Indian writing, in which the enabling means of expression, and of the creation of a self, are also deeply implicated in the destruction of any self rooted in the traditional past" (79). The two times of the text, the past which must be forgotten even as it is remembered, and the present which must be constructed as an overcoming and a forgetting, dismember the unities of nation and self.

Copway's own lack of psychological and cultural coherence is reflected in the text's confusing array of premises and styles. He begins by both asserting and denying his authorship, for instance. "It would be presumptious in one, who has but recently been brought out of a wild and savage state; and who has since received but three years' schooling, to undertake, without any assistance, to publish to the world a work of any kind. It is but a few years since I began to speak the English language" (vi). His claim is that he planned and wrote the work himself but that a "friend" (referred to as a man but possibly his wife) corrected the most egregious grammatical errors, "leaving the unimportant ones wholly untouched, that my own style may be exhibited as truly as possible." Here the announcement of "mistakes" serves the purpose of establishing the self-in-transition as "authentic."

Copway's insistence on stylistic identity, however, makes little sense. The text is an amalgam of labored English phrasing (as in the first sentence quoted above), high-flown Romantic rhetoric, sarcasm, earthy humor, quotations from canonical English poets, biblical reference, self-inflation, and self-denigration; withal it conveys little real sense of Copway as "one of Nature's children," the description he proffers in his opening self-presentation.[1] If anything, Copway comes across here as a prime example of Homi Bhabha's category of the mimic as one of the parodists of history: a man who, despite his intentions, "inscribe[s] the colonial text erratically" in a narrative "that refuses to be representational," at least so far as the aim of that representation is "the desire to emerge as authentic, . . . through a process of writing and repetition" ("Mimicry," 128–29).

Problems beset the reader who attempts to find in Copway an authorial voice, even as what we have called (using Krupat's phrase) "a willed line of informed approach." These problems are partly spelled out in the most complete discussion of Copway's life and work, Donald B. Smith's "The Life of George Copway of Kah-ge-ga-gah-bowh (1818–1869)—and a Review of His Writings." Smith believes that "evidence in the manuscript indicates that he [Copway] did supply the information himself" (18). Though identifying his role as one of supplying "information" might lead one to look for other presences in the text such as a scriptor or an editor, Smith shies away from concluding that someone else actually composed most of the English sentences, preferring to believe that "the defrocked minister [Copway] had an acute market sense—he took advantage of his Christian Indian identity, and at the age of twenty-nine wrote his life story for a white audience" (17).

Nevertheless, Smith advises "Reader beware!" and for good reason. In any given passage the writing may be Copway's or it may not be. When Copway's autobiography appeared in 1847 (self-published and registered December 9, 1846, in Albany, New York), it became quite popular and went through seven editions. On the strength of its popularity, Copway traveled through the Eastern United States giving a series of lectures. He was apparently a dynamic speaker. As one journalist described him: "His voice was strong, clear, and full, with nothing whatever disagreeable in enunciation. With a fine commanding figure, and suitable gestures, and a thorough acquaintance with his subject, he appeared and spoke to great advantage" (quoted in Smith, 19). But even this receptive member of his audience had to admit: "To be sure he did not evidence a knowledge of the strict rules which govern the English language, but the deficiency in this particular, was more than compensated by his figures of rhetoric and his thrilling incidents" (19). Such reservations concerning Copway's mastery of his adopted language became even stronger after he lost his reputation. By late 1850 his public had grown tired of George Copway, and his speech at the Frankfurt Conference for World Peace in Germany dismayed even the man who invited him, Elihu Burritt, who wrote: "the Indian Chief Copway made a long, windy, wordy speech, extremely ungrammatical and incoherent" (quoted in Smith, 24).

Though the autobiography is by no means flawless, and it is incoherent, its presentation suggests if anything an over-conscientious imitation of nineteenth-century literary modes. It is hard to connect its style(s) with these descriptions of Copway's stumbling grammar in his public speeches. Take, for instance, another passage from the "Word to the Reader":

All along, have I felt my great deficiency; and my inadequacy for such an undertaking. I would fain hope, however, that the kind Reader will throw the mantle of charity over errors of every kind. I am a stranger in a strange land! And often, when the sun is sinking in the western sky, I think of my former home; my heart yearns for the loved of other days, and tears flow like summer rain. How the heart of the wanderer and pilgrim, after long years of absence, beats and his eyes fill, as he catches a glance of the hills of his nativity, and reflects upon the time when he pressed the lips of a Mother, or Sister, now cold in death. Should I live, this painful pleasure will yet be mine. (vi–vii)

Though the punctuation in this passage (for instance, in the first sentence) is nonstandard, the rhetoric is all too recognizable as a version of the romantic sentimentalism to be found in many newspapers and magazines of the day. Read aloud, this passage would hardly strike most auditors as the composition of one who learned English but recently or who needed further training in how to put a sentence together.

One possibility is that Copway's wife, a white woman named Elizabeth Howell, composed sentences such as these. Smith mentions that she published a number of articles in Canada and the United States. "Lacking a good command of written English himself, George valued her assistance and advice. His well-read consort possibly suggested the quotations from Shakespeare and Pope" (14). On the other hand, Smith describes her writing style as "easy and agreeable," terms which do not quite capture the effect of *The Life of Kah-Ge-Ga-Gah-Bowh*, much of which seems labored to a modern reader.

The fact that Copway's first writing project was a translation (of the Gospel According to Luke from English to Ojibwa) is suggestive. His works (which in addition to the autobiography include ethnographic studies of the Ojibwa and travel sketches) contain many Ojibwa words and even some picture writing; Copway is careful to inform his white audience how to read them, while, as we will see at a later point, he insists upon the untranslatability of many Indian expressions. My point is that, unlike Black Hawk, he seems very much aware of the text as a mediation between reader and writer, and often he tries to second-guess his reader's response.

For example, at one point he recounts a long dream in which he saw his cousin leaving the earth for the afterlife. When he awoke, one of his stepbrothers arrived to tell him of his cousin's death. Many Indian writings contain such material. (Black Hawk too mentions that reliable information came to him first through dreams.) But George Copway feels the necessity to apologize for this material in the text, seemingly attempting to mediate between Indian and white culture. He says: "My readers will, I trust, excuse me for having inflicted upon them this dream. It is even now so vivid in my recollection, and being somewhat curious and peculiar, that I have ventured to give it. It is but a dream, and I wish it to go just for what it is worth, and no more" (151).

But what is it worth? What does the author wish us to believe it is worth? Clearly, Copway (for by default we must somehow take him as the "author") is of two minds about this. In an earlier passage he seems to be soliciting acceptance of dream material while at the same time denying that he any longer relies upon such superstition. In recounting his early life before his conversion, he comments: "I relied much on my dream, for then I knew no better. But, however little reliance can be placed in dreams, yet may not the Great Spirit take this method, sometimes, to bring about some good result?" (51).

This passage reveals the sometimes abject aspect of subjugated discourse which I have chosen to call Copway's "surrender." He first asserts a temporal distinction: then I relied on dreams, now I know better. Almost immediately, however, he equivocates with words like "but," "however," "yet," "sometimes," "some." In one sense Copway hasn't accepted the sacrifice of his earlier beliefs and refuses to turn them over. The double temporality of what was once believed and of what is now believed, because both are present simultaneously, creates an instability which is both the problem and to some degree the enriching potential of this form of subjugated discourse, because it preserves the frisson of *ressentiment* and, following Rey Chow, we can see that, like the gaze of the native, it "bears witness to its own demolition."

It is significant that this passage is immediately followed by a non sequitur, a discussion of the introduction of swearing (forswearing?) by white men. It ends angrily: "I have seen some *white faces*, with *black hearts*, who took delight in teaching them [the Indians] to profane the name of God. O merciless, heartless, and wicked white men, may a merciful God forgive you your enormous turpitude and recklessness!" (51). The abject apology concerning the value of dreams, because of the sacrifice of earlier beliefs it entails, seems to elicit the subsequent angry denunciation of white people who lead Indians to profane what before they held sacred in more ways than one.

Throughout the autobiography Copway veers wildly between adulating white culture and denouncing whites for perfidy. Donald Smith comments that "the contradictions of the man abound" (6), and indeed it would be hard to conclude otherwise. A Canadian by birth, George Copway migrated to the United States and founded a newspaper called *Copway's American Indian*. In England he claimed to be proud of his Canadian / British heritage. In his autobiography he expresses considerable bitterness about the Canadian government and presents America as the locus of his new self. Though in some ways a foreigner in the United States, he joined the Know-Nothings, a nativist (that is, nationalist, not Indian) Euro-American group that denounced both Catholics and immigrants.

As Dale T. Knobel has admirably demonstrated, the Order of United Americans and their ilk (dubbed Know-Nothings by the press) were quite friendly to Indians in the 1850s, and several of their American Party political leaders—Millard Fillmore, Senator John B. Thompson, and Congressman Thomas R. Whitney—used their political clout to oppose Indian removal. Many of the secret societies which were part of this movement used Indian names (Order of the

Red Men, Choctaws), Indian icons, and Indian titles (sachems, chiefs) in their rituals. The Indian was useful to them as an example of native republican virtue and the importance of slow acculturation through environment and institutions.[2] In 1852 George Copway was voted into the New York Chapter of the O.U.A. as a "real North American."

Copway, for his part, made speeches and wrote articles throughout the 1850s supporting the Know-Nothings' "American Party" and displaying a heightened sense of patriotism. Knobel describes his behavior at this time in these terms: "He loaded his effusive, romantic prose with paeans to America—to home and soil—and to the natural patriotism of the original 'native Americans.' 'All natives love their country,' Copway editorialized in the *American Indian*, 'I adore my own soil. . . . Did I say because it was my own country, yes!'" (195). Copway enjoyed the laughter he elicited in his public speeches when he called himself a "native American." By 1851 he seems to have forgotten his earlier devotion to the British crown.

Similarly, Copway vacillated in his religious orientation as well. In his written works, he sometimes presents native medicine (and the sacred medicine bag) as examples of ignorant superstition. Yet near the end of his life he returned to Canada, settling in Quebec and performing miraculous cures with bark, leaves, flowers, and roots. In a final grand volte-face, after a lifetime of associating himself with Methodism, and after joining the violently anti-Catholic Know-Nothings, Copway became a Roman Catholic shortly before he died.

One index of Copway's vacillations, symbolic of the circumstances which gave rise to his use of subjugated discourse, is his attitude toward elders. He is by turns extravagantly filial and covertly anti-authoritarian. Like Apess and Black Hawk, he is at pains to tell us that his father, whose grandfather founded the Rice Lake Band, was an elevated man in the tribe, a hereditary chief. "My father still lives; he is from sixty-five to seventy years old, and is one of the chiefs of Rice Lake Indian Village" (15). He also dutifully recounts a long speech that his father makes to him to the effect that he must always reverence the aged. "'If you reverence the aged, many will be glad to hear of your name,' were the words of my father" (27).

Yet unlike Black Hawk and Apess, Copway repeatedly found himself in conflict with his elders. He was charged with embezzling money from funds raised to establish an Indian school. After this he was regarded with suspicion by the Ojibwa and expelled from the Canadian Conference of the Wesleyan Methodist Church. Twice he was jailed for debt. Even in his early years as a young minister-trainee, he struck some as headstrong and vain, refusing to follow humbly in the footsteps of older and wiser men. In a key incident he compromised, by misrepresenting, both the governor-general and the famous mixed-blood preacher Peter Jones whom at one time he called his spiritual father.

Significantly, when he later came to propose that the American Indians unite in Dakota and petition the government for state status, he advocated removing the power from the tribal elders and investing it instead in younger educated Indians like himself. In his 1850 work *The Traditional History and Characteristic Sketches of the Ojibway Nation*, he argues: "Gradually the chiefship, which is hereditary, would cease to exist, for this is one of the greatest barriers to their civilization. By giving the rule and authority to the well educated, their improvement would be rapid, but, heretofore, the elder Indians have ruled, and their prejudicial views of education, have ever unfitted them to become a fit medium of instruction to their people" (277).

Throughout his life, George Copway sought power, and he was not above misrepresenting himself (and others) in order to obtain it. In his travels through the United States, he claimed to be an Indian chief and a Methodist minister when in fact he was never accorded the status of a chief in his tribe and he had already been expelled from the Methodist ministry. He once wrote a letter to a Baptist minister in Sault Sainte Marie saying that he would soon travel west in the company of Miss Jenny Lind, the "Swedish Nightingale," and the American poet Nathaniel Willis, a fantasy Copway created entirely on his own. As Donald Smith comments, "Continually he twisted facts to place himself in the best possible light" (21). He even plagiarized an epic poem entitled *The Ojibway Conquest* written by former Indian agent Julius Taylor Clark.[3]

For all of these reasons, it is difficult to know where George Copway is in his texts and who "the author" might be taken to be. David

Murray's comment about Indian publications in the nineteenth century, that they are inevitably "stage-managed" by whites, seems appropriate to his case, not because translators and editors intervened in any clear way but because his mimicry continually performs the presence of white power as a frame. Here it may be characterized in the terms Fredric Jameson uses, paraphrasing Gramsci, to describe "subalternity," namely, as "the feelings of mental inferiority and habits of subservience and obedience which necessarily and structurally develop in situations of domination" (76). But this is not all there is to say about George Copway's work because it also evidences the return of the repressed in characteristically discordant moments where his arguments seem to fall apart or exemplify the opposite of their declared intention. This too is a feature of the discourse of subjugation.

Having established that Copway was a problematic figure and that his texts are distinctly fractured and polyvocal, I will turn, then, in the remainder of this chapter to examining, first, his form of subjugated discourse, with all of its wild vacillations, particularly in passages where Copway characterizes "nation" as "culture." Second, and more briefly, we will take note of Copway's views of the nation-state and his vision of an Indian political entity within the borders of the larger nation. Finally, we will once again consider "the subject of America" in Copway's self-presentation as the personification of American virtue, the ironies of that representation, and its potential for challenging postmodern notions of national identity as "the people in flux."

It will be remembered that in chapter 1 "subjugated discourse" was characterized by its insistent attention to differential power relations in a mode that is metropolitan, particularizing, interventionist, vertical, and strategic. Copway's work follows this definition closely. Indeed, his emphasis on vertical movement, for example, is so pervasive that it might almost be seen as parodic. At one point Kah-ge-ga-gah-bowh visits Boston and views the city and its surround from the top of the State House. His vista is filled with the works of the white man: towns, ships, steamboats, railroad cars, and factories. Predictably his feelings are mixed. "As I saw the prosperity of the white man,

I said, while tears filled my eyes, 'Happy art thou, O Israel, who is like unto thee, *O people saved by the Lord!*'" (134). Nostalgia for a lost Indian past afflicts him (he includes a poem purportedly of his own composition on this topic). Yet when he then goes down and visits the Missionary Rooms of the American Board, where some Indian artifacts are displayed—bead work, moccasins, porcupine quills, and war clubs—he thinks to himself, "if Brother Greene had seen as much of war clubs as I had (for I have seen them stained with blood and notched according to the number of individuals slain), he would conceal them from every eye" (135).

The fundamentally hierarchical nature of subjugated rhetoric, as opposed to the horizontal dimension of transpositional rhetoric, is everywhere present in Copway's discourses on the nation, by which he *usually* (but not always) means the cultural community. The whites (whom he calls here the "people saved by the Lord") are represented by their cultural artifacts as the Indians are by theirs. Copway's gaze, however, never stays still but is always traveling up and down, as he switches perspective, assessing one culture by the terms of the never equally powerful other. Symbolically, he views his surroundings in Boston from the *bottom of Bunker Hill* one minute (133) and from the top of the State House the next (134).

Similarly, Copway's self-presentation is by turns abject and supercilious. He calls himself "an unlearned and feeble Red man—a mere worm of the dust" (93) when he is first invited to join the Methodist ministry, and his use of the worm sounds more typically salvationist than Apess's because it is paired with the adjectives "unlearned" and "feeble." But this view of himself is then overwritten; for instance, when he tells the reader of his appointment by the President of the General Council of the Ojibwa Nation, July 4, 1845, as the primary agent to raise subscriptions for a manual labor school. There follows an ego-boosting transcription of the document of his appointment in which he is presented as anything but an unlearned and feeble red man.

As Copway surveys the body of Christian Indians who have come together at this time to petition the British-Canadian government for help, he inevitably thinks in vertical terms. "Never was I more delighted than with the appearance of this body. As I sat and looked at them, I contrasted their former (degraded), with their present (elevated) condition. The Gospel, I thought, had done all this" (194). The words in parentheses encapsulate Copway's emphasis on verticality and upward mobility. When Copway leaves Canada to seek greater opportunities in the United States, he again thinks in vertical terms of "raising up" the downtrodden. His litany is like a ladder, rising from the foul rag-and-bone shop of Indian reservation life to the stars of his imagination.

The Menomenees in Wisconsin, the Winebagoes and Potawatamees in Iowa, the warlike nations of the Sacs and Foxes, the Osages, Pawnees, Mandans, Kansas, Creeks, Omahas, Otoes, Delawares, Iowas, and a number of others elsewhere, must perish as did their brethren in the Eastern States, unless the white man send them the Gospel, and the blessings of education. There is field enough for all denominations to labor in, without interfering with each other. It is too late in the day to assert that the Indians cannot be raised up out of their degraded state, and educated for God and heaven. (217)

To some extent, of course, this language is biblical; "raising up" is something God does in recognition of the faithful. However, the persistence of hierarchical language, of lowering and raising, bottom and top, is not so characteristic of other converted Indians such as William Apess or Sarah Winnemucca, for instance. More than a theme in Copway's work, upward mobility becomes a performative of cultural desire. As an Indian and for Indians, he insists upon moving *up,* all the while attempting to obscure or overwrite his many real descents. In contrast, Apess's autobiography tells of many backslidings. Though Apess also seeks education and acculturation, he keeps both ends in play, so to speak, self-consciously mixing transpositional and subjugated modes of discourse.

The tension in Copway, by contrast, is part of what Homi Bhabha calls "dissemiNation": "Cultural difference is to be found where the 'loss' of meaning enters, as a cutting edge, into the representation of the fullness of the demands of culture" (*Nation and Narration,* 313). When Copway speaks of nation, it is at once an hereditary boundary, a construct born of his migration, and a mythical vision at the political horizon. Such confusions bleed into the national image, and, to quote Bhabha again: "the national narrative [becomes] the site of an ambivalent identification: a margin of the uncertainty of cultural meaning that may become the space for an agonistic minority position" (317).

The shock of oxymoron, of "painful pleasure" as Copway terms it (vii), provides a moment of fruitful reflection for the reader wishing to ponder what Jameson calls "the national allegory" implicit in this example of Indian writing. Though one may question Jameson's insistence that "the story of the private individual destiny is always an allegory of the embattled situation of the public third-world culture and society" (69), one cannot help but read Copway as simultaneously writing about himself and about the agonistic situation of "the nation." Indeed, the dedication of *The Life of Kah-Ge-Ga-Gah-Bowh* calls attention to this very simultaneity of reference: "To the Clergy and Laity of the American and British Dominions, this brief History of a Child of the Forest and of His Nation, is most respectfully and affectionately Inscribed by the Author" (n.p.). In the original typefaces, the enlarged words are "THE CLERGY AND LAITY," "HISTORY OF A CHILD OF THE FOREST," and "HIS NATION." Copway includes many passages from the autobiography in *The Traditional History and Characteristic Sketches of the Ojibway Nation* (1850)[4] (called by Smith "the first tribal history in English by a North American Indian," 22), thus presenting himself as both ethnographer and exemplar. However, behind the story of national reconstruction one hears another story of dismemberment and loss.

Though in personifying the Ojibwa in himself, Copway adopts the posture of the representational figure, it is also true that self and (Indian) nation become oxymoronic in his work where he speaks disparagingly of the practices of his people. This criticism stands in sharp contrast to Black Hawk's "I am a Sac. my forefather was a Sac! and all the nations call me a SAC!!" For Black Hawk the traditional past is still the locus of his identity; his sense of his own nation is fixed. In sharp contrast, Copway speaks of the past with horror. "In the days of our ignorance we used to dance around the fire. I shudder when I think of those days of our darkness" (34–35). This sense of horror (a response that Julia Kristeva calls "abjection" in the sense that it throws the self aside) converges with Copway's hints that Indian-ness is itself a cause of shame.

Take, for example, the story he tells in the autobiography about Ojibwa-Sioux conflicts which have been going on "from time immemorial" (114). One day the young Methodist minister is traveling through the forest with a group of his fellow Indians, speaking to them about religion. He recounts the following episode.

On our way, the Indians pointed to the battle grounds of the Ojebwas and the Sioux. How dreadful and awful was their description. The Chief, pointing to a certain spot, observed, "There I killed two Sioux, about thirteen winters ago; I cut open one of them; and when I reflected that the Sioux had cut up my own cousin, but a year before, I took out his heart, cut a piece from it, and swallowed it whole. I scooped some of his blood, while warm, with my hand, and drank as many draughts as the number of friends who had perished by their hands." As he spoke, the fierceness of the Indian gleamed from his countenance. (114)

Does "the fierceness of the Indian" refer to this particular Indian or to Indian-ness? The bulk of the evidence points to the latter. In *The Traditional History* Copway praises Christianity for bringing radical changes, using his typical vertical language: "It has dethroned error, and has enthroned truth. The fact is enough to convince any one of the unjustness and falsity of the common saying, that, 'the Indian will be Indian still' " (vii). Apparently, for Copway, it was preferable not to "be Indian still," in the sense of being equated with the ferocity of traditional Indian culture.

There are several moments in the autobiography, however, where Indian-ness is presented more positively. One occurs, surprisingly, in a passage about alcohol. It is commonplace in Indian publications in English to find denunciations of whites for their introduction of alcohol into Indian culture. Black Hawk's autobiography includes several, although apparently he was not above an occasional indulgence himself. George Copway curses the Evil Demon in a number of places in the autobiography, in one such declaring: "O! why did the white man give it to my poor fathers? None but fiends in human shape could have introduced it among us" (41). Therefore, the reader is likely to be caught off guard when Copway lightens the ideological load of his narrative by telling the following funny story.

A certain Indian once teased a Mrs. F. for whiskey, which he said was to cure his "big toe," that had been badly bruised the previous night. Mrs. F. said, "I am afraid you will drink it." He declared he would not drink it; and after much pleading, she handed him some; he took it, and looking first at his toe, and then at the liquor, alternately, all of a sudden he slipped the whiskey down his gullet, at the same time exclaiming, as he pointed to his toe, "There, *whiskey*, go down to my poor big toe." (52–53)

Though this story is framed by conventional Methodist sentiments concerning the evils of alcohol, its effect is not entirely offset by them. The wedge of humor here splits the narrative, making room for the emergence of a countereffect. Whose role in the story is the most engaging, we might ask, the teetotaler Mrs. F.'s or the wily Indian's who circumvents her? The story is reminiscent of trickster tales about the wily figure "Coyote." If the reader laughs appreciatively at the trick, can s / he then return to the dismal head-shaking over the folly of Indians set up by Copway's earlier stories about intoxication where it leads to tribal murder? This is only one of many places where the autobiography insists upon the superiority of European principles only to undercut that evaluation by what seem to be moments of genuine appreciation for the now derided Indian character. "Oh! the heights and depths of the goodness and mercy of God!" (53) he exclaims at the end of this page, quoting a brief passage from a poem called "The Indian's Regret."[5]

We might well call this passage an eruption of the uncanny, because what happens here, as elsewhere, is an incursion into the frame narrative of material that cannot easily be assimilated into the monologism of salvationist discourse. The past, one might say, in which traditional culture—not equatable with consumption of alcohol but identifiable perhaps as the centralizing of native resourcefulness and survival techniques—haunts the national narrative and challenges formulations such as "savage benightedness" or "Euro-Christian liberal enlightenment."

It is important to recognize that such moments of uncanny reflection are more disorienting for the reader than the simple, straightforward attacks upon white perfidy, for these can be made as appeals to the genuine spirit, the basic principles, of human justice embodied in the philosophy of the Enlightenment or in Christianity. Disorienting or not, however, such passages need not be seen as exceptions to subjugated discourse but rather as reversals inevitable in the rhetoric of the colonized. In the whiskey story, we find a momentary reversal of power relations but no real leveling of the playing field. If we turn our attention now to considering several places where Copway seems to wish to reappropriate traditional culture, we can see that this is characteristic of such moments: their fragility is inscribed within them.

At the beginning of the autobiography, power relations are established where Copway in his preface presents himself as an Indian endeavoring to "win the favorable notice of the white man" for those who "were once the lords of the land on which the white man lives" (5). Though the reader is immediately confronted with Copway's double self-presentation—his humility and his pride—he emphasizes his role as performer of the abject. His motto is—"My poor People" (6). The preface is a supplication. "Pray for us—that *religion and science* may lead us on to intelligence and virtue; that we may imitate the good white man, who, like the eagle, builds its nest on the top of some high rock—*science;* that we may educate our children, and turn their minds to God" (6). In this preface Copway prepares the reader for a conversion story, notifies us of his present commitments to Christianity and "science" (western education), and invites us to see him as a man who has left traditional culture behind.

The story does not unfold quite as expected, however, for in his evocation of his life "in Nature," we find many places in which the past seems the abode not of darkness and ignorance but of enlightenment and virtue. The religion he learns at his father's side reverences all aspects of the creation; the customs of the tribe demand that one honor one's father and mother, care for the poor, share one's wealth, and observe the golden rule. "Never use improper medicine to the injury of another, lest you yourself may receive the same treatment" (41). Though Copway does not make this point, it is impossible not to feel that the essential teachings of Christianity are already present in his life before he becomes converted, with the exception of the attitude toward killing and revenge. That sense of inner peace, of the heart at home, that marks the Christian transformation recalled in so many Euro-American conversion narratives, seems to belong to Copway *before* his conversion rather than after.

Yet Copway cannot linger long in this realm of nostalgia. After listing the moral principles of Ojibwa culture, he comments: "These are a few specimens of the advice given by our fathers, and by adhering to their counsels, the lives, peace, and happiness, of the Indian race were secured; for then there was no whiskey amongst them" (41). Thus, though traditional culture and its benefits are remembered and venerated, we always know the end of the story. One is reminded of Giannina Braschi's remark: "Nostalgia is a fruit with the sting of distance in its pit" (24).

Secure for a moment in his role as ethnographer, Copway sees no problem with comparing Indian culture to western modes on the grounds of their similarity rather than their difference. While discussing the principles of government of the Ojibwa in his *Traditional History*, he says casually: "The law of the nation, like that of ancient Greece, has been enacted with a view to the health of its subjects" (53). Where he dwells lovingly and amusingly on the pastimes of the people, he again suggests parallels. In the "Maiden's Ball-Play" the young women of the tribe play a form of baseball or lacrosse. "The young women of the village decorate themselves for the day by painting their cheeks with vermilion, (how civilized, eh!)" (49), he comments in a humorous aside. Yet these similarities are effective precisely because Copway knows he can depend upon his reader's assumptions of difference, of the facts of subjugation. The irony conveyed by "(how civilized, eh!)" would not work in a transpositional context where the writer was arguing fundamental parity.

The starting point of the pastimes chapter is a quotation from John Cotton: "Fantastic, frolicksome and wild, / With all the trinkets of a child" (42), and an implicit comparison between Indians and children is made again at the beginning of the chapter on Indian legends where Copway uses this quotation:

> 'Tis a story,
> Handed from ages down; a nurse's tale,
> Which children open-eyed and mouthed devour,
> And thus as garrulous ignorance relates,
> We learn it, and believe. (95)

Presumably the point of this epigraph is to undercut Indian belief in superstitions. Nevertheless, Copway seems to relish repeating the legends that follow, so we are left once again with a sense of incoherence. Indeed, that sense is deepened where, toward the end of the *Traditional History*, Copway writes bitterly, "In former years, the American governors were more kindly disposed to us than they have been of late, yet the name of 'children' is applied to us. The government and its agents style us 'My children.' The Indians are of age—and believe they can think and act for themselves. The term 'My children' comes with an ill grace from those who seem bent on driving them from their fathers' house" (201).⁶

Donald B. Smith suggests a partial explanation for this kind of inconsistency where he claims that the *History* shows greater effects of collaboration than the autobiography, in part because so much of it is made up of quotations from other sources, "nearly 100 pages (in a 298 page book)" (23). He hypothesizes that the quotations from English poetry are the work of Copway's wife. However, Copway's vacillations cannot simply be written off as the work of others because they permeate everything we know about the man's life and work.

Language, often characterized as a defining principle of nation, is a particularly tangled issue in Copway's mind. He begins the chapter on "Their Language and Writings" in the *Traditional History* with a quotation from Shakespeare: "Here are a few of the most unpleasant words / That ever blotted paper" (123). Since this quotation is immediately followed by the sentence "The Ojibway language, or the language of the Algonquin stock, is perhaps the most widely spoken of any in North America," it is reasonable to assume that these words (foreign to the white American reader) are the ones characterized as "unpleasant." We soon see that such is not the case, however, and the epigraph therefore comes to seem ironic, whether intentionally so or not.

Copway moves almost immediately into a discussion of translation. It too carries the force of dramatic irony as Copway chooses to reference H. R. Schoolcraft rather than his own work in translation in order to elicit belief on the part of the reader concerning the nature of Indian language. Copway thus participates in what Eric Cheyfitz in *The Poetics of Imperialism* describes as "the romance of translation" in which "the other is translated into the terms of the self in order to be alienated from those terms" (15). Here, however, the romance of translation is being performed for the reader by the other, who is himself simultaneously a "native speaker" and an alienated "self" adopting the posture (and the language) of those who regard him as alien. His double role is again uncanny, as where he says: "I cannot express fully the beauty of the language, I can only refer to those who have studied it as well as other languages [why does this not describe his own position?], and quote their own writing in saying, 'every word has its appropriate meaning, and with [*sic*] additional syllables give additional force to the meaning of most words.' " As he goes on, however, we find that he does see himself as able to make comparative judgments, for he reflects: "After reading the English language, I have found words in the Indian combining more expressiveness. There are many Indian words which when translated into English lose their force, and do not convey so much meaning in one sentence as the original does in one word" (124–25).

In this chapter Copway moves back and forth several times between representing his nation's language and traditions as worthy and calling them "absurd," "unpleasant," or improperly performed. "The softness of the language is caused, as I have before said, by the peculiar sounding of all the vowels; though there is but little poetic precision in the formation of verse, owing to the want of a fine discriminating taste by those who speak it" (126). The language itself may be beautiful but those who speak it (presumably Indians?) lack the finesse to demonstrate its potential.

And for those who wish to preserve Indian language use, there is more bad news to come. Copway's ambivalence in this chapter turns decisively toward rejection of language preservation as a national principle where, toward the end of the volume, he advocates educating the new generation in English. Like the ethnocentric Know-Nothings, he sees English as becoming "the universal language in all lands" (260–61). But in a passage that again destabilizes the nation, Copway reflects: "Our language perpetuates our own ideas of civilization, as well as the old usages in our nation; and, consequently, how limited our field of acquiring knowledge! On the other hand, by giving [Indian students] an English education, you introduce them into the endless field of English literature, and from the accumulated experience of the past, they might learn the elements which would produce the greatest amount of good to our nation" (260). The peculiar aspect of this passage is that he seems perfectly aware that the nation is grounded in language; and yet, in order to "produce the greatest amount of good to our nation," he is prepared to forego even bilingual instruction and have Indian education take place entirely in English, thus destabilizing the nation itself.

From this we may turn to George Copway's views of national political identity which likewise follow a zigzag path, in many ways mirroring his notions of cultural identity. As we have already seen, the dimensions of his conception of nation are fluid. In chapter 17 of the autobiography, he informs us that the Ojibwa (or Chippewa) nations "are within the bounds of the two governments—the American and the British" (203). Though he proposes to give a separate account of each, the distinction between the American Ojibwa, which he numbers about twenty-five thousand, and the British-Canadian Ojibwa, who number only about five thousand, soon blurs for the reader. It does not in fact seem feasible to distinguish between them except by locating certain bands (or tribes) geographically. Much that is said about the nation seems to refer equally to northern and southern tribes, and even to the broader classification of North American Indians such as Copway believed them to be. Perhaps for this reason he felt comfortable establishing a newspaper entitled *Copway's American Indian* claiming to speak for many Indian nations.

On the other hand, Donald Smith notes that when Copway was sent to missions in present-day Wisconsin and Minnesota, he was regarded as something other than a real Indian. Smith recounts: "At the same time the Indians in the Lake Superior and Upper Mississippi region regarded George as culturally alien. When he, his cousin John, and Peter Markson, for example, had met Sioux Indians near Fort Snelling in 1837, one Sioux perceived these men dressed in European clothes to be 'Frenchmen,' persons of European culture, who incidentally happened to be Indian" (14). Such responses demonstrate that Copway's Pan-Indianism was more mythic than existential. For these American Indians, cultural practice rather than biological heritage determined one's national identity, and Copway should have known this.

Copway equally blurs the identity of the nation to which the autobiography is addressed. Much of it is concerned with petitions to the British Canadian government. On the other hand, the focus of Copway's attention moves away from British Canada and toward the United States. At the end of the text, Copway includes a speech predicting disaster if Native Americans are not treated fairly. Help is needed to "ward off the terrible retribution which must, sooner or later, unless it be averted, fall upon this nation" (224). The last word of the text, then, the word "nation," refers to America.

The *Traditional History* is even more preoccupied with defining the nature of nation and concludes with an even grander and more mythic vision. By 1850 Copway had spent considerable time away from Canada, though he proposes here a reformulation of the Canadian chiefs' petition to the governor-general to set aside a territory where all the Indians (or all the converted Indians, it is unclear) can settle in Saugeen and develop a civilized agricultural community unmolested.

By this point Copway seems to have accepted an American nationality. As we know, he would go on to work for the American government, first offering his services (unsuccessfully) in the effort to expel the remaining Seminoles from Florida and then working as a Union Army recruiter. As Donald Smith discovered, "According to a report of the Canadian Indian Department dated October 8, 1864, 'two Indians named David and George Copway, the former belonging to the Rice Lake Band and the other from the United States [!]

have unlawfully enticed & carried away by false pretenses to the United States several young Indians and enlisted them in the American army' " (27).

Smith sees evidence of growing mental instability in George Copway in the last decade of his life. His wife eventually insisted upon a permanent separation. In Detroit he took up the role of the medicine man (a role his father had at one time occupied and about which Copway is typically ambivalent in his writings).[7] In 1868 he returned to Canada. A year later he was baptized a Catholic; but, as ever, living out the symbolism of his situation, he died a few days later before celebrating his first communion. Clearly George was seeking a cure not just for himself but for his people. Sadly, he never found an effective instrument for this cure, not in nation, religion, science, writing, or politics.

Nevertheless, the man whose life and work exemplify such internal dissension gives us one of the most eloquent appeals for unity in nineteenth-century Indian writing. "I want to make the great family of the Indians ONE, should I live long enough—*one* in interest, *one* in feeling, *one* while they live, and *one* in a better world after death" (*History*, 282). In the *Traditional History* he lays out a proposal for bringing all the Indians together in a territory in present-day South Dakota. They would be supervised by a white governor and an Indian lieutenant-governor and hold their land in perpetuity. (Copway is scathing about the continuous removals to which the Indians are subjected.) Eventually he hoped this territory would become a state with rights of citizenship for its people equal to those enjoyed by others in the Union. His vision of nation here is a projection of his desire for a resolution to all the conflicts which have plagued him and his people.

The American government has addressed us like different nations, instead of addressing us as an Indian nation, and as one family; they have in this way perpetuated our differences towards each other.—The same law which governs the masses of people of all nations (civilized) among the pale faces, in some degree would then keep them at peace with each other. The law of necessity—the law of common interest—the law of love, are so many influences which ought to have operated on them before. . . . The tribes, being weakened by their hostilities, can never prosper. But collect them in a large body by themselves, and commence rationally to adopt a system of pupilage which will be well adapted for the young; and one good man would be like a light-house in a storm, who would warn and guide the rest. (270–71)

This "one good man" brings us at last to George Copway's use of personification. During his lifetime he sought various personifications of virtue in both whites and Indians. To Americans he offered William Penn as a model of Indian-white reconciliation, calling him in a letter to the *Saturday Evening Post* "that personification of Christianity" (*History*, 280). In another occasional piece, he wrote: "We trust that the time may come when the Indians of the far West will have it in their power as it is their inclination to erect a monument to the memory of Gen. Washington as to that of William Penn" (quoted in Knobel, 184). Among Indians he recommended Pocahontas, insisting: "I admire her character [and] think her name merits a place among the great of earth" (quoted in D. Smith, 22). Given her uncertain status within the Indian community, Copway's advocacy of Pocahontas may seem strange, but it is all of a piece with his desperate search for individuals who seemed to him to bridge the two cultures. This search even comprehended people like Colonel McKenney and Francis Parkman, who from other points of view were deeply implicated in the denigration of Indians, the disruption of Indian nations, and the decrease of their members.

Though he was willing to flatter and fawn upon men such as Parkman, Copway was outraged by the ideology of the vanishing American. "The pale face says that there is a fate hanging over the Indian bent on his destruction. Preposterous! They give him liquors to destroy himself with, and then charge the great Good Spirit as the author of their misery and mortality" (*History*, 93–94). Yet when he looked around, he found himself at a loss for leaders who could deal effectively with both cultures and thus create for the Indians a prosperous and happy future.

Clearly Copway hoped that he himself might be such a leader and part of the project of his autobiography is self-promotion. The name he proposed for his Indian state, Kahgega—meaning "Ever to be"—is, as Donald Smith notes, a variation on his own name, as though nation and self might both achieve authenticity at the same time. But Copway ends up personifying the incoherence of the American subject more than anything else.

Much of what Homi Bhabha has to say about minority discourse in "DissemiNation" (*Nation and Narration*) has relevance to George Copway, whose discourse about nation keeps "adding on" without, as Bhabha says, "adding up." In one way we might see this as its enriching potential because it destabilizes such abstractions as "the people," the nation, and Copway's final point of reference: "every true American" (*History*, 283). As with Bhabha's example of the Turkish *gastarbeiter* in John Berger's *A Seventh Man*, "the final return [to the nation] is mythic, we are told, 'It is the stuff of longing and prayers . . . as imagined it never happens. There is no final return' " (*Nation and Narration*, 316).

Once we acknowledge that Copway could not "return," and was therefore consigned to mythologizing, we are left with the incommensurability between his desire to imagine the people as one and his multiple distanciations, ambivalences, temporalities, national identities: the multiple writings of George Copway as meaning and text. A purely dismissive response to his work seems too simple, however. It is not adequate to say that Copway was crazy, that he sold out, that he was naive, a pawn, or not a "real Indian." Though some might argue that Copway is not representative, I would suggest, to the contrary, that his work is highly representative of a certain tendency, not only in Indian writing but in the writing of many "minorities" including postcolonials, immigrants, and even some mainstream Americans. It is the agonistic tendency to juxtapose the fragmented experience of the individual with the dream of a significant polis or group, without being able to resolve the emergent contradictions. Can this kind of writing do significant political work?

For Homi Bhabha the answer must be yes. Antagonistic to the pacifications implied by the notion of a "pluralistic" society, Bhabha prefers streaming to mainstreaming.

Once the liminality of the nation-space is established, and its "difference" is turned from the boundary "outside" to its finitude "within," the threat of cultural difference is no longer a problem of "other" people. It becomes a question of the otherness of the people-as-one. The national subject splits in the ethnographic perspective of culture's contemporaneity and provides both a theoretical position and a narrative authority for marginal voices or minority discourse. They no longer need to address their strategies of opposition to a horizon of "hegemony" that is envisaged as horizontal and homogeneous. The great contribution of Foucault's last published work is to suggest that people emerge in the modern state as a perpetual movement of the "marginal integration of individuals." ("Mimicry," 301)

Yet Bhabha's contention that we are all exiles, like Foucault's image of the nation as the people in flux, somehow fails to address the significance of the longing for political identity that provides the pathos of Copway's work. In Bhabha's mind "the people" can never be anything but a strategic illusion. For Copway, the Order of United Americans was appealing precisely because it promised "to renationalize the United States" and "to nurture and protect the 'peculiar character' of the republican citizenry" (Knobel, 192). It provided a promise of unity and coherence.

A view of "the people" as simply a conglomerate made up of infinitely maneuverable parts seems to me to be a sign of the triumph of what we might call a capitalist mentality. As Jameson puts it: "Thus the primordial crime of capitalism is exposed: not so much wage labor as such, or the ravages of the money form, or the remorseless and impersonal rhythms of the market, but rather this primal displacement of the older forms of collective life from a land now seized and privatized. It is the oldest of modern tragedies, visited on the Native Americans yesterday, on the Palestinians today" (84). Even postmodernists may participate in such displacement.

If we compare Black Hawk's use of transpositional narrative with George Copway's resort to subjugated discourse, Copway seems from one point of view an ineffective spokesman for Indian welfare. Black Hawk's comparatively consistent use of stable juxtapositions provides a fundamental moral challenge to the ideology of Manifest Destiny. From another point of view, however, because Black Hawk totally refuses to confront the logic (as opposed to the effects) of power relations, he has to be seen as a utopian visionary with the limitations implicit in that role.

Copway bespeaks the dilemma of the modern Indian caught between a traditional culture which is no longer viable in the old sense and an alien culture which is both destructive and empowering at the same time. Copway's performance of the unresolvable tensions of this position is deeply interesting. As the next chapter will indicate, it has affinities with the work of John Rollin Ridge. It is also the position from which many twentieth-century Indian writers speak. In *From the Deep Woods to Civilization* (1916) by Charles Eastman (Santee Dakota), we can hear echoes, not consistent but nevertheless distinct, of the earlier work of George Copway. "I am an Indian: and while I have learned much from civilisation, for which I am grateful, I have never lost my Indian sense of right and justice. I am for development and progress along social and spiritual lines, rather than those of commerce, nationalism, or material efficiency. Nevertheless, as long as I live, I am an American" (quoted in Murray, 78).

As Kenneth Lincoln comments in *Native American Renaissance:* "These new mixtures of being 'now day Indi'n' (or American) are no less 'native' than changing conditions ever left people in North America" (186).

George Copway (Ojibwa). *Courtesy of Donald B. Smith*

William Apess (Pequot). *Courtesy of the American Antiquarian Society*

John Wesley Jarvis's portrait of Black Hawk and Whirling Thunder (Sauk and Fox). *Courtesy of the Thomas Gilcrease Museum, Tulsa*

John Rollin Ridge (Cherokee).
Courtesy of the Bancroft Library

Sarah Winnemucca (Paiute);
1878 photograph sent to her
brother. *Courtesy of the Nevada
Historical Society*

Sarah Winnemucca; 1880s photograph, probably from her last stage
performance. *Courtesy of the Nevada
Historical Society*

6. John Rollin Ridge
and the Law

In the previous chapter on the work of George Copway, we examined some of the material about nation that was buried in Copway's ethnography. In this chapter we will be undertaking a similar process, rerouting material from one discourse to another by looking at the understandings of nation that develop in John Rollin Ridge's thematics of law.

Ridge's most extended prose work, *The Life and Adventures of Joaquín Murieta* (1854), is the first American novel known to have been written by an Indian, but its status as an Indian text is generally reduced to a brief mention in histories and bibliographies of Native American literature.[1] The reasons for this are many, and they go to the heart of what one means by both "Indian" and "Indian text." Briefly stated, John Rollin Ridge (or Yellow Bird), though of Cherokee descent, was a metropolitan, acculturated Indian who migrated from Indian Territory to California and upheld views repugnant to those who wished to maintain traditional Indian cultural practices. He was a journalist, wrote in English, and worked against the (also mixed-blood) leader generally preferred as a Cherokee spokesman, John Ross. Furthermore, his novel is not "about" Indians in the sense that its protagonist, Joaquín Murieta, is a Mexican outlaw. Native Americans appear only briefly; for instance, when Murieta's depredations on the inhabitants of California in the early 1850s lead him to be momentarily captured by the indigenous Tejon Indians about whom Ridge makes a number of satirical remarks. Nevertheless, one can read it (and the life-text of Ridge himself) as a form of native national narrative similar in some respects to George Copway's. This is what I propose to do in this chapter, which will examine further the exfoliation of Native American texts within American culture and the consequent destabilization of the notion of national "identity"—all the while attempting to keep in mind the importance and benefits of that notion as we have seen them represented by figures such as Black Hawk.

The Life and Adventures of Joaquín Murieta can be read as a novel about the law, for by representing its protagonist as an outlaw but as a figure designed to engage our sympathies, Ridge continually puts pressure on the question of what is "lawful." Opposing a concept of natural law to mere legalisms, at times making law the opposite of justice, and generally insisting that honor requires individuals not protected by the law to transgress its boundaries even to the extent of murder, Yellow Bird speaks as much as an Indian as he does as a voice of white culture.

Chees-quat-a-law-ny (Yellow Bird) or John Rollin Ridge (known as Rollin) studied law briefly after coming to California but gave it up due to his frustration with the tedium of its applications. According to Farmer and Strickland in their introduction to *Yellow Bird's Essays on the North American Indian* (1981), Ridge noted in a letter: "The general science of the law I admire—its everyday practice I dislike" (26). Instead, he turned to a career in journalism, following in the footsteps of his illustrious cousins, Elias Boudinot and son.[2] Like George Copway, John Rollin Ridge felt that it was essential for the Indians to have their own press, and his earnest desire was to found an Indian newspaper. However, lacking the requisite funds, Ridge went to work for other papers in California—including the *Sacramento Bee*—expounding his views on the law from those venues instead. Patriotic in his writings concerning the United States, Ridge considered "the rule of law" one of the most important contributors to national stability, and in his mind the constitution of the nation as a legal entity was essential to its longterm viability.

Given Ridge's early experiences as a Cherokee, it is hardly surprising that he became preoccupied with the law. Born in Georgia, Rollin Ridge was part of an Indian family which had been acculturated for several generations. His grandfather, Major Ridge,[3] owned slaves and lived the life of a Georgia planter, sending his son north to Connecticut for his education where he subsequently married a white woman from Cornwall. The Ridge family was prosperous. Most of them spoke and wrote English and initially considered themselves protected by the laws governing the Cherokee Nation. Several members of the family became lawyers.

The Cherokee, like other Native American nations, had not always had written laws. Deloria and Lytle explain: "Although tribes used precedent for making their decisions, punishment was often devised to reflect the best solution for the community at that time and was not always dependent upon following the former resolution of the problem. Because of this great flexibility, there was no need to formulate a rigid set of laws, and there was little inclination to make precedents absolute in the same way that the Anglo-Saxon legal tradition found necessary" (18). Nevertheless, as Theda Perdue recounts, the Cherokee came to believe in the value of written laws:

Written laws dated from 1808 when the council passed and recorded a law establishing a national police force, commonly called the lighthorse guard, for the purpose of suppressing 'horse stealing and robbery of other property.' Two years later the council abolished clean revenge, and in 1822 the Nation established a Supreme Court. The process of political centralization and the formalization of legal and judicial institutions culminated in 1827 with the organization of a republic under a written constitution patterned after that of the U.S. federal government. (56)

Designed to give the Cherokee a legal basis upon which to remain independent, the Cherokee Constitution situated the nation as an "imperium in imperio"—a state within a state—much like the status of the American colonies before the Revolution. It furnished the Cherokee with a collective identity separate from, while remaining connected to, the United States. However, as Priscilla Wald describes it, "The Cherokee's becoming like but not of the United States political entity, mirroring without acceding to its claims, seems to threaten the terms of that identity [the United States]. And the threat it literally embodied by the 'mixed-bloods' who trouble both white exclusionists and integrationists in their *physical,* as well as *legal,* uncanniness" (89). Therefore, it was in some ways not surprising that Georgia would move to abolish the claims of the Cherokee Nation within its borders, thereby embroiling the Ridge family in a controversy that tarnishes its reputation to this day.

In several landmark cases before the Supreme Court, Chief Justice John Marshall laid out the terms under which the independence of the Cherokee Nation would be constructed.[4] The first of these actually preceded the adoption of the Cherokee Constitution and probably inspired it as a countermove. *Johnson v. McIntosh* (1823) invoked the "Doctrine of Discovery," a euphemism that granted Euro-American immigrants preeminent authority over Indian territory by virtue of the claims of imperialism. According to another principle remembered at this time, the so-called Rights of Conquest, the dominant European power had the right to trade with the natives, to send missionaries into areas occupied by indigenous peoples, and to quell uprisings. Though brought back into play now, these notions really belonged to an era when various European powers—principally Britain, France, and Spain—were carving up North America into what amounted to "spheres of influence." A key element of this case, argued by the defense, was the statement that "the Indians never had any idea of individual property" (quoted in Wald, 85) and therefore could not sell the land upon which they resided. Though jurists disagreed about these matters, more than one argued that Indian tribal organization exempted natives from inclusion in "the family of nations" and even from representation within the American legal system (see Wald, 84). Marshall's view, however, was that "a weak state, in order to provide for its safety, may place itself under the protection of one more powerful, without stripping itself of the right of government, and ceasing to be a state" (quoted in Deloria and Lytle, 17). As Vine Deloria and Clifford Lytle note: "A good deal of the subsequent history of conflict between the United States and Indian tribes has revolved around the question of preserving the right to self-government and the attributes of Indian sovereignty as suggested by Marshall's decision" (17).

In the countermove of establishing their own constitution, the Cherokee had attempted to position themselves as a composite American subject whose lands, though jointly owned, were not annexable by the United States. Furthermore, as Arnold Krupat recounts, "Correctly anticipating that President Jackson's First Annual Message to Congress . . . would strongly support their removal from the east, the

General Council of the Cherokee Nation met in November 1829 to draft a 'Memorial' to both Houses of Congress petitioning for their right to remain" (*Ethnocriticism*, 151). This Memorial like its successor would emphasize the legal status of the Cherokee Nation and appeal to the United States on the grounds of its own understanding of legal procedure. Unfortunately, however, these maneuvers proved entirely ineffectual.

Foreseeing that further clarification of tribal relations with the United States was necessary, John Marshall, in the subsequent "Cherokee Cases" of 1831 and 1832, attempted to find legal grounds for keeping the Cherokee in a special category, thus shielding them from the threat posed by the terms of the Indian Removal Act of 1830, a piece of legislation passed by Congress providing for "an exchange of lands with any of the Indians residing in the states and territories, and for their removal west of the river Mississippi" (Churchill and Morris, in Jaimes, 14). President Andrew Jackson was eager to support Georgia's desire to take possession of the fertile and well-developed properties of the Cherokee (upon which gold had been discovered) and generally favored clearing the eastern United States of all Native Americans.

Marshall opposed this wholesale appropriation of Indian lands. In the so-called Cherokee Cases, he attempted a compromise under which Indian tribes like the Cherokee would hold the status of "domestic dependent nations." In the words of his decision, "Their relation to the United States resembles that of a ward to his guardian. They look to our government for protection; rely upon its kindness and its power, appeal to it for relief to their wants; and address the president as their great father" (Wald, 90). However, if Marshall thought that by appealing to such notions of paternalism he could prevent Georgia from an act of blatant imperialism, he was wrong. When he heard of Marshall's attempt to limit the aggression of the state, President Jackson reportedly grumbled: "John Marshall has made his decision. Now let him try to enforce it" (Jennings, 332).

One of the reasons that the Cherokee cases caused so much controversy, especially in New England where the appropriation of Indian lands for a cash settlement was regarded (by Emerson, for instance) as scandalous, was that the Cherokee (one of the "five civilized tribes") were living in many respects just like white people. The Ridge family was thoroughly assimilated, and, in fact, they had a role (along with John Ross) in creating the Cherokee Constitution. However, they went against Ross—the designated chief—in signing the highly controversial New Echota Treaty of 1835, agreeing to the imperialistic demands of the state of Georgia that insisted upon the removal of the indigenous people west to Indian Territory. To this day the voluntary compliance of the Treaty Party—who acted, from their point of view, out of a sense of necessity and in order to protect the lives of the people in a era of Indian massacres—is regarded with contempt by other Indians. The Ross Party continued to petition Congress and to raise legal objections to the terms of the treaty long after it had been signed. As M. Annette Jaimes (Juaneño / Yaqui) and Theresa Halsey (Standing Rock Sioux) describe the situation in their essay in *The State of Native America* (1992):

Despite much groveling by the 'sellouts,' Andrew Jackson ordered removal of the Cherokees—as well as the Creeks, Choctaws, Chickasaws, and Seminoles. . . . [After the removal], the assimilationist faction continued to do substantial damage to Cherokee sovereignty. Although John Rollin Ridge, the Major's grandson, was forced to flee to California in 1850 and was unable to return to Cherokee Country until after the Civil War, Stand Watie ([Elias] Boudinot's younger brother) managed to lead a portion of the Cherokees into a disastrous alliance with the Confederacy from which the nation never recovered. (321)

The removal of the Cherokee took place in two stages. The first group, who were mostly propertied landowners and received a "settlement" from the government, left voluntarily in 1836 (the Choctaws had migrated in 1832), settling primarily in Arkansas. The other sixteen thousand were removed by force in 1838 and marched at bayonet point across the country to "Indian Territory" in Oklahoma. This "Trail of Tears"—in which the old, the infirm, little children, men and women were forced to travel fifteen hundred miles under conditions of the greatest hardship—remains one of the most egregious examples of American use of force against nonthreatening (and legally entitled) native peoples. As two recent demographers describe it: "Even by [James] Mooney's usual low-counting estimation, at least 25 percent of those forced to walk the 'Trail of Tears' died of disease, exposure, and malnutrition along the way. [Russell] Thornton's much more thorough computations reveal that approximately eight thousand—or nearly 50 percent of the entire Cherokee population remaining after earlier epidemics had caused severe attrition—failed to survive the Trail" (Stiffarm and Lane, in Jaimes, 33).

The Ridge clan did not walk the Trail of Tears. Having received a cash settlement, they went ahead to Indian Territory, where they hoped to regain their financial footing with the help of their slaves.[5] This created extremely hostile feelings among the Resistance Party headed by John Ross. On June 22, 1839, several Ross supporters broke into the Ridge household, dragged John Ridge out, and in front of his wife, son Rollin, and servants stabbed him to death. On the same night a cousin, Elias Boudinot (the elder), and Rollin's grandfather, Major Ridge, were also murdered.

This traumatic night haunted Rollin Ridge for the rest of his life. Though, like the young Elias Cornelius Boudinot, he was sent north after the killings, he did not take to the environment that nurtured his father. He returned south again, receiving most of his education from the New Dwight Mission School in Arkansas which emphasized literature and the classics in a program dedicated to purifying the Indians of their "savage" ways and indoctrinating them with the views of white culture; Ridge married a white woman, Elizabeth, who lived in the territory of the Cherokee Nation. In an 1844 letter written during this period, which unfortunately has not survived intact, he wrote: "If there is no law in a Nation to [*missing word, punish?*] those who take the lives of their fellow men it [is impos?]sible to have justice done . . . unless it is [*missing text*] ties of kindred blood to the slain" (quoted in Parins, 37). Though the wording is uncertain, this letter suggests his disillusionment with current law enforcement procedures and sets the stage for his novel, written ten years later.

It also lends support for the idea that the outlaw Joaquín Murieta is a man with whom the reader may be asked to sympathize. There are a number of links between Murieta's band and Indian outlaws. Perdue informs us that in the wake of the murders, members of the Treaty Party (including Stand Watie, Rollin's cousin) conspired to create a gang "for the purpose of killing and robbing the most prominent men of the opposite party" (74). Perhaps this is the force of retributive justice Ridge had in mind in his letter.

Furthermore, in "The Cherokees—Their History—Present Condition and Future Prospects," an article first published in the Clarkesville, Texas, *Northern Standard* (Jan. 20, 1849), Ridge describes the Cherokees as divided into three groups: the Old Settlers party, the Ross Party, and the Ridge or Treaty Party. He also mentions a group of malcontents (he calls them "banditti") both red and white, who "bid defiance to society and law" (Farmer and Strickland, 51). Ridge claims that "although their daring-wickedness was everywhere acknowledged, yet so numerous were the relations and friends of these lawless men" that they essentially operated unopposed.

The postremoval chaos that afflicted the Cherokee community was a cause of great concern to Rollin Ridge who, on the one hand, sympathized with some of the outlaws and, on the other, felt that such lawlessness undermined the nation itself. "Prejudice and Hatred, instead of Justice, hold the scales," he laments in his 1849 article. Ridge said further that such problems would persist "until a strong arm is extended over [the Cherokee Nation]—I mean the laws of the United States" (Farmer and Strickland, 52).

Fleeing the law himself, after killing a man who attacked him in an incident suggesting further foul play by the Ross faction, John Rollin Ridge made his way to California in 1850. In 1854 he published *The Life and Adventures of Joaquín Murieta, the Celebrated California Bandit*, a haphazard narrative written in dime novel format. Full of hairsbreadth escapes and brutal killings, it contains all the elements of melodramatic romance. Ridge seems to have written it primarily to make money, since none of his occupations thus far—as trader, miner, hunter, and deputy clerk—had provided much income. According to his own reports, he realized little profit on the novel, though he may have underreported his earnings in order to enlist the sympathies of his cousin Stand Watie to whom he repeatedly turned for money. In any case, the story of the Romantic Bandit, who has the clothes, women, horses, and bulging wallet Rollin craved, was more of a fantasy than a serious literary undertaking. (Yellow Bird also wrote poems and short stories that show his more reflective side.) Nevertheless, this narrative, brightened by moments of wit and humor, is still engaging to read. Though it occasionally descends into mere bathos and bravado, weirdly lit by flashes of lurid violence, *The Life and Adventures* presents a fascinating picture of a multicultural frontier America where defiance of the law is common.

As a "national narrative," however, the novel must be read as much for what it points to as for what it says. Focusing on outlaws and exiles, it bespeaks a longing for law and homeland of the sort that Homi Bhabha describes as typical of diasporic populations. Indeed, for those who focus on the endless circulation of cultural meanings by writers in exile, writers who tell us of "home" while living "abroad," who insist upon "the people" as a significant category while living the experience of the diaspora, who—to use Bhabha's phrase—"enter in" without themselves being contained by that entry, John Rollin Ridge, in this work in particular, might stand as an example of the metropolitan postmodern.

Nothing, for instance, could be more postmodern than the fate of Ridge's story about Joaquín Murieta. Why he chose a Mexican character to represent certain problems confronting the Indians remains a mystery[6] for, according to his biographer James Parins, Ridge himself supported "settlerism"—that is, the taking of land from Mexican aristocrats in California by American settlers given small land grants. He further advocated annexing Sonora with or without the consent of the Sonorans. Nevertheless, his tale of the Mexican bandit became the basis for subsequent nationalistic narratives in Chile, Spain, and Mexico itself; Mexican-American families have preserved the tale of Joaquín Murieta, the lovable bandit, for generations.

It has also been taken up enthusiastically by Chileans. In 1967 Pablo Neruda wrote *Splendour and Death of Joaquín Murieta* arguing that "Joaquín Murieta was a Chilean. I have proof" (author's foreword). The "Poet's Voice" at the end of the play claims: "A sleeping nation awoke to its need on the reddening path of this soldier: the murderer who murdered the murderers and died for our honor"

(143), that is, the honor of Chile, not Mexico, the Cherokee Nation, or the United States. Unfortunately for those who have believed Neruda, there is no such proof. The work Neruda elsewhere references as his source—*The Last of the California Rangers*—was based on files that themselves may be traced back to Ridge's novel (see Jackson, xli ff.).

There are, however, some facts of the case still accessible. When Ridge wrote his novel, California had been for several years the scene of guerrilla attacks upon white settlers by bands of Mexicans whose cultural setting had been disrupted by imperialistic immigrations, the war with the United States, the Gold Rush, and the annexation of California. As Joseph Henry Jackson describes the situation, in his introduction to the 1955 edition of the novel, the great "ranchos" had supported large families of dependent Mexicans who were subsequently displaced, reduced to menial status, and forced to find new ways of supporting themselves, as the Indians had been in the East. Jackson concludes:

It is easy, then, to see how, in the mind of the Spanish-Californian, patriotism was equated with outlawry. Here were men cut adrift by forces of which they had no notion, excepting that anybody could see that it was the fault of the *gringo,* wherefore it was perfectly reasonable to hate him for it. Moreover, this hatred was fostered by Mexicans who had fought the Yankee in the war just past, and who, when the war was lost, wandered northward into California to join the native in his struggle against the new-come American who had done him down. This injection of patriotism into the business makes it clear why even Mexican-Californians who remained honest, somehow found work to do, and were peaceably inclined, were yet friendly to outlaws, gave them information, and helped to confound the Yankee law-officers whenever possible. (xvii–xviii)

Mexican gangs roamed the countryside, running off cattle, holding up travelers, stealing horses, and even sometimes resorting to murder. Between 1850 and 1853, reports flooded into the authorities of a leader known as Joaquín, though, according to several sources, there were at least five Joaquíns engaged in such business: Carrillo, Valenzuela, Bottilier, Murieta, and Ocomoreña. Subsequently a price was placed upon "Joaquín's" head and the ironically named Captain

Harry Love went out with a posse to bring back the outlaw dead or alive.[7] Surprising a group of Mexicans in the region of the Panoche Pass, Love and his men became engaged in a gun battle which led to the deaths of the Mexican leader and one of his henchmen, identified as Manuel García or "Three-Fingered Jack," a known thief and murderer with a reputation for brutality. In order to provide evidence of the killings and thus collect the reward, the leader's head was cut off and preserved in a jar of alcohol. Jack's three-fingered hand met a similar fate.

Of course, no one knew precisely which of the Joaquíns, if any, had been killed, but Captain Love received his reward and was even voted a bonus by the California legislature. The head and the hand were placed on display and drew crowds of spectators. To at least one Californian, the editor of the San Francisco *Alta*, the whole thing was deeply suspect. This editor even insisted that the man who had been killed was definitely not Joaquín Murieta. But the problem was, and is, that there is no reliable information about Murieta, no records we can trace of either his life or his death. (Even Neruda admits that all birth and death records have been lost.)

Ridge's biographers are unanimous in believing that John Rollin Ridge invented most of the story about Joaquín Murieta though he claimed to have done extensive research. His tale was so compelling that it was subsequently pirated in 1859 by the *California Police Gazette* and from there it made its way around the world, turning up in slightly altered forms—forms that recognizably echo Ridge's novel—in Chile, Spain, and Mexico, where the bandit Joaquín Murieta is each time presented as a kind of national hero: "El Bandido Chileño" in Chile, for example. In the late nineteenth century, two historians, Hubert Howe Bancroft and Theodore Hittell, used John Rollin Ridge's account in their histories of California. As Jackson tells it: "A few conscientious county historians in the 1880's and 1890's tried to call a halt, but to no effect. *The Overland Monthly* and *The Argonaut*, now beginning to print the recollections of pioneers, both published 'recollections' of Murieta, usually in language oddly resembling Ridge's. As the century closed, Murieta, clear in outline now as Ridge had drawn him, had become a 'fact' " (xxxviii).

In retrospect, one can see that the peculiar literary fate of Ridge's protagonist was indeed due in part to the way he drew him. As a man with only the slightest hint of cultural particularity, Joaquín was available for transformation and reproduction as the hero of various nations. Unlike Black Hawk who rooted himself in Sauk culture, unlike William Apess and George Copway whose Indian heroes were firmly tied to their historical circumstances, John Rollin Ridge's Joaquín Murieta has few traits that limit his circulation. He is a man who has been wronged, who turns in rage and despair to a life of "revenge," but who preserves elements of nobility, loyalty, sentiment, and magnanimity in spite of the brutality of his career. Consistent with Ridge's own preoccupations, Joaquín Murieta and his men, who ride hundreds of miles up and down California, camping in the woods and canyons with their horses, could be Indian as easily as Spanish Mexican.[8]

Nevertheless, the novel begins with a statement about Murieta's ability to personify certain elements in *American* culture, as though he should be seen as both heroic (special) and representative (typical). He says: "The character of this truly wonderful man was nothing more than a natural production of the social and moral condition of the country in which he lived, acting upon certain peculiar circumstances favorable to such a result, and, consequently, his individual history is a part of the most valuable history of the State" (7). Ridge invites us to read the novel as an allegory, but not simply as an allegory of the unhappy fate of an "outsider inside." Rather he seems to have in mind an allegory of the American character, seen here as the effect of a chaotic social determinism. In short, Ridge opens the way for a vision of national character as essentially contentless, postmodern in its chameleon-like tendency to act according to circumstances rather than inherent nature or cultural background.

Given this historical context, then, it behooves us to examine the man and his novel as pondering questions of law and nation. One theme of the novel is the necessity of establishing within the nation the rule of law. A contrary theme, however, concerns the code of honor which, according to the laws of nature, provides a motive to go against the legal system when one's own are threatened and justice is denied.

Near the beginning of the novel, Ridge inserted "Mt. Shasta, Seen from a Distance," which Parins describes as the best-known of Yellow Bird's poems. Though written in 1852 as an independent piece, it appears again in the novel, at a point where Murieta's band is heading north toward the California border. At first this long blank-verse poem seems a mere digression inserted for picturesque Romantic effect, but it also serves a purpose beyond that of mere window dressing because it focuses the reader's attention on the allegorical use of California "landscape"—an analog of history—in the discussion of law. The poem begins:

> Behold the dread Mount Shasta, where it stands,
> Imperial midst the lesser hight [*sic*], and like
> Some mighty, unimpassioned mind, companionless
> And cold. The storms of heaven may beat in wrath
> Against it, but it stands in unpolluted
> Grandeur still; and from the rolling mists up-heaves
> Its tower of pride e'en purer than before. (23)

Mt. Shasta epitomizes the spirit of the Sublime: "We may not grow familiar with the secrets / Of its hoary top, whereon the Genius / Of that mountain builds his glorious throne!" (24). Ridge presents the peak supreme over both time and human feeling. The "broad / Dominions of the West . . . lie beneath / His feet." The gigantic hills "in the long review of distance / Range themselves in order grand." It is an "icy mirror" that seems designed to reflect an eternal order impervious to human desire.

> Itself all light, save when some loftiest cloud
> Doth for awhile embrace its cold forbidding
> Form—that monarch-mountain casts its mighty
> Shadows down upon the crownless peaks below,
> That, like inferior minds to some great
> Spirit, stand in strong contrasted littleness!

Shasta seems to represent the law of Nature but a far more Nietzschean Nature than what we find in either Emerson or Wordsworth, or, for that matter, in most other Indian texts. In fact, this 1852 poem (inserted into the 1854 text) looks forward to Naturalism's discourse about forces in the universe beyond good and evil. It is difficult to imagine how human society could incorporate the truths represented by this "icy mirror," unapproachable as they are, in the daily administration of justice. Nevertheless, Ridge ends the poem by suggesting this very application of the mountain text.

> And well this Golden State shall thrive, if, like
> Its own Mount Shasta, sovereign law shall lift
> Itself in purer atmosphere—so high
> That human feeling, human passion, at its base
> Shall lie subdued; e'en pity's tears shall on
> Its summit freeze; to warm it, e'en the sunlight
> Of deep sympathy shall fail—
> Its pure administration shall be like
> The snow, immaculate upon that mountain's brow! (25)

This is quite peculiar from many points of view. Rollin Ridge's own problems with the law, and the problems of his people, had precisely to do with the cold way it trampled upon human feeling and was impervious to pity's tears. Would one want to create a legal system in which even "deep sympathy shall fail"? How is justice to be understood if it is thus represented as beyond questions of application?

One can accept the idea that law must be above individual passions and desires but surely not above all consideration of human interest as it appears here. Interestingly enough, this view of law has virtually nothing to do with the motivations of Joaquín Murieta, a man whose actions are justified entirely by his capacity for deep feeling. Its closest analog in the text is to the soulless bandit Luis Vulvia, a member of Murieta's band:

A tall, dark-skinned man sat in the middle of the room, with a huge log chain around one of his legs. His brow was tall and massive, and his large grey eyes looked forth with that calm, cold light which unmistakably expresses a deep, calculating intellect, divested of all feeling and independent of all motives which arise from mere impulse or passion—an intellect which is sole in itself, looking at the result merely in all its actions, not considering the question of right and wrong, and working out a scheme of unmitigated villainy as it would a mathematical problem. (92)

But Vulvia is far from the hero of the narrative. His is a minor role, seemingly designed like that of Three-Fingered Jack to suggest the dark possibilities to which injustice in America gives rise.

Nothing in the novel fully reproduces the paean to supreme and soulless law of "Mount Shasta." So what is its purpose? One possibility, and I think an important one, is that the poem offers a reference point against which other conceptions of the law appear, not in fact in subjection, not as lesser, but in postmodern juxtaposition, each invoking the context in which its force appears appropriate. The icy elevation of this "mountain-monarch" is appropriate not to time but to eternity. It bears some similarity to Darwinian conceptions of evolution, about which I will have more to say later. Furthermore, by invoking the law of Mount Shasta, Ridge universalizes subjugation, as though pondering with Ishmael in Melville's *Moby Dick*, "Who aint a slave?" The context of universal subjugation makes individual experiences of oppression transpositional, thus, perhaps, leveling the playing field.

Nevertheless, this is not the perspective from which we are asked to view the character of Joaquín Murieta. Despite his allegorical outlines as "the Robin Hood of El Dorado,"[9] there are particular circumstances of oppression that make understandable his turn to a life of revenge. Murieta is born in Mexico and lives through the Mexican-American War. "Disgusted with the conduct of his degenerate countrymen" (8), he decides to try California, which is now part of the United States, because he has formed a good opinion of Americans. Why we do not know. He begins as a miner and is making fair headway when he is run off his claim by a band of thugs. Ridge writes: "This country was then full of lawless and desperate men, who bore the name of Americans but failed to support the honor and dignity of that title. A feeling was prevalent among this class of contempt for any and all Mexicans, whom they looked upon as no better than conquered subjects of the United States, having no rights which could stand before a haughtier and superior race" (9). One might well see this passage as applying equally to the situation of Native Americans confronted with the doctrine of the Rights of Conquest. And Ridge continues:

The prejudice of color, the antipathy of races, which are always stronger and bitterer with the ignorant and the unlettered, they could not overcome, or if they could, would not, because it afforded them a convenient excuse for their unmanly cruelty and oppression. A band of these lawless men, having the brute power to do as they pleased, visited Joaquín's house and peremptorily bade him leave his claim, as they would allow no Mexicans to work in that region. (9–10)

When he relocates, "a company of unprincipled Americans" once again "coveted his little home surrounded by its fertile tract of land" (10) driving him off. His mistress is raped before his eyes. Through a misunderstanding concerning a stolen horse, he is tied up and publicly whipped; his half-brother is lynched. Having endured all these experiences of injustice, Joaquín Murieta finally commits himself to revenge. "He had contracted a hatred to the whole American race, and was determined to shed their blood, whenever and wherever an opportunity occurred" (14).

In this tale of injustice, Ridge does not mention the way California law colluded with such racism and oppression. In 1850 the California legislature had passed the "Foreign Miner's Tax Law" in order to limit the profits from the Gold Rush to whites. Many Latin-American, Mexican, and Spanish-speaking Native Californians were panning for gold and succeeding very well. In a bizarre construction of the terms "native" and "foreign," the legislature insisted that such people were "foreigners" and had to pay an oppressive and disabling tax from which "Americans"—who included by consent French, German, and even Australian miners—were exempt. In 1851 the Supreme Court intervened and declared the law unconstitutional, but in the meantime many miners had been driven from their claims. It was another version of what the Cherokee had faced in Georgia.

Rollin Ridge makes this racist policy the actions of "lawless men" instead of the law. Since most of his readers would have known about the miners' law, the California legislature itself comes to seem "a band of lawless men," a nice turn. Ridge plays with the terms of this law at the point in the narrative where Joaquín refuses to let his men kill some Germans whom they have robbed, joking that at a later point he might want to collect taxes from them for "Foreign Miners' Licenses" (130). Of course, Germans didn't have to pay the taxes and Mexicans, even those born in California, did.

If legislation does not constitute the law, one must then ask how the law is to be understood in the novel. The code of honor represents an alternative "law" or rule, which is sometimes observed by Murieta and at all times respected by the narrator. Indeed this code—which also governs Black Hawk's narrative—is a more reliable touchstone of justice and moral value in this novel than either legal codes or ethnic identity (for many of the Mexicans violate the codes of honor and some of the Americans abide by it).

An example of the latter is Captain Ellas. "A chivalrous son of the South, he had grown up under a discipline that taught him that honor was a thing to be maintained at the sacrifice of blood or of life itself; that fear was a feeling too base to harbor in a manly breast, and that *he* was a coward who would not give the question of his rights to the *arbitration* of steel or of the deadly ball" (second emphasis added, 111). The deputy sheriff of Calaveras County, Captain Ellas sets out to apprehend Murieta and his men. Significantly, he is not limited to legal measures which, the narrator suggests, is all to the good. "At a juncture so important as the period of which I speak, a man like Ellas was most naturally looked to as a leader and intrusted with a large amount of discretionary power, so necessary to be used in perilous times when the slow forms of law, with their snail-like processes, are altogether useless and inefficient" (111).

Southerners, though white, are more likely to display this sense of honor in the novel than Euro-Californians. Another young man, originally from Arkansas, is caught in a trap by Murieta and his men. He and his friends are hunters and are invited to Murieta's fire under false pretenses, only to be confronted by the grisly band. Murieta contemplates killing them because they have discovered his hideout. At this point the young Southerner steps forward to argue that it would be cowardly to murder unarmed men who had never done

him any harm. He pledges secrecy, saying "Under different circumstances, I should take a different course, but *now*, I am conscious that
to spare our lives will be an act of magnanimity on your part, and I
stake my honor, *not as an American citizen*, but as a man, who is simply
bound by justice to himself, under circumstances in which no other
considerations can prevail, that you shall not be betrayed" (emphasis
added, 78). It is interesting that Ridge has him bind himself "not as an
American citizen" but "as a man."

As whites are sometimes seen to abide by the code of honor rather
than the laws of the nation, so Joaquín justifies his own actions
this way and is also at times thus justified by the narrator. When he
lays out his plan of wholesale robbery and murder, he insists: "My
brothers, we will then be revenged for our wrongs, and some little,
too, for the wrongs of our poor, bleeding country" (75). One of his
men, his mistress's brother Feliz Reyes, is characterized as a younger
version of his chief. A youth of sixteen, he "had read the wild romantic lives of the chivalrous robbers of Spain and Mexico until his enthu-
siastic spirit had become imbued with the same sentiments which
actuated them, and he could conceive of nothing grander than to
throw himself back upon the strictly natural rights of man and hurl
defiance at society and its laws" (17).

Ridge several times connects the laws of nature, in which self-
preservation figures prominently, with the code of honor.[10] Indeed,
self-preservation may be expanded to include dark deeds undertaken
to "preserve"—that is defend and even revenge—the honor of the
group (family, nation) to which one belongs. In a proleptic passage in
the first half of the narrative, Ridge refers to an honorable deed which
will close Joaquín's career and "show him aftertimes, not as a mere
outlaw, committing petty depredations and robberies, but as a *hero*
who has revenged his country's wrongs and washed out her disgrace
in the blood of her enemies" (80).

However, it remains unclear to the reader which deed Ridge has in
mind. Furthermore, the narrative perspective vacillates about Joaquín, at times rendering him heroically and at other times presenting
him as a kind of Byronic antihero whose nobility is a thing of the past.
He is accompanied by men who seem to represent a range of his own

attributes or instincts, positive and negative. If Feliz Reyes reflects his chivalrous side, and Vulvia his lonely intellect, the brutal Three-Fingered Jack is his murderous id. The targets of the band's crimes are not simply "Americans" but a hodgepodge of different groups always referred to by their national origin: Frenchmen, Germans, Dutchmen, Americans, and frequently the Chinese. Jack is particularly bloodthirsty toward Asians, who never provide any resistance but are nevertheless slaughtered in droves. Jack comments: "I love to smell the blood of a Chinaman. Besides, it's such easy work to kill them. It's a kind of luxury to cut their throats" (64). In one scene 150 Chinamen are killed, and the narrator comments: "The miserable Chinamen were mostly the sufferers, and they lay along the highways like so many sheep with their throats cut by the wolves. It was a politic stroke in Reis to kill Chinamen in preference to Americans, for no one cared for so alien a class, and they were left to shift for themselves" (97).

Clearly, there is nothing in the slightest bit honorable about these massacres, and Joaquín himself generally disapproves of them, restraining Jack from several savage attacks. However, at one point he concludes that for safety's sake they had better kill six Chinamen whose camp they have entered in order to rob the inoffensive inhabitants. The narrative then takes a grisly turn.

Three-Fingered Jack, by a nod from Joaquín, stepped up to each one and led him out by his long tail of hair, repeating the ceremony until they all stood in a row before him. He then tied their tails securely together, and drawing his highly-prized home-made knife, commenced, amid the howling and shrieks of the unfortunate Asiatics, splitting their skulls and severing their neck-veins. He was in his element, his eyes blazed, he shouted like a madman and leaped from one to the other, hewing and cutting, as if it afforded him the most exquisite satisfaction to revel in human agony. (133)

This is undoubtedly the most horrifying scene in the novel. The emphasis upon hair suggests the behavior of renegade Indians on the war-path, murdering and scalping their victims, but from another point of view we might read the Chinese as standing in here *for* the Indians, who were also slaughtered in large numbers even when they did not resist.[11] This form of "splitting" in which one group (here the Chinese) may be seen as occupying two positionalities simultaneously is also true, of course, for Joaquín and his men. Here, however, we are told nothing about Jack to explain, let alone justify, this violence. Unlike Indian war parties, Jack is not motivated by revenge but by sheer psychopathology, an aberration in which Joaquín himself is partly implicated. It seems as though we are meant to believe that injustice gives rise to madness which cannot then be controlled, or, as Ridge puts it at the end of the novel, "there is nothing so dangerous in its consequences as *injustice to individuals*—whether it arise from prejudice of color or from any other source; that a wrong done to one man is a wrong to society and to the world" (158).

Here the law of cause and effect comes into play in the reference to dangerous consequences. What is missing in this moral summing up is any reference to nation which seems to have dissolved in an acid bath of proliferating violence. In the final scene the unity of the band breaks down and Joaquín tells them to scatter, "every man for himself" (152). Mexican solidarity also breaks down as one of the outlaws who has been captured is kidnapped from the jail and hanged in the middle of the night. "The Americans knew nothing of the hanging, so that the most rational conjecture is that he was put out of the way by Mexicans to prevent the damning revelations which he would certainly have made" (157). So much for group solidarity and the code of honor.

How might we read this narrative as a novel about Indians and the United States? A seemingly minor incident just prior to the final shootout is suggestive. Joaquín dispatches one of the peaceful Digger Indians to town to get a bottle of liquor. However, growing uneasy lest the Indian betray his position, he overtakes him (without a shred of evidence to support his supposition) and kills him. It is an illegal as well as dishonorable act which, like the murder of the Chinese, the novel seems to present as dishonorable. But it mirrors the many so-called "California trials" that occur throughout the novel when Mexicans—innocent and guilty—are summarily lynched without any opportunity to defend themselves. At one point the narrator interrupts the narrative to comment on public hangings with a certain bitterness: "Bah! it is a sight that I never like to see, although I have been civilized for a good many years" (138). The notion of civilization as embroiling one in previously unknown forms of savagery was a key feature of Native American discourse throughout the nineteenth century. Ridge seems to be recalling this here as a way of indicting the so-called civilized social formations characteristic of "American" culture.

If we read these episodes as part of the American national narrative, it seems that America is a place of lawlessness rather than of law. If we then connect that lawlessness to the fate of the Indians, we find the implication that the disruption of nations and traditional morality—so often a feature of "Americanization"—created societies governed by a degree of murderous anarchy that threatened the whole fabric of life in the United States. In this sense, Joaquín can operate as both "American" and anti-American, a would-be patriot whose loyalty is to the ideal rather than the degraded reality. We have already seen such feelings expressed by William Apess and George Copway.

In this novel, too, race is no guarantee of good conduct. Two Cherokee "half-breeds" hang one of the Mexican outlaws by the side of the road with the tacit approval of Captain Ellas. The whole frontier scene may be said to be transpositional to the extent that groups such as Mexicans, Indians, Germans, Frenchmen, and Americans—seem to function interchangeably as both purveyors and targets of violence. California is a landscape in flux where "Jew-peddlers, almond-eyed Chinamen, and deplorably ragged-looking Frenchmen" (134) are all "on the road," jostling one another for a living and having to fight to survive. Even the women in the novel are both victims and perpetrators, presented as naturally nurturing but also just as "naturally" predatory.[12]

Only two groups are singled out as fundamentally nonaggressive—the Chinese and the Digger Indians—and both are treated ironically, even, one might say, dismissively. Like the Tejons who briefly capture Joaquín and several of his men—stripping them naked, tying them up, beating them, and then letting them go (to the enormous amusement of Joaquín himself)—the Diggers are targets of humor. They will "travel a considerable distance for a small piece of bread, fresh meat, or a ragged shirt" and are thus used as messengers, a form of communication called "Digger-Express." Ridge comments: "They are extremely faithful in this business, having a superstitious dread of that mysterious power which makes *a paper talk without a mouth*" (emphasis in original, 130). In the novel they are considered basically cowardly, like the Tejons, and are therefore not to be taken seriously.

Similarly, the narrator describes the Tejon chief, Old Sapatarra, as "seated upon his haunches in all the grandeur of 'naked majesty,' enjoying a very luxurious repast of roasted acorns and angle-worms" (36). The Tejons, however, are more cunning than the Diggers, and, when Sapatarra is offered a reward if he catches Joaquín, we are told: "The cupidity of the old Chief and his right-hand men was raised to the highest pitch, and they resolved to manage the matter in hand with great skill and caution; which last, by the way, is a quality that particularly distinguishes the California Indians, amounting to so extreme a degree that it might safely be called cowardice" (37).

Though Americans are also sometimes targets of humor, it may seem odd that John Rollin Ridge, an Indian himself, should make sport of Indians such as the Tejons and the Diggers. The answer to this puzzle, however, lies in his essays, where Ridge argues that the Indians are a distinct race but that cultural differences distinguish the tribes east of the Rockies from those west of them. The California Indians he sees as particularly abject. "Were these Indians like the genuine North American red man, in the times of the bloody frontier wars of the United States, brave, subtle, and terrible in their destruction, it would be a different matter. But they are a poor, humble, degraded, and cowardly race" (Farmer and Strickland, 62).

However, Ridge was appalled at the treatment of the Diggers in the 1850s; the "it" he refers to above concerns the violence inflicted upon them. Bands of American "cowboys" shot down even women and children in cold blood, sometimes surrounding whole villages and incinerating the inhabitants in the middle of the night. According to Ridge, Digger children were stolen and sold in other parts of the country. Rollin published several essays to draw attention to the "Oppression of the Digger Indians." When he was supporting himself as a hunter in 1852, he learned some of their language and conversed with them. "We had acquired a sufficient knowledge of the Digger tongue to express ourselves understandably, although we would give a word occasionally an extra American touch that would set our critical friends in a roar" (Farmer and Strickland, 55–56). Here he speaks indulgently of Indian humor even when deployed against him and his friends.

In most of these essays Ridge presents himself as an educated metropolitan figure who sees himself as an "American." In fact, like George Copway, Ridge made a Fourth of July speech, in 1859, "earnestly enjoining the cultivation of a broad national patriotism" (Parins, 146). Though he was almost denied voting privileges because he was an Indian, he took an active interest in politics, both American national politics and the situation of the Cherokees back in Oklahoma. After the end of the Civil War, he went to Washington to negotiate a new relationship between the United States and the Cherokee, many of whom had supported the Confederacy. He hoped that the Cherokee Nation would at some future time be admitted into the Union as a state with full rights of citizenship for its people (see Farmer and Strickland, 52).

Yet his attitudes were split along many lines. He saw himself as an Indian but also as an American when the two identities were not easily conjoined. Furthermore, his commitments mired him in contradictions. On the one hand, he put his faith in "the law." On the other, he justified lawlessness. The whole discourse about cowardice (and its binary, courage) suggests that in his hierarchy of values honor supercedes the law. Even Indians, when they are not aggressive—"the genuine North American red [men]" being "brave, subtle, and terrible in their destruction"—are "degraded."

According to Parins, Ridge saw himself as a Cain figure, cursed by dark thoughts (presumably murderous ones if we take the reference seriously). Throughout his work there is a sense of isolation, of being "an exile." In his short story "The Harp of Broken Strings," he recreates himself as a Byronic hero whose self-concept has been shaken by the tragic events of his life and upon whom a "doom" has settled.

At times his character (alter ego?) Joaquín is described as a man in the hands of Fate, over whom a dark necessity seems to brood, but he is also, through most of the narrative, seemingly protected by what Ridge calls a "guardian fiend": "His guardian fiend seemed never to desert him, and he came forth from every emergency in triumph. The following incident is but one among many which shows the extraordinary success that attended him, and would almost lead us to adopt the old Cherokee superstition that there were some men who bear charmed lives and whom nothing can kill but a silver bullet" (139).

However, at the end of the novel, Ridge pulls back from these metaphysical notions of Fate and supernatural protection. In a highly significant passage at the time of Joaquín's death—not by a silver bullet but at the hands of Love and his men—Ridge comments: "While their beloved leader was proudly submitting to the inexorable Fate which fell upon him, if we may call it Fate when it was born from his own extreme carelessness *in separating himself from the main body of his men* and in a habitual feeling of too much security at his rendezvous, his followers were struggling for their lives" (emphasis added, 153). In this event and in a prior incident, where Joaquín breaks faith with a fellow Mexican, saying, "This is not my fight—this is Bill's fight" (120), we witness a breakdown in the law of community, a breakdown everywhere duplicated on the American scene.

The polyglot frontier population has no unifying principle to exact loyalty or create community, being made up of brutal Americans, subversive Mexicans, and "so alien a class" as the Chinese. In one description of a frontier town preyed upon by Joaquín's men, Ridge writes: "Men were murdered, and the bloody hand remained unseen. Yet everyone knew that thieves and murderers walked unknown in the midst of the community. A strange dread hung over every face and gave vigilance to every eye" (110). One of the reasons Joaquín is able to avoid capture is that the population is so full of transients that no one knows who actually belongs to the community.

In some ways Ridge applauded this rootlessness and mobility, seeing California as a place of democratic opportunity, a crucible of American culture that could produce positive change in a short space of time. In one letter he wrote, "California still goes ahead, reversing the old order of things. . . . The beggar of today is the prince of tomorrow, and the aristocracy of wealth smells of every trade and calling from a butcher to a perfumer" (Farmer and Strickland, 23).

Like George Copway, Ridge was drawn to the cities, to Sacramento and San Francisco. There he was regarded with respect and was able to live a sophisticated if not entirely comfortable life. For example, he attended the famous literary salons of Ina Coolbrith who, during her long residency in the San Francisco area, entertained such luminaries as Joaquín Miller, John Muir, Jack London, and Mark Twain. Ridge thrived in this kind of atmosphere. In his novel the city is even presented at times as a social form resembling Mount Shasta. At the release of Joaquín and his group by the Tejons, the narrator comments: "Poor fellows! They went forth into the wilderness as naked as on the day they were born and stricken with a blanker poverty than the veriest beggar on the streets of London, or New York, or any other proud city that raises its audacious head above the sea of crime and wretchedness into the pure light of Heaven" (39–40). Here the city seems to transcend its own capacities for violence and inequality as, in other places, the United States as a nation is said to do. It partakes of the ideal in the face of the dismaying reality.

John Rollin Ridge never knew the kind of wilderness life that nurtured Black Hawk and George Copway. Even in Georgia Ridge had no real roots in uncultivated nature, which makes the publisher's preface to his novel especially amusing when it claims that *The Life and Adventures of Joaquín Murieta* is the work of a " 'Cherokee Indian,' born in the woods—reared in the midst of wildest scenery—and familiar with all that is thrilling, fearful, and tragical in a forest life" (2). The Georgia plantations of his family hardly corresponded to this description.

But Rollin Ridge's metropolitanism does not tell the whole story. The year before he wrote his novel, he confessed his loneliness in a letter, referring to "the bent of my mind which leads me back to my own people and to my own country" (Parins, 92). In 1854, the year of the novel's publication, he was thinking about founding an Indian newspaper and also about writing "the history of the Cherokee Nation as it should be written and not as white men will write it" (Parins, 112). In an emotional statement characteristic of his passionate nature, he claimed: "If ever there was a man on earth that loved his people and his kindred, I am that man" (Parins, 114).

Therefore, it seems highly significant that Joaquín's death is brought on by his "carelessness in separating himself from the body of his men," that it occurs in a scene of dispersal (diaspora) where it is "every man for himself." John Rollin Ridge had also separated himself from the Cherokee community and thus he felt cut off, isolated, an exile. As Farmer and Strickland put it: "Ridge's writings speak eloquently of the past, the present, and the future condition of Native Americans and yet they represent not so much the old Indian way as the growing national spirit" (13) of assimilated Indians. Though critical of certain decisions made by the American government, Ridge advocated citizenship for Native Americans, giving them the status of a territorial government first, and then ultimately that of a state with its own representatives in Congress.[13]

Nevertheless, Ridge's focus seems to be more on the rights of the individual than on tribal polity. The "growing national spirit" is one that Ridge equated with "liberty" more than anything else.[14] But liberty as individualism, as Ridge himself seems to know at some level, undermines the force of nation in which Indian life was traditionally rooted.

Unlike George Copway, Ridge "had confidence in the working out of America's Manifest Destiny" (Parins, 124). He believed that societies and nations evolve. Though western nations were, in his estimation, at a higher stage than others, he praised the cultures of the Inca and the Aztec. It is clear from his "Poem" on what makes a nation great (see Parins, 147–51) that race is not the issue. Cultures of varying kinds and colors may emerge as great in the long history of time. Furthermore, both individuals and groups change and progress. Yet, as he puts it in "The Atlantic Cable," "Man is Man in every age and clime." There are no hierarchies of value implicit in nature itself; culture creates the basis for distinctions.

In terms of Indian culture, however, America's evolutionary process might well mean the end of indigenous nations as such. Ridge believed Indians must become amalgamated with white society or risk being wiped out, and this view of historical progression takes us back to the landscape imagery in his poem on Mount Shasta where the hills "in the long review of distance / Range themselves in order grand." If we transform this spatial image into a temporal one, we might see Ridge proposing here a law of history in which different cultures succeed one another in the order of Time. But we must recognize that this image, like the view of Nature this poem proposes, is not very comforting. The Sublime evokes a good deal of terror and dismay and we can see in the poem no clear benefit from it for human beings rooted in local, temporal situations, except a sense of awe.

> The herdsman
> Oft will rein his charger in the plain, and drink
> Into his inmost soul the calm sublimity;
> And little children, playing on the green, shall
> Cease their sport, and, turning to that mountain,
> Old, shall, of their mother ask, "Who made it?"
> And she shall answer, "God!"

But since the summit of Mount Shasta is said to freeze pity's tears and subdue human sympathy, it is hard to know how it can stand as "the guarantee of health and happiness" (25). The humans who live in the shadow of Mount Shasta are like children playing about the feet of a giant, always in danger of being stepped on.

As though uncomfortable with the implications of this grandiose (and inhumane) vision of Nature placed at the beginning of the novel, Ridge later introduces another set of associations which seem at odds with the discourse of the Sublime as "Manifest Destiny" and closer to Romantic Sentimentalism or even, perhaps, to later conceptions of Existentialism.

All-loving Nature is no respecter of persons, and takes to her bosom all her children when they have ceased their wanderings, and eases their heartaches in her embracing arms. We may go down to our graves with the scorn of an indignant world upon us, which hurls us from its presence—but the eternal God allows no fragment of our souls, no atom of our dust, to be lost from his universe. Poised on our own immortality, we may defy the human race and all that exists beneath the throne of God! (54–55)

Here enters the anarchic transpositional principle I mentioned at the beginning, in light of which all principles of human community dissolve but may be assumed to reemerge in the community of souls reconfigured at the throne of God. As is perhaps obvious, it has some affinities with the view of "law" we are given in the poem to Mount

Shasta, for human beings are equalized in their relation to a higher order of being.

Yet one also feels in this passage the longing for acceptance and the isolation of the "exile," as though Ridge, jostled between white culture and Indian affiliation, in some ways contemptuous of both, were seeking a final truth or principle of law to which he could give his allegiance and which would release him from the politics of contestation and violence. If, as has been argued in this chapter, each conception of the law (and of Nature) is contradicted by another, what remains for the individual to believe in? What is the final effect of these juxtapositions? In each category—Nature, Law, and Nation—John Rollin Ridge evokes an unrealizable wish for the resolution of contradiction by means of an absolute, but such absolutes operate of necessity *outside* the realm of human experience. Thus, the ultimate effect of John Rollin Ridge's work is tragic. In his inability to find an experiential model of justice and virtue, Ridge comes to seem a lonely exile forever cast out from the realm in which communal meanings make sense of a fragmented world.

And his life only echoed this sense of displacement and loss. Rollin Ridge died at the age of forty of "softening of the brain," afflicted by gout, alcoholism, and syphilis. Four years later the third edition of *The Life and Adventures of Joaquín Murieta* was published, but the author was forgotten while the myth survived. Today Ridge is little noticed, even by historians of Native American literature, as though, having "separated himself from the main body of his men," he was left to suffer the same indignity as his notorious character.

Like Copway, Ridge's example demonstrates that the deconstruction of national identity has its costs as well as its benefits. All his life Ridge wanted two incompatible things: stability and opportunity, the nation's hoop and the American ladder, what David Hollinger calls "roots and wings."[15] *The Life and Adventures of Joaquín Murieta* reveals by its absent presence his dream of amalgamation *under the law* but at the same time vividly realizes his recurrent nightmare of the breakdown of national culture, with all the disastrous results such a breakdown inevitably entails.

7. Sarah Winnemucca's Mediations

Gender, Race, and Nation

It may be useful at this point to be reminded of where we have been so far in our exploration of Native American constructions of the nation by means of discursive strategies we have named transpositional and subjugated. Black Hawk and George Copway furnish the purest examples of these types, Black Hawk projecting an independent, egalitarian vision of the Sauk vis-à-vis America and Copway envisioning a pan-Indian state in the Dakotas (Kahgega) where Native Americans would be educated in English, supervised by white men and westernized Indians rather than hereditary chiefs, and, with the help of the Gospel, would move up the ladder into positions of power in the existing structure of the United States.

By contrast, William Apess and John Rollin Ridge, as we have seen in the case of Ridge and will see in the case of Apess, both personify America in "outlaws," Ridge in Joaquín Murieta, Apess in King Philip. They use mixed modes of transpositional and subjugated discourse principally to criticize America as a nation of institutionalized injustice, though each presents as well a vision of an idealized nation within which Native Americans would be protected from injustice through law and provided with opportunities to thrive. By focusing on the contradictory aspects of transpositional and subjugated discourse we can see more clearly where the tensions in these documents come from.

If we turn now to Sarah Winnemucca, the picture becomes more complicated because Winnemucca positions herself on the border, advocating accommodation rather than assimilation, preservation of Indian traditions and language but transformation of the hunter-gatherer culture into an agricultural one. Like Copway and Ridge, she wanted citizenship for Native Americans and congressional representation, but, like Black Hawk, she fiercely defended her own people and their culture as fundamentally equal (or even superior) to the whites.

Not surprisingly, Winnemucca's principal literary achievement—
Life Among the Piutes (1883)—is also a hybrid text, rhetorically both
transpositional and subjugated. If we can say that John Rollin Ridge's
use of mixed modes, like George Copway's but to a greater degree
mixed in Ridge, leaves him in the position of an exile, accepting the
loss of a basic conception of national unity even as he continues to
long for it, Sarah Winnemucca's movement between transpositional
codes and forms of subjugation in *Life Among the Piutes* has a far
different effect. Ridge's work leans toward postmodernity, with all of
its possibilities and problems, but it may also be seen as Romantic—
emphasizing the fate of the individual as the contested site of national
identity and justice. In contrast, Sarah Winnemucca's orientation is
tribal. Though her work is an autobiography of sorts, its title is suggestive: *Life Among the Piutes: Their Wrongs and Claims.* It is the
Northern Paiute (this spelling is more usual) community for whom
she seeks justice, not herself alone. Her purpose in writing the book
was distinctly political. According to her biographer Gae Whitney
Canfield, she wrote it to influence Congress to pass legislation that
would improve the condition of her people, and, though she failed in
her larger aims, she succeeded in publicizing the plight of the western
Indians and in moving many individuals to become involved in their
welfare.

This fundamentally political thrust might lead us to conclude that
Life Among the Piutes: Their Wrongs and Claims must necessarily be
an example of subjugated discourse which, as we have said, often
takes oppression as its theme, is political (that is, concerned to effect
changes in power relations) and operates within a hierarchical system
of values according to which Indian writers seek to "move up," at-
taining in time the blessings already enjoyed by white people. However, this last element describes Copway and Ridge to a much greater
degree than it does Sarah Winnemucca. Some critics have argued
recently that the autobiography is "heavily biased by [Sarah Winnemucca's] acculturated and Christianized point of view" (Bataille
and Sands, 21).[1] However, the text itself is outspokenly critical of the
assumption that white culture is superior to the culture of the Indians,
and it is far from delicate in its condemnation of professing Christians. Indeed, Winnemucca did *not* advocate complete assimilation.

There is a wonderful zest in Sarah Winnemucca's writing that seems to come from nothing so much as her firmly held belief that, if only the truth were known, she and her people would be seen as every bit as good as Euro-Americans, indeed in many respects better. As Brumble says: "Winnemucca does not seem to see any . . . fundamental differences between her Indian people and the whites. Certainly she is aware of different customs; she is outraged at how dishonest the whites are, and she contrasts this with the honesty of her own people; she realizes that her people have to learn a great deal in order to become self-supporting farmers, but she nowhere suggests that there are *essential* differences" (64). I would go further than this to say that Sarah Winnemucca insists that the *value* of the two peoples is equal. In short, the premise of the autobiography may be the position of subjugation, but its argument is often distinctly transpositional.

Sarah Winnemucca moves back and forth with surprising ease between the assumptions of white culture (with which she was partly raised) and the beliefs and practices of her own people. In this chapter we will examine Sarah Winnemucca's mediations—both literary and experiential—in the discursive realms of gender, race, and nation. Winnemucca was canny in her use of motifs belonging to what Shirley Samuels has called "the culture of sentiment," but she never fully assimilated; indeed, she died in Bannock Indian Country in Idaho where she had gone to join her sister who was living in a log cabin at Henry's Lake, a far cry from the urban environments where William Apess and John Rollin Ridge ended their lives. At her death she was eulogized by General Howard (for whom Howard University is named). In his short biography of Sarah, he emphasized her role as a native mediator and an American heroine: "She did our government great service, and if I could tell you but a tenth part of all she willingly did to help the white settlers and her own people to live peaceably together I am sure you would think, as I do, that the name of Toc-me-to-ne [Sarah's Indian name, Shell-Flower] should have a place beside the name of Pocahontas in the history of our country" (Canfield, 259).

Sarah Winnemucca's principal value to the American government was as a translator. She spoke three Indian languages as well as Spanish and English. In this role she served both the Indian agents on the reservations and the U.S. Army. It is typical of her desire to bring peoples together and allow passage of ideas from one group to another that she served in this capacity, mediating between various Indian groups and also between whites and Paiutes. However, this role also put her in jeopardy because she became the voice of the American government to her people; since the government was unreliable, her own position was far from secure. Nevertheless, for a long time she continued to believe that she could negotiate effectively by spelling out in detail the issues at hand. In *Life Among the Piutes* she explains: "We Indians never try to rule our people without explaining everything to them. When they understand and consent we have no trouble" (91). Some of the worst problems developed, as Sarah and other Indians have noted, because of inept translators. "Some of the interpreters are very ignorant, and don't understand English enough to know all that is said. This often makes trouble. Then I am sorry to say these Indian interpreters, who are often half-breeds, easily get corrupted, and can be hired by the agents to do or say anything. I know this," she adds, "for some of them are my relatives" (91).[2] Sarah was adept at translation, but even she could not completely avoid the imputation of collaboration with the enemy, especially since at times she worked as a scout for the army. Nevertheless, her main energies were always engaged in the support and defense of the "Numa," as the Paiutes call themselves, using an Indian word that simply means "the People." Though she admits to making some mistakes, many of her efforts were nothing short of heroic.

Sarah Winnemucca was born around 1844—the exact date is not certain—in an area of present-day Nevada where life was hard and white people were scarce. She presents her grandfather (known as Captain Truckee) as the tribal chief, though in fact he was but one of many respected members of the Northern Paiute group and had no unique official standing. Captain Truckee believed that white men were his brothers and therefore adopted an early attitude of acceptance and accommodation toward them. When whites were first spotted in the area, he told the following story about the origins of the human race and the division that followed:

In the beginning of the world there were only four, two girls and two boys. Our forefather and mother were only two, and we are their children. You all know that a great while ago there was a happy family in this world. One girl and one boy were dark and the others were white. For a time they got along together without quarreling, but soon they disagreed, and there was trouble . . . and then our father took the dark boy and girl, and the white boy and girl, and asked them "Why are you so cruel to each other?" They hung down their heads and would not speak. They were ashamed. . . . So he separated his children by a word. He said, "Depart from each other, you cruel children;—go across the mighty ocean and do not seek each other's lives."

So the light girl and boy disappeared by that one word, and their parents saw them no more, and they were grieved, although they knew their children were happy. And by-and-by the dark children grew into a large nation; and we believe it is the one we belong to, and that the nation that sprung from the white children will some time send some one to meet us and heal all the trouble. Now, the white people we saw a few days ago must certainly be our white brothers, and I want to welcome them. (6–7)

It is worth noting that in this story whites and Indians begin on an equal footing. The white people are the exiles, forced to migrate from their homeland in order to avoid bad feeling. However, as is typical of transpositional stories, each group might occupy the position of the other. There is no particular reason why the whites go across the sea and the Indians stay at home.

Captain Truckee was persuaded that no intrinsic factors prevented the unification of the two groups. He saw the arrival of the whites as fortuitous, but at first Sarah was terrified by them, and her grandfather had to insist that she accompany him to the white settlements. Eventually she was even taken to California, where, in the Santa Cruz area, she became fluent in Spanish by the age of ten. It was here that she had the little formal education she received, a brief stint in a convent school. Then she returned from the coast and settled in Stockton, living with white families (one of which she later said "adopted" her), learning English, and dressing in American clothes. She had to work in the white households where she lived, but the labor was not strenuous compared to life among the Paiutes, and with the Ormsbys—who housed her for a considerable time—she was treated almost like a daughter, went to frontier-style dances involving both Indians and whites, and met many important local people.

Then in 1865 a man named Captain Wells, angered by cattle stealing and the murder of two miners, led a surprise attack on an encampment of Paiutes—old men, women, and children—at Mud (or Winnemucca) Lake. Old Winnemucca was off hunting with the younger men. In the middle of the night Wells surprised the Indians, killing out of the thirty in camp all but one, Sarah's sister, who managed to get away. It was a horrifying massacre and, unfortunately, soon to be followed by others. As Sarah describes it: "After the soldiers had killed all but some little children and babies still tied up in their baskets, the soldiers took them also, and set the camp on fire and threw them into the flames to see them burn alive. I had one baby brother killed there" (78).[3] In the year following, disease spread among the Indians, and Sarah lost her mother and the sister, Mary, who had escaped the massacre.

In the wake of these devastating events, Sarah decided to leave white society and return to live with her people at Pyramid Lake Reservation. This was only one of many such movements she made in her life, going back and forth between Indian and white settlements. By now what was called the "Humboldt Code" was in effect among whites: "kill and lay waste everything pertaining to the tribes, whenever found—no trials, but at arms; no prisoners; no red tape" (Canfield, 49). In 1867 Truckee John, Sarah's uncle, who had built a cabin, fenced land, and was raising good crops, was summarily murdered on the reservation because he reminded a white man of one of the hostiles in the recent Pyramid Lake uprising. There seemed to be nowhere for Sarah and her people to go. However, in 1868 Captain Jerome contacted Sarah and her brother Natchez, offering the Indians safety at Camp McDermit in exchange for bringing in Old Winnemucca who had disappeared into the hills after discovering the murders of his family and friends. Sarah accepted the invitation, Old Winnemucca and his people were brought in, and they spent several years of peace and relative prosperity at Camp McDermit.

However, life at Camp McDermit required Sarah to return to the basic Paiute way of living which she had not experienced for a long time. It meant sleeping on the ground, digging for roots, wearing dusty, rarely washed clothes, and occupying the traditional Paiute shelter of branches covered with tin, canvas, and blankets called a "nobee." During this time, she was interviewed by a reporter from the Sacramento *Record* who published these remarks: "She said: I am glad to see you, although I have not now a parlor to ask you into except the one made by nature for all. I like this Indian life tolerably well; however, my only object in staying with these people is that I may do them good. I would rather be with my people, but not to live with them as they live. I was not raised so" (Canfield, 65). Though Sarah was not used to the ruggedness of Indian life, she got along well with the women and readily returned to their hardscrabble form of existence. Throughout her life, when she was away from her people and living with whites, she would long for the pine nuts that were a principal part of the Paiute diet. Sometimes she would beg her brother to send her some just so she could have a taste of home.

During the Bannock War, when the Paiutes split into "hostile" and "friendly" camps, Sarah went to work for the American Army. Most of her people were not involved in the hostilities and Sarah felt that she could serve a useful function by helping to limit the war. Taking on a role usually reserved for men, she liberated her father (and other "friendlies") from the camp of the hostiles and rode hundreds of miles through enemy territory, the only person (along with her sister-in-law Mattie) who was willing to undertake this dangerous mission. She translated between the two camps and helped to end the war.

Most of Sarah's life was spent dealing with fraudulent Indian agents and attempting to raise the consciousness of the American people concerning the terrible conditions under which Indians in the West were living. Her first "performance" was with Old Winnemucca in San Francisco where she participated in "Indian scenes" to raise money for the Paiutes. Later she made many trips across the country, lectured widely, met with presidents and public officials, all in an attempt to bring justice to the Numa. Though she was not able to overcome all the obstacles facing her or her people, she left a vital record of her efforts in *Life Among the Piutes,* a work which has only recently been republished by University of Nevada Press (1994).

After her final visit to the East, when she gave hundreds of lectures to packed crowds in many cities[4] and published her book, Sarah returned with little to show for her efforts. Her last husband (Lewis Hopkins) gambled away her money and then fell ill, requiring expensive medical care. She could not get the support from the government or private donors that would have made possible a new life for her people. So instead she went home to the reservation. "She slept in a *nobee* on the ground with a couple of blankets, having given most of her belongings and clothing to destitute friends and relatives. She returned to the old diet of pine nuts and fish" (Canfield, 218). Sometime during this period, she caught a fever (possibly malaria) which plagued her for the rest of her life, and she became half-paralyzed with rheumatism. The Indian women placed her in piles of warm ashes with blankets to try to offset her chills. It was a far cry from the life she had led in the East where she was called a "princess," ate her meals in private homes and hotels, and wore elaborate and expensive clothes. But it was typical of her ability to live in both worlds, Indian and white, an ability not shared by other acculturated Indians such as George Copway and John Rollin Ridge who spent most of their lives apart from their tribes, living like white men.

At the end of her life, however—after the death of Old Winnemucca, the separation of the people on several reservations, and the failure of her efforts to raise money and reunite them—Sarah was rejected by many of the Numa and left to construct a new community on a smaller scale. She settled with her brother Natchez who was attempting to farm near Lovelock, Nevada, on a piece of land owned by the railroad but donated for farming, probably by Leland Stanford. Here she established the Peabody Indian School (named after the tireless though now elderly reformer Elizabeth Peabody) and taught bilingual courses to twenty-six Indian children—an almost unknown form of Indian education at that time.

In this project, too, we can see her attempts at mediation, for it was her intention "to create a school taught by and for Indians, where

they would not be separated from the Indian life-ways and languages, as they were in the government boarding schools, which
were miles from their homes" (Canfield, 226–27). The Bureau of
Indian Affairs, to their great discredit, refused to give any money to
the kind of education Sarah provided. This was partly due to her
ongoing battles with them (about which more will be said below) and
partly due to their conscious decision to support educational programs that would fundamentally alter Native Americans, assimilating
them into white society.

Earlier examples of Indian schools were mainly of two types:
manual labor schools which ran day programs that required the Indians to do extensive work on the reservations, thus reducing the
amount of government money required to support them, and local
mission schools where Indians were indoctrinated in Christianity and
forbidden to practice their own spiritual traditions.[5]

After the Dawes Act of 1887 passed the Congress—a piece of
legislation that Sarah herself had supported because it provided land
ownership for Indians—the "boarding school" concept was put in
place, an idea Sarah deeply disliked. The Dawes Act was the offspring
of Senator Henry L. Dawes who had taken a great interest in Sarah
when she was in the East. It appealed to her initially as an alternative
to the reservation system because it allowed Indian families to become self-sufficient. They were to be given 160 acres of land, and
after twenty-five years they would receive title to the property and
American citizenship. All of this was part of the move to "assimilate"
Native Americans and break up the old tribal structures. Since Sarah
favored agricultural self-sufficiency, she supported it at first, but
when she understood the threat it represented to communal traditions and to Indian families, she bitterly opposed its educational philosophy. Her school was the alternative she offered.

Two Indian schools already had a national reputation for their
success in "civilizing" the Indians: the Carlisle School in Pennsylvania (where Zitkala-Sa—Gertrude Bonnin—would someday teach)
and the Hampton Institute in Virginia. "General Samuel Chapman
Armstrong, the head of the Hampton Institute, believed that the
sooner Indian children were taken from their parents, their lan-

guages, and their cultures, the sooner they would be 'Americanized' "
(Canfield, 239). With the passage of the Dawes Act, the government
decided to place all of its resources for Indian education behind this
disruptive scheme, and consequently Indian children (when they
could be found) were taken, even without their parents' consent, and
shipped hundreds, sometimes thousands, of miles away to schools
where they were not allowed to speak their languages, visit their
parents, practice their religion, or in any other way assert an "Indian"
identity. Zitkala-Sa was herself educated according to this plan.

Sarah was opposed to it, however, and knew that her people
deeply resented the idea of having their children virtually kidnapped
and sent away. Since she spoke three Indian languages fluently, she
was in a good position to give her students training in both English
and Indian tongues. She made great headway with her scholars,
wrote everything on the board and explained it carefully in their
native language, and had her students copy the English phrases and
learn them by heart. According to Canfield, "Sarah told Elizabeth
that her students never forgot those words, but wrote them all over
fences in Lovelock" (232). Many people visited the school and were
impressed by her teaching and her students. Nevertheless, like so
many of Sarah's projects, it came to nothing when the school had to
be closed in 1888. Her last husband, Lewis Hopkins, had used up not
only all her money but her brother's as well, causing a rift in the
family.

When Lewis died, Sarah and her brother were reconciled, but the
Peabody Indian School experiment came to an end. Natchez eventually left farming (where his struggles with his white neighbors
proved debilitating) and returned to the reservation. Sarah spent the
last three years of her life with her sister Elma in Idaho where she
died, probably due to complications associated with her "fever,"[6] in
1891 at the age of forty-seven.

She had published a book, become notorious in Washington for
her opposition to the Bureau of Indian Affairs and its reservation
system; she had engaged the interest and support of white feminists
such as Mary Mann and Elizabeth Peabody; she had earned the respect of General Howard; indigenous people throughout Indian terri-

tory knew her name. Even today she is accorded an honorable place in the history of Native American women. In their essay on this topic, M. Annette Jaimes and Theresa Halsey mention *Life Among the Piutes* respectfully as playing an important and influential role in "the adoption by Indians of written articulation as a mode of political action" (327).

Life Among the Piutes was certainly a strategic text, and there is little doubt that it was composed by Sarah Winnemucca. Mary Peabody Mann, who edited the manuscript and corrected the spelling, wrote to a friend that she was deeply moved by the simple honesty of Sarah's storytelling.

I wish you could see her manuscript as a matter of curiosity. I don't think the English language ever got such a treatment before. I have to recur to her sometimes to know what a word is, as spelling is an unknown quantity to her, as you mathematicians would express it. She often takes syllables off of words & adds them or rather prefixes them to other words, but the story is heart-breaking, and told with a simplicity and eloquence that cannot be described, for it is not high-faluting eloquence, tho' sometimes it lapses into verse (and quite poetical verse too). I was always considered fanatical about Indians, but I have a wholly new conception of them now, and we civilized people may well stand abashed before their purity of life & their truthfulness. (Canfield, 203)

Mary Mann and her sister Elizabeth Peabody undertook to raise money for the publication of the manuscript and Elizabeth made sure that it got into the hands of many prominent politicians. At her death Mary Mann left most of her small estate to Sarah.

Though there is little evidence of editorial "tampering" with the text, beyond what would be expected from an editor, there is considerable evidence of influence. In particular, one can see the way Winnemucca's argument is positioned within the context of the "culture of sentiment" that had nourished Elizabeth Peabody and Mary Peabody Mann for half a century. Both women had been abolitionists, and they also worked for educational reforms, especially those affecting women and children. After the death of Horace Mann, Mary's husband, she and Elizabeth lived together in modest rented rooms in

Boston. Often they did not even have a fire but sat in their cold quarters writing letters and raising money for charitable causes. Sarah's connection to them and the book she produced under their auspices represent the ongoing influence of sentimental reform ideology, its emphasis upon compassion and sacrifice in the face of an increasingly selfish and materialistic society.

One passage from the book will serve to orient us to Winnemucca's rhetorical style. It appears toward the end, at a point in the story when Sarah has become deeply frustrated with the cruelty and intransigence of Agent Wilbur at the Yakima Reservation where part of her people are being held. In the form in which Sarah chooses to address the reader, we can see her tendency to combine outrage with sentimental appeal:

Oh, for shame! You who are educated by a Christian government in the art of war; the practice of whose profession makes you natural enemies of the savages, so called by you. Yes, you, who call yourselves the great civilization; you who have knelt upon Plymouth Rock, covenanting with God to make this land the home of the free and the brave. Ah, then you rise from your bended knees and seizing the welcoming hands of those who are owners of this land, which you are not, your carbines rise upon the bleak shore, and your so-called civilization sweeps inland from the ocean wave; but, oh, my God! leaving its pathway marked by crimson lines of blood, and strewed by the bones of two races, the inheritor and the invader; and I am crying out to you for justice, — yes, pleading for the far-off plains of the West, for the dusky mourner, whose tears of love are pleading for her husband, or for their children, who are sent far away from them. Your Christian minister [Agent Wilbur of Yakima] will hold my people against their will; not because he loves them, — no, far from it, — but because it puts money in his pockets. (207)

Here we see how gender (the "dusky mourner"), race (inheritor vs. invader), and nation (epitomized in both the Paiutes and the Puritan beginnings of America) are all constituted through the experience of wounding and sacrifice. As *Life Among the Piutes* demonstrates at length, the "nation" for Sarah Winnemucca is the community for whom and with whom one will suffer.

In what follows, we will examine Sarah Winnemucca's role as sacrificial intermediary, an advocate of *both-and* rather than *either-or*. She took on both male and female roles, advocated cooperation between red and white, and tried to position the Paiute nation as a viable entity in the heart of America. Inevitably she presented herself (and her family members, Truckee, Old Winnemucca, and Natchez) as individuals embodying American ideals: republican liberty, military courage, Christian compassion, and democratic justice. Thus in the "home of the free and the brave"—"the cradle of liberty"—"God's chosen instrument" achieves a greater degree of concreteness and reality in the figure of Sarah Winnemucca herself than in the presidents, government employees, or Indian agents who might otherwise be expected to embody these American ideals. Sarah, like Black Hawk, becomes both the personification of her own Indian nation and the quintessentially American underdog, a personification of America as a land of possibility. "When I think of my past life," Sarah begins, "and the bitter trials I have endured, I can scarcely believe I live, and yet I do; and, with the help of Him who notes the sparrow's fall, I mean to fight for my down-trodden race while life lasts" (6).

If in the long quotation given above we can see the construction of gender, race, and nation as sacrificial bodies, we can also see the presence of both transpositional and subjugated rhetoric. The bones of two races mingle as inheritor and invader lie side by side in true transpositional fashion. Nevertheless, Winnemucca pleads as a subjugated, colonized individual for the liberation of her people from Yakima, using phrases, such as "the land of the free and the brave" and "the dusky mourner," that clearly mimic the dominant discourse in the hope of bringing about political change. Sarah speaks as a wounded representative of her people in an effort to effect a reciprocal "wounding" in her reader, hoping to open up through this double discourse a gash in the kind of hegemonic national narrative that tends to close down possibilities for Native Americans by allocating to them a merely passive and historic role.

Much of this discourse can be understood with reference to "the culture of sentiment" which, as Shirley Samuels shows, "is literally at the heart of nineteenth-century American culture" (4). Though one response to sentimentalism in the (white) reader could be a sort of passive sympathy, people on the margins—slaves, Indians, immigrants, for example—found it useful because it was also capable of doing serious political work. Many of the narratives written by ex-slaves—for example, Harriet Jacobs, William Wells Brown, Frederick Douglass—made use of sentimental rhetoric, because, as Samuels says: "As a set of cultural practices designed to evoke a certain form of emotional response, usually empathy, in the reader or viewer, sentimentality produces or reproduces spectacles that cross race, class, and gender boundaries" (4–5). By foregrounding the problem of the body politic—the refusal of raced, classed, and gendered bodies to stay in their places in the national narrative—minority sentimental literature in general, and *Life Among the Piutes* in particular, gives us a new story, imagining what Samuels calls "the nation's bodies and the national body" in a new way.

Clearly, nineteenth-century feminism played a major role in the culture of sentiment, and through Mary Mann and Elizabeth Peabody, Sarah became aware of its force. For example, she added to her repertoire one particular lecture—"for women only"—on sexual mores and domestic culture among the Paiutes. Elizabeth, who attended a great many of these public performances, claimed that it was "a lecture that never failed to excite the moral enthusiasm of every woman that heard it" (Canfield, 203). When Mary Mann came to write her Editor's Preface to the volume, she stressed that "it is of the first importance to hear what only an Indian *and an Indian woman* can tell" (emphasis added, n.p.).

It is impossible to know to what extent Sarah was influenced by women's literature, in particular the sentimental novel, when she wrote *Life Among the Piutes*. Her formal education was scant, amounting to only three weeks at a convent school in San Jose from which she and her sister were removed when the parents of white students complained about their presence. According to Fowler, upon her return "she spent a goodly proportion of her meager earnings [as a domestic] on books" (37). Nevertheless, in *Life* Sarah claims that she has always had difficulty "reading writing" (82).

A. LaVonne Ruoff speculates that Sarah Winnemucca (like Apess and Copway) may have absorbed sentimental ideas from the culture itself rather than from specific texts. "To gain the attention of their audiences, they structured their narratives to reflect not only native oral traditions but also the forms and themes to which their readers would respond. The presence of aspects of popular literature in their autobiographies may reflect the narrators' responses to their non-Indian audiences, spouses, friends, and editors. Consequently, these parallels may well mirror the taste of the age rather than the literary background of the narrators" ("Three Nineteenth-Century American Indian Autobiographers," 269).

Nevertheless, it is tantalizing to compare *Life Among the Piutes* with a sentimental novel such as *Uncle Tom's Cabin*. Both works emphasize the agony felt when families are separated, on the one hand, by the reservation system and, on the other, by slavery. Both value tears. When the Bannock War splits the tribe and some are forced to return to the reservation supervised by the heartless Indian agent Rinehart, Sarah comments, "You should see how my people love each other. Old and young were crying at parting with each other" (201). When members of the tribe are reunited, they fall weeping into one another's arms: "It is the way we savages do when we meet each other," Sarah comments sarcastically, "we cry with joy and gladness" (101). Elsewhere she again makes the point that "Although we are savages, we love one another as well as the fairest of the land" (129).

Both Sarah and her brother Natchez try to engage white sympathies by means of affecting transpositional rhetoric emphasizing parallels between Indians and whites. When they go to Washington to meet with Secretary of the Interior Carl Schurz, Natchez says: "Oh, Good Father, have you wife or child? Do you love them? If you love them, think how you would feel if they were taken away from you where you could not go to see them, nor they come to you" (219–20). Harriet Beecher Stowe uses the same kind of appeal in some of her direct addresses to the reader.

Sarah clearly links such tears to feminine sensibilities among Anglo-Americans. White women cry but white men do not. At the end of the autobiography, Sarah confronts President Rutherford B.

Hayes, whom she has already seen briefly in Washington about Indian affairs. Her story once again reflects the conventions of women's literature and mirrors the situation of the slaves in *Uncle Tom's Cabin:*

> When I was in Vancouver, President Hayes and his wife came there, and I went to see them. I spoke to him as I had done in Washington to the Secretary, and said to him, "You are a husband and father, and you know how you would suffer to be separated from your wife and children by force, as my people still are, husbands from wives, parents from children, notwithstanding Secretary Schurz's order." Mrs. Hayes cried all the time I was talking, and he said, "I will see about it." But nothing was ever done that I ever heard of. (246)

Sarah is careful to show us that, despite the prejudices of racist whites, she herself is as emotional as any white woman. In one scene, where Sarah in desperation is pleading for her people who are starving, Colonel Wilkinson says to her: "Why, Sarah, what are you crying about? You are only an Indian woman. Why, Indian women never cry" (243). Obviously he is wrong.

Along with their capacities for empathy, women, according to Sarah Winnemucca, can serve their people politically as well. Among the Paiutes, she says, women as well as men contribute to the decision-making process: "The women know as much as the men do, and their advice is often asked. We have a republic as well as you. The council-tent is our Congress, and anybody can speak who has anything to say, women and all" (53). Just as we see in *Uncle Tom's Cabin* that Senator Bird's wife is potentially a better legislator than her husband because she connects her feelings to her judgment, Winnemucca writes: "If women could go into your Congress I think justice would soon be done the Indians" (53).

Though Sarah posed for publicity pictures that emphasized a "feminine" appearance,[7] and the reviews of her lectures describe her self-presentation as "feminine" and "womanly," *Life Among the Piutes* gives a far more flexible version of the roles women can play. Paiute women do strenuous manual labor. When a woman marries, "She is to dress the game, prepare the food, clean the buckskins, make his moccasins, dress his hair, bring all the wood—in short, do all the household work. She promises to 'be himself,' and she fulfills her promise" (49). To prepare herself for marriage, a woman must pile up wood, fifteen stacks a day for twenty days.

Sarah Winnemucca herself was married at least three, possibly four times, each time with disastrous results.[8] With the exception of Lewis Hopkins, who was merely an inveterate gambler, she left her husbands because they proved to be abusive or alcoholic. At least three of the husbands were white. Though according to all accounts, she was actively heterosexual, Sarah is sometimes referred to as "ber-dache," that is, a third-gender or mixed gender person. In his classic work on this subject, *The Zuni Man-Woman*, Will Roscoe defines female berdaches as "women who assumed male roles as warriors and chiefs or engaged in male work or occupations" (5). This was certainly true of Sarah as she does not hesitate to inform her white readers in *Life Among the Piutes*.

During the Bannock War, she spent hard days in the saddle riding between the warring parties. "This was the hardest work I ever did for the government in all my life,—the whole round trip, from 10 o'clock June 13 up to June 15, arriving back at 5:30 P.M., having been in the saddle night and day [mostly without eating]; distance, about two hundred and twenty-three miles. Yes, I went for the government when the officers could not get an Indian man or a white man to go for love or money. I, only an Indian woman, went and saved my father and his people" (164). The act of saving Old Winnemucca occurred when she and her sister-in-law Mattie, in disguise, entered the camp of the hostiles and managed to free many of the Paiutes being held there against their will.

Sarah is not shy about letting the reader know that her role in the tribe was considered equal to that of a man. Once again her activities as a mediator put her in the position of uniting opposing categories: male and female, red and white. Sarah includes a speech, supposedly given by her father, at the time of her daring rescue. In her account, he says to his men:

I am much pained because my dear daughter has come with the fearful things which have happened in the war. Oh, yes! my child's name is so far

beyond yours; none of you can ever come up to hers. Her name is everywhere and every one praises her. Oh! how thankful I feel that it is my own
child who has saved so many lives, not only mine, but a great many, both
whites and her own people. Now hereafter we will look on her as our
chieftain, for none of us are worthy of being chief but her, and all I can say to
you is to send her to the wars and you stay and do women's work, and talk
as women do. (193)

Though she was ready to do more than "women's work," one
issue that concerned Sarah deeply was sexual assault. When she and
her sister were young, they were left in a white community by Captain Truckee. "The men who my grandpa called his brothers would
come into our camp and ask my mother to give our sister to them.
They would come at night, and we would all scream and cry; but that
would not stop them" (34). Finally, they are saved by being able to
live with a white family. But again and again women are raped. The
Bannock War begins when "One of the Indians had a sister out digging some roots, and these white men went to the women who were
digging, and caught this poor girl, and used her shamefully. The
other women ran away and left this girl to the mercy of those white
men, and it was on her account that her brother went and shot them"
(139). At another place she reports: "Sometimes [white men] would
throw a rope over our women, and do fearful things to them" (228).
Sarah herself is not about to put up with such treatment. She thus
asserts her belief that a woman should fight fire with fire to prevent
herself from being raped. "If such an outrageous thing is to happen to
me, it will not be done by one man or two, while there are two women
with knives, for I know what an Indian woman can do. She can never
be outraged by one man; but she may by two" (228). In fact, Sarah
did carry a knife, and she used it on more than one occasion. Canfield
points out that "As an Indian she had no legal protection of her
person or property" (78). Once she was actually jailed for cutting a
man who tried to interfere with her, but the charges were dropped
when the size of her knife (which was very small) was revealed.
According to her biographer, Sarah Winnemucca got into physical struggles with both men and women. She sometimes gambled and

drank to excess. In these ways she did not fit the stereotypes of Victorian womanhood, but she was fierce in her defense of herself as a moral person. *Life Among the Piutes* includes a number of testimonials to her character because she was a target of character assassination by the Bureau of Indian Affairs. Corrupt Indian agents, whose evil behavior she had exposed, tried to ruin her reputation; their journal in Washington, *The Council Fire and Arbitrator,* published scurrilous accounts of the "Amazonian champion of the Army [who] was being used as a tool of the army officers to create public sentiment in favor of the transfer of the Indian Bureau to the War Department" (Canfield, 204). According to them, "She is so notorious for her untruthfulness as to be wholly unreliable. She is known . . . to have been a common camp follower, consorting with common soldiers. It is a great outrage on the respectable people of Boston for General Howard or any other officer of the army to foist such a woman of any race upon them" (204).

Such imputations of immorality made Sarah furious, and she certainly intended *Life Among the Piutes* as a defense of her character. But even more important to her was its function in documenting racial injustice. Winnemucca repeatedly uses the term "race" to refer to her Indian people. In the passage quoted above, she says "I mean to fight for my down-trodden race while life lasts" (6). When her brother Tom died on the reservation, she published in a local paper a despairing account of the situation she was facing by 1885, two years after the publication of her book. With their people divided among several reservations from which they were not allowed to move, and the many promises Sarah had received from Washington all unfulfilled, the Indians had become apathetic and even hostile toward her. She had come to an impasse:

Now I desire to say here that I have no personal feelings against Mr. Gibson [the Pyramid Lake Reservation Agent]. I have fought him and all other agents for the general good of my race, but as recent events have shown that they are not disposed to stand by me in the fight, I shall relinquish it. As they will not help themselves, no one can help them. "Those that would be free must strike the blow themselves." I have not contended for Democratic,

Republican, Protestant or Baptist for an agent. I have worked for freedom, I have laboured to give my race a voice in the affairs of the nation, but they prefer to be slaves so let it be. (Canfield, 231)

This passage is particularly interesting because it establishes the sacrificial perspective as it relates to race and nation. Sarah presents herself as having demonstrated her loyalty by her acts of sacrifice. She also relates the Indian cause to "the affairs of the nation." Those who wish to preserve the tribe as one of "the nations within," must be willing to accept a sacrificial role.

Just as the sentimental novel helps us to see the way in which gender in *Life Among the Piutes* both adheres to and departs from white female norms, so we can see here that slave narratives (also a major feature of the "culture of sentiment") provide a helpful comparison to Sarah Winnemucca's presentation of Indian affairs. The emphasis on the word "race"—which is not used in earlier Indian texts in the same way—suggests that Winnemucca was aware of the discourse of race as it grew out of abolition and postwar African American discussions. She calls her people "slaves," and she quotes (inaccurately) a passage from Byron's *Childe Harold's Pilgrimage*, also used by Frederick Douglass as an epigraph to part 4 of his novella *The Heroic Slave*: "Know ye not / Who would be free, *themselves* must strike the blow" (60).

Like William Apess, Sarah Winnemucca sometimes suggests that people of color share common ground as victims of white oppression. For example, at an early point in *Life Among the Piutes*, she tells us that her grandfather would not travel with a party of white men because their captain was "whipping negroes who were driving his team" (23). However, at other points she implicates black men along with whites as engaging in immoral behavior toward white women. "I am so proud to say that my people have never outraged your women, or have even insulted them by looks or words. Can you say the same of the negroes or the whites? They do commit some horrible outrages on your women, but you do not drive them round like dogs" (244).

Here, echoing racist beliefs about black men, she seems more than willing to make exceptions to the premise that people of color are united by their position as victims of white oppression. Similarly, Captain Truckee, who fought in the Mexican War, exempts Mexicans from his usual belief in universal brotherhood. "They are not my brothers" (28), he says. Sarah herself makes disparaging remarks about the Umatilla Indians and the Flatheads.

Even the terms "black" and "white" do not necessarily denote stable racial categories or moral evaluations. Oytes, a Paiute who refuses to go along with the reservation system even as directed by the kindly agent Samuel Parrish, insists that he is "black": "I cannot call that white man my father. My father was black, like myself, and you are all white but me, and, therefore, tell him I quit my country" (113). However, we do not really know what Oytes means when he calls himself "black" and the others "white." It is not likely that Oytes means his father was African American because on a subsequent page he links himself with Sarah who is a full-blooded Paiute. He says to her, " 'You and I are two black ones. We have not white fathers [*sic*] lips.' I said, 'No, we are two bad ones. Bad ones don't need pity from anyone' " (114).

The tale of racial oppression that Sarah tells, often quite horrifying in its brutality, is one in which white men such as the Indian agents insist upon racial binaries that her own narrative serves to complicate. As we see from her stories, there are good Indians and bad Indians; there are good white people and bad white people. In her comments about the corrupt translators, she adds: "There are unprincipled men in all tribes, as I suppose there are among all people" (216). This statement reflects the deeply transpositional nature of Sarah Winnemucca's thinking. She was a mediator. As Gae Whitney Canfield summarizes her position: "She was an integrated, but complicated, person who understood the realities of her situation as well as anyone and yet had a romantic attitude toward life. She wanted to believe in the wisdom and sincerity of the whites and to have their respect. She also wanted to believe in the natural intuitive wisdom and goodness of her people and to continue to command the Paiutes' respect" (191).

It will be remembered that transpositional narratives are generally reciprocal, egalitarian, ethical, utopian, horizontal, and direct. In what sense is it fair to call Sarah Winnemucca's thinking "utopian" since it is also clearly "political," and we have for purposes of ideal integrity tended to oppose utopian visions to political maneuvering?

The utopian aspect of Winnemucca's project may be seen in her efforts at "translation." At no point does she seem to recognize that the "language" of one culture inevitably renders the assumptions of another culture opaque to some degree. In Sarah's mind a clear representation of suffering must undo a system based upon institutionalized disempowerment. Therefore, for most of her life she believed that her exposition of the truth must prevail. All that was needed was a powerful enough representation. The benefits of "civilization" and the ethical strength of "native tradition" might exist side by side. At one point she breaks out: "Oh, my dear good Christian people, how long are you going to stand by and see us suffer at your hands? Oh, dear friends, you are wrong when you say it will take two or three generations to civilize my people. No! I say it will not take that long if you will only take an interest in teaching us" (89).

Though it focuses upon suffering, this passage is utopian because it assumes the possibility of the easy coexistence of the two cultures, and it ignores the threat to Indian traditions posed by "Americanization." Similarly, Sarah seemed to believe that she could be a Christian and also participate in Wovoka's Ghost Dances performed in order to usher in the Indian millennium.[9] Wovoka's vision was itself utopian because it prophesied the return of Indian supremacy in the West without use of force. According to the prophet, white people would simply fade away, and then all the world's peoples would henceforth live in harmony.

Sarah Winnemucca had no clear political plan for preserving the integrity of her people within the larger nation of the United States. Unlike Copway and Ridge, she did not advocate statehood as a political strategy, though she did believe in the importance of congressional representation. Sometimes she linked Native Americans to other marginal groups who, she felt, were better treated. For example, one newspaper quoted her as saying, presumably with heavy irony, that "if she possessed the wealth of several rich ladies whom she mentioned [perhaps Emma Lazarus, the author of the poem on the Statue of the Liberty, was one],[10] she would place all the Indians of Nevada on ships in our harbor, take them to New York, and land them as immigrants, that they might be received with open arms, blessed with the blessings of universal suffrage, and thus placed beyond the necessity of reservation help and out of the reach of Indian agents" (Canfield, 224).

As we all know, no such warm welcome greeted those who disembarked at Ellis Island in the late nineteenth century. Furthermore, immigrants like Indians were expected to give up their traditions and assimilate as soon as possible. However, Sarah Winnemucca and her family seemed to believe that one could give one's allegiance to America and still preserve one's traditional culture. Captain Truckee taught his people to sing "The Star-Spangled Banner" and salute the American flag. He saw no particular conflict in the Paiutes continuing as an Indian nation and also declaring loyalty to the larger national body called the United States. Old Winnemucca marched in parades, wearing, like Black Hawk, an officer's coat provided by the whites. Sarah interprets this transpositionally, saying: "The Indian is like my white brother Emperor Norton: he likes epaulets" (Canfield, 36).

Though we might say she was overly optimistic, she was also stubborn. As further evidence of Winnemucca's resistance to engulfment by the dominant culture, one might educe her beliefs about religion as presented in *Life Among the Piutes*. If we compare that text with the works of converted Indians such as William Apess and George Copway, we can see that Sarah Winnemucca—despite her own Methodist conversion—makes far fewer concessions to the superiority of white religion. The traditional beliefs of her nation are presented positively with no apology when they diverge from Christianity. When, as a child, Sarah is frightened by the Methodist minister's portrayal of hell, her mother tells her "that it was only here that people did wrong and were in the hell that it made, and that those that were in the Spirit-land saw us here and were sorry for us. But we should go to them when we died, where there was never any wrongdoing, and so no hell." Sarah presents this to the reader with the summary comment "That is our religion" (55). In contrast to George

Copway's hesitations about the value of dreams, Sarah provides three separate examples in which dreams tell Indians something that has just happened or will happen shortly. She merely comments: "Many of my family have seen things in their dreams that were really happening" (185).

By her lights, it seems, native religion is not in conflict with Christianity: "But the whites have not waited to find out how good the Indians were, and what ideas they had of God, just like those of Jesus, who called him Father, just as my people do, and told men to do to others as they would be done by, just as my people do" (51). Transpositional rhetoric here—"just as my people do"—finds an equivalence like Black Hawk's between the *professed principles* of the two cultures if not between their actual practices.

In what sense does this add up to a "new" vision of the body politic along the lines suggested by some versions of sentimentalism? Sarah's vision of the nation is not atomistic but familial. The community must be held together by loyalty and reciprocity; if necessary individuals must be prepared to sacrifice their own well-being for the good of others. New ideas and new people may be incorporated into the group but the position of chief should remain inherited. (Remember George Copway's opposition to inherited chiefships.) Winnemucca writes:

My people, and I think . . . Indian people [in general], [do not] feel the same respect for a *made* chief. Sometimes chiefs are chosen by others and set over tribes. That breaks up the family life that is the best thing for Indians. I do not like to think of my people as separated from each other. Their love for their chief holds them together and makes them do right. A tribe is a large family. If a chief appoints sub-chiefs to help him take care of his people, they are respected unless they do wrong; but as I said before, no man can be a leader among Indians who is not a good man. (194)

Of course, from one point of view this is not a new vision of the body politic at all. In his speech aboard the *Arbella*, John Winthrop insisted that the Puritans should see themselves as similarly knit together by the bond of love: "We must delight in each other, make others' conditions our own, rejoice together, mourn together, labor and suffer together, always having before our eyes our commission and community in the work, our community as members of the same body" (McMichael, 67).

What distinguishes Winnemucca's view from Winthrop's is that the communal family (or nation) is theoretically open to all people not just to those, like Winthrop's Christians, who have bound themselves together through a covenant. Sarah says: "there is no word so endearing as the word father, and that is why we call all good people father or mother; no matter who it is, — negro, white man, or Indian, and the same with the women" (39). Thus, the communal "family" is not defined according to principles of gender hierarchy or racial inheritance. Its boundaries are more flexible.

Perhaps it was the very amorphousness of Sarah Winnemucca's vision of the nation that kept it from being viable, however. The Paiutes themselves were decentralized, with Southern Paiutes a quite separate group speaking a different language and Northern Paiutes spread out over a vast territory congregating around several different leaders. The people Sarah speaks for come together as a "nation" mainly in her text and mostly in opposition to the actions of the American "state." We see little of America except through the acts of its government agents and little of the governmental structure of the Numa except as it is overpowered by the American state. Nation and state are here opposed and mutually constituting.

As we survey the nationalism of native peoples in works such as this one, we confront a paradox: the impossibility but nevertheless the necessity of bringing divergent ideas of polity together in one national narrative space. However, the postmodern model of a decentered nation in perpetual motion seems politically vulnerable. Articulated political action that goes beyond more than a few individuals is impossible from the position of pure diaspora.[11] There must be some center. But there must also be a recognition of the incoherence, the instability, the inevitably exclusionary nature of all such centers. It is these features of "nation" that Native American writings such as *Life Among the Piutes* help us to see most clearly.

8. Personifying America

Apess's "Eulogy on King Philip"

It may seem peculiar, as indeed in some respects it is, to conclude an investigation of nineteenth-century Native American literature with one of its earliest examples, William Apess's "Eulogy on King Philip," delivered in Boston as a sermon, published in two editions (1836 and 1837), and then all but forgotten.[1] However, from the perspective of considering nationalist rhetoric, there is no nineteenth-century Native American text more engaging, tantalizing, or challenging. Therefore, I turn to it now as a way of bringing closure to our discussion of personification, transpositional and subjugated modes of discourse, and mirroring—these strategies of national narrative that have principally occupied us in this study.

The "Eulogy on King Philip" was the last text Apess published before he disappeared from view. (The last legal entry for him was the attachment of his goods for debt by the Barnstable Court of Common Pleas in 1838.)[2] Though the eulogy (even after O'Connell's orthographic cleansing) contains many grammatical errors and many sentences that are more than a little confusing, it remains a monument to Apess's imagination and rhetorical energies. In it he constructs a devastating critique of republican national discourse while at the same time generating, in the very face of history, a revised vision of the nation using the same components—Christianity, nature, and liberty—that framed this national rhetoric.

In this, his work parallels the implications of Sarah Winnemucca's *Life Among the Piutes,* which also transfers American ideals from a Euro-American to a Native American context. However, Apess is far more directly concerned with the discourses of nationalism. Both political and utopian, both subjugated and transpositional, the "Eulogy on King Philip" holds the national mirror up to American patriots. Whether one sees there the face of George Washington or, superimposed upon it, the face of King Philip, the seventeenth-century Wampanoag Indian, depends, Apess argues, upon your point of view.

The centerpiece of the eulogy is the figure of King Philip (or Metacomet) himself, with whom Apess here and in *A Son of the Forest* claims kinship. In the earlier text Apess insists that Philip was "king of the Pequot tribe" (3) despite historical evidence to the contrary.[3] In another challenge to contemporary views, he begins the eulogy by reversing his white audience's associations of King Philip with the devastating eponymous war (1675–76), which killed what may have been five thousand Indians as well as many colonials. Beginning by invoking comparisons with Philip of Macedon, Alexander the Great, and George Washington. Apess elevates King Philip to the status of a hero, only to go on to insist that, though Philip (like them) was indeed a skillful warrior, Apess has no wish to eulogize the Indian chief for his military talents because he does not believe in war as a means of resolving conflict or "civilizing the world."[4] Since the reputations of Philip of Macedon, Alexander the Great, and Washington are heavily dependent upon their military prowess, and since in each case their military exploits led to subjugating indigenous peoples for the purpose of "civilizing the world," Apess's refusal to valorize war seems designed to set aside their claims as it elevates King Philip's.

Instead of emphasizing militarism, he tells us, he will bring before this audience "beings made by the God of Nature, and in whose hearts and heads he has planted sympathies that shall live forever in the memory of the world, whose brilliant talents shone in the display of natural things, so that the most cultivated, whose powers shone with equal luster, were not able to prepare mantles to cover the burning elements of an uncivilized world" (277). Even for a careful reader (and certainly for an audience simply hearing these remarks read to them), it is difficult to follow the twists and turns of Apess's language here. Who are these beings whose sympathies "shall live forever in the memory of the world"? Who are the "most cultivated, whose powers shone with equal luster"? Who is being called civilized in this series of implied binaries? Is it a good thing or a bad thing "to cover the burning elements of an uncivilized world"?[5]

Such questions, I would argue, are precisely what Apess wishes Americans to ponder, forcing us to struggle with the contexts in which such evaluations are made. Civilized men, he goes on to say, are responsible for slaughtering tens of thousands of Indians and "think it no crime to wreak their vengeance upon whole nations and communities, until the fields are covered with blood and the rivers turned into purple fountains" (278). If the "uncivilized" Indians respond in kind, is it any wonder? In an elaborately ironic passage, Apess holds the words "civilized" and "uncivilized" up to the light: "Now, if we have common sense and ability to allow the difference between the civilized and the uncivilized, we cannot but see that one mode of warfare [uncivilized?] is as just as the other [civilized?] for while one is sanctioned by authority of the enlightened and cultivated men [civilized?], the other is an agreement according to the pure laws of nature [uncivilized?], growing out of natural consequences" (278) and thus sanctioned by God. By reversing the sequence of implied terms — uncivilized, civilized is presumably followed by civilized, uncivilized — Apess's chiasmus undermines the stability of these signifiers. What might be called civilized in one context appears uncivilized in another. Similarly, in another artful deconstruction, Apess's use of the word "cultivated" takes on aspects of Rousseau's critique of civilization as the cultivation of false values; those who are uncultivated and closer to nature come to seem less barbaric, their lives more in keeping with God's will.

Much of the eulogy focuses upon history as memory. Whose memories are recorded and thus reinforced? Whose point of view is represented as history? Having told us that the pure sympathies God has planted in the beings Apess wishes us to contemplate "shall live forever in the memory of the world," Apess seems to reverse himself: "Those noble traits that marked the wild man's course lie buried in the shades of night; and who shall stand? I appeal to the lovers of liberty" (277). Again, the vagueness of reference — "noble traits," "lovers of liberty" — seems intended to remind us of American national rhetoric while at the same time insisting upon a different frame of reference in which Indians occupy the spaces previously reserved for European-Americans. "Who shall stand" (presumably, Apess) allies his task with that of the faithful Christian.[6]

When Apess announces his project as one of refreshing historical memory, this strategy is intensified through the trope of personification:

But those few remaining descendants who now remain as the monument of the cruelty of those who came to improve our race and correct our errors—and as the immortal Washington lives endeared and engraven on the hearts of every white in America, never to be forgotten in time—even such is the immortal Philip honored, as held in memory by the degraded yet graceful descendents who appreciate his character; so will every patriot, especially in this enlightened age, respect the rude yet all-accomplished son of the forest, that died a martyr to his cause, [which] though unsuccessful, [was] yet as glorious as the *American* Revolution. (277)

Again the rhetorical turns make progress through the passage difficult. Yet we cannot fail to see the central point: if European-Americans revere Washington as "the father of his country," Indians revere King Philip as the hero of their nation. Furthermore (and here is the surprising turn), *every patriot* (not just Indians) *in this enlightened age* should follow the Native Americans' example. For, as we will go on to see, Apess is offering King Philip as a personification not only of Indian America but of the nation America should aspire to become, a nation of justice for both whites and peoples of color.[7]

Before we continue with an analysis of the "Eulogy on King Philip," it is worth noting that Apess was not the only American writer thinking about King Philip at this time. Others such as Washington Irving (*Sketch-Book*), James Eastburn and Robert C. Sands (*Yamoyden*), and John Augustus Stone (*Metamora*) also returned to the story of King Philip's War to reinterpret that conflict and connect it with the new nation. Thus, King Philip himself, though an obscure figure to most twentieth-century Americans, was not so obscure in William Apess's day. Nineteenth-century Americans knew of him as the son of friendly Massasoit; Philip was a strong leader, but he failed in his attempt to organize all the tribes against the white invasion. Though he was eventually defeated, and assassinated by an Indian, King Philip's War killed or wounded a greater proportion of the white population living in the New England colonies than any subsequent military engagement including the Revolutionary War.[8] It was a watershed in colonial history, bound to excite the interest of American historians. Even more important, by the 1830s Indian wars had come to seem central to the building of the nation.

In 1804 Jedidiah Morse and Elijah Parish published *A Compendious History of New England Designed for Schools and Private Families.* As was often the case in this early national period, the Indian was presented there as a noble savage whose tragic end, though inevitable, should teach all Americans to respect the Native American past. Morse and Parish describe "the character of Phillip," as that of "a deep politician, with a heart glowing with love of his country, and burning with indignation against the prosperous strangers, who were extending themselves over the inheritance of his fathers" (261) Thus, his claims are seen sympathetically even if (as will prove to be the case) these claims must in the end capitulate before those of civilization. Furthermore, Morse and Parish portray Philip as a tragic hero who attempted to engage the Maquas (Mohawks) in his battle against the English but whose trick (killing a Mohawk and blaming it on the Puritans) backfired. Morse and Parish conclude:

Thus Phillip himself was the means of turning the fury of the Maquas from the English against himself and his people. The despairing monarch fled to his former dwelling, a most unfortunate, unhappy man, deserted by his allies, assaulted by a powerful neighbour, on whose help he had depended, his own people discouraged and scattered, suffering and dying, strangers triumphing in his distresses, and seizing his possessions. [Nevertheless] Had his father possessed his foresight and courage, perhaps his posterity might long have enlivened the palace at Mount Hope. (261–62)

Thus Philip is allowed a certain limited heroic status. (Note the language of European aristocracy in words associated with "King" Philip such as "monarch" and "palace"; Apess also uses such language.) Morse and Parish allow one to speculate here that the destruction of Native Americans was not inevitable, since they propose that if Massasoit had had Philip's talents, Indians might have remained secure in Massachusetts. However, in recounting the death of King Philip in a subsequent passage, they negate this possibility: "So fell one of the most valiant captains of the New World; and so will the arts of civilized men always triumph over the simple savage" (263). It was this kind of attitude, claiming as inevitable the subjugation of the "simple savage," that William Apess set himself to correct.

Even closer to Apess's work in time of publication are Samuel G. Drake's *Biography and History of the Indians of North America* (1832) and *Chronicles of the Indians of America from Its First Discovery to the Present Time* (1836). In these works the American historian is sympathetic to the Indians in some respects. He notes Puritan insensitivity and failure to abide by the conditions of some treaties. He even calls Philip "this truly great man" (*Biography,* iii, 45). However, his main theme is war; the only form of history he takes seriously is political history. In contrast to Parish and Morse's use of tragic motifs, Drake's chronicle is a list of "facts"; he details the land sales and the battles Philip engaged in without attempting to analyze the Indian's motives. Drake's King Philip is heroic only to the extent that he repeatedly manages to escape ambush by the English.[9]

What we can see, then, is a pattern of stories written by whites in which at first Philip occupies the role of the "talented warrior," the "passionate leader," only to dissolve into the "vanishing American," a figure who must be sacrificed to make way for the building of the civilized nation. In contrast, William Apess portrays King Philip as the hope of that nation, the embodiment of Christian forbearance, expressing charity toward all, and turning to war only as a defensive strategy. He is, in fact, the epitome of what America insists it represents, practicing the principles of Christianity in harmony with nature and in defense of liberty.

Apess emphasizes that Philip was the son of Massasoit, one of the Indians most helpful to the Puritans in their early struggles. Though Massasoit was not one of the so-called "Christian Indians" converted by John Eliot, he represents for Apess (as Captain Truckee did for Sarah Winnemucca) the principles of Christian forbearance: "for injuries upon injuries, and the most daring robberies and barbarous deeds of death that were ever committed by the American Pilgrims, were with patience and resignation borne, in a manner that would do justice to any Christian nation or being in the world—especially when we realize it was voluntary suffering on the part of the good old chief" (278). The phrase "voluntary suffering" even evokes a connection between Massasoit and Jesus Christ.

At a later point in the essay, Apess will go on to argue that Philip also displayed this attitude of Christian forbearance and forgiveness of his enemies, though upon taking power he was already pessimistic about the future. "When he came into office it appears that he knew there was great responsibility resting upon himself and country, that it was likely to be ruined by those rude intruders around him, though he appears friendly and is willing to sell them lands for almost nothing" (290). Even the land sales, which other commentators interpret as indicating Philip's naïveté or greed, become for William Apess signs of King Philip's generosity of spirit. He then calls Philip "the greatest man that ever lived upon the American shores" (290).

Now it is obvious from this remark, and from many other statements in the essay, that Apess is deliberately using strategic techniques (here hyperbole) that will challenge his audience's assumptions. Precision seems to be less important—from his point of view— than getting his audience to engage emotionally and intellectually with the issues. In fact, one feels repeatedly that his whole approach is designed to stir up controversy rather than to persuade by subtle and intricate argument as he attempts elsewhere. If one accepts that Apess consciously chose what we might describe as a primarily Romantic mode, it is easier to understand why he got so many of his "facts" wrong.

Clearly, Apess was working with at least one historical source because he gives a very detailed account of each property King Philip sold, when he sold it, and how much he received for it. At one point (279) he references Drake's 1832 *History of the Indians* mentioned above. However, despite having such a source or sources at his disposal, Apess makes glaring errors, such as insisting that Philip and Massasoit were part of the Pequot tribe (instead of Wampanoags, who were enemies of the Pequots). He also runs together historically distinct events and persons such as the Pequot War (1637) and King Philip's War (1675–76). If he had worked closely with Drake's text as he seems to have done (for he quotes the Lord's Prayer in Wampanoag straight out of Drake), he could not have made these errors unknowingly. So what is the explanation for them?

One reading of the "Eulogy" suggests that William Apess was interested less in accurate history than in enabling fictions, less in colonial chronicle than in national allegory. The basic thrust of his argument is to tell the truth and to promote the good, but telling the Truth, that is, the larger truth, might be quite consistent with juggling the facts.

From some points of view, William Apess did inherit the mantle of Massasoit and King Philip whether he was from the same tribe or not. He, like they, first wished for accommodation with whites, but he also wished to change the political configuration of power. "Power," he says, "was not given us to abuse each other, but . . . delegated to us by the King of heaven, a weapon of defense against error and evil; and when abused, it will turn to our destruction. Mark, then, the history of nations throughout the world" (279). Apess chose the power of the English language to do his political work, and at all times he seems to maintain a "national" perspective. Indeed the eulogy may be read as a stunning example of national invention in which the word "nation" reverberates throughout.

Though sentences here and there are hard to follow,[10] the essay contains a great deal of effective wordplay. For instance, Philip is described as "active as the wind, as dexterous as a giant, firm as the pillows of heaven, and fierce as a lion," a series of comparisons that begins and ends with clichés while in the middle puzzling us with surprises. Under what conditions might a giant (usually thought of as clumsy) be described as dexterous? When he has the gigantic force of nature behind him? Is it because Philip showed "Christian" restraint and forgave his oppressors before he undertook to defend his people that he is described as "firm as the pillows of heaven"? In Christian theology God is gentle and supporting but also firm. And Philip, like Massasoit, is repeatedly described as paradigmatic of the Christian leader. "It might well be said he was a pattern for the Christians themselves; but by the Pilgrims he is denounced, as being a savage" (283).[11]

In addition to tantalizing us with intriguing images, Apess at times dramatizes scenes to engage his audience in the action.

Upon this news, one Standish, a vile and malicious fellow, took fourteen of his lewd Pilgrims with him, and at midnight, when a deathless silence reigned throughout the wilderness; not even a bird is heard to send forth her sweet songs to charm and comfort those children of the woods; but all had taken their rest, to commence anew on the rising of the glorious sun. But to their sad surprise there was no rest for them, but they were surrounded by ruffians and assassins; yes, assassins, what better name can be given them? (284)

In this passage he pauses to set the scene in which women and children will be awakened by Standish and his men. The "deathless silence" that derives from nature taking her rest will be broken by the shrieks of those threatened with violence and death.

Apess uses a number of rhetorical techniques to emphasize his points, but the two which he uses most effectively are direct address to his audience and mirroring. Of the former the essay abounds in examples. Apess takes up the role of gadfly, provoking us with statements such as the following: "And do you believe that Indians cannot feel and see, as well as white people? If you think so, you are mistaken. Their power of feeling and knowing is as quick as yours. Now this is to be borne, as the Pilgrims [supposedly] did as their Master told them to; but what color [H]e was I leave it. But if the real sufferers say one word, they are denounced as being wild and savage beasts" (285). In "An Indian's Looking-Glass for the White Man," Apess spells out his argument that Jesus Christ as a Jew was a man of color (see Apess, 160).

The use of mirroring, which is also present throughout the eulogy, is particularly effective, however, because it plays with the terms of national discourse, exposing its racist exclusionism. As Barry O'Connell comments in his introduction: "By taking over the patriotic language of the dominant culture and switching its referents he could disrupt the almost seamless ideology of a racist republicanism that cloaked itself in universalist language" (lxxiv).

As we have already seen, Christian foundationalism was the first battleground upon which William Apess engaged his audience, attacking both Puritans and later Americans for attempting to build a nation of the faithful upon principles of injustice. "And as the seed of iniquity and prejudice was sown in that day, so it still remains; and there is a deep-rooted popular opinion in the hearts of many that Indians were made, etc., on purpose for destruction, to be driven out by white Christians, and they to take their places; and that God decreed it from all eternity" (287). This is a view Apess is at pains to attack, countering with an Enlightenment appeal to the study of nature. "If such theologians would only study the works of nature more, they would understand the purposes of good better than they do: that the favor of the Almighty was good and holy, and all his nobler works were made to adorn his image, by being his grateful servants and admiring each other as angels, and not, as they say, to drive and devour each other" (287).

We must remember that William Apess was a Christian minister himself, a man who deeply resented the use of Christianity for oppressive purposes. Though a convert, he was forced to endure insults by Christians because he was an Indian, struggling against a hegemonic discourse which insisted that the health of the Christian nation was dependent upon the removal of the heathen, a term applied to all Indians, Apess notes, whether professing Christianity or not. As Francis Wagner states in *Nation-Building in the United States: The American Idea of Nationhood in Retrospect* (1985): "Protestantism played an all-important role during the natal phase of the historical process of nationmaking" (22). But often the Christian spirit did not include protecting the rights of indigenous peoples.

Apess comments bitterly: "We hope we shall not hear it said from ministers and church members that we are so good no other people can live with us, as you know it is a common thing for them to say Indians cannot live among Christian people; no, even the President of the United States tells the Indians they cannot live among civilized people, and we want your lands and must have them and will have them" (306–7). Apess imagines that if the legislators spoke the truth they would say: "We want your land for our use to speculate upon; it aids us in paying off our national debt and supporting us in Congress to drive you off" (307).

Nevertheless, though he is critical of both Christians and legislators, the author of the "Eulogy" does not wish to undermine Christianity itself any more than he wants to abolish the U.S. Congress as the body governing the territory previously owned and inhabited by the Indians. Instead he proposes that truly Christian principles be the basis of conduct toward peoples of color and that the rights of citizenship be extended to all. "And he that will not set his face against [slavery's] corrupt principles is a coward and not worthy of being numbered among men and Christians—and [guilty of] conduct, too, that libels the laws of the country, and the word of God, that men profess to believe in" (301).

One should note here that Apess preserves the connection between nation and religion (laws of the country and the word of God) though he seeks to transform the way this connection is understood. Even at the end of the essay, Christianity continues to be part of Apess's national vision, though he implies that it is not the only important element. "I say, then, a different course must be pursued, and different laws must be enacted, and all men must operate under one general law. And while you ask yourselves, 'What do they, the Indians, want?' you have only to look at the unjust laws made for them and say, 'They want what I want,' in order to make men of them, good and wholesome citizens. . . . That is not only to make Christians of us, but men [i.e., legally recognized adults], which plan as yet has never been pursued" (310).

Mirroring in this passage operates in a powerfully transpositional mode: Apess tells his audience, you have only to say "They want what I want" in order to uncover the operations of injustice and move toward a more just society. This is a Christian principle, in Apess's thinking, because it follows the Golden Rule: Do unto others as you would have them do unto you. But it is also consistent with the natural order. Apess's God is the Enlightenment God of Nature. In nature we are created equal. "Every white that knows their [*sic*] own history knows there was not a whit of difference between them and the Indians" in the state of nature (305).

Ever since J. Hector St. John de Crèvecoeur in his *Letters of an American Farmer* penned the now famous formula *ubi panis, ibi patria* (where there is bread, there is the homeland), American writers have emphasized the importance of the North American landscape and its natural abundance to their conception of nation. If Christianity is the first element of national rhetoric taken on by Apess in this essay, nature is the second. Apess shows that nature, though most congenial it would seem to the "son of the forest," is appropriated by whites as part of a rhetorical strategy to displace the Indian.

As an example of the abuse of language for ideological purposes, he quotes the Reverend Nahum Gold concerning the settlement of the Far West: "Let any man look at this settlement, and reflect what it was three years ago, and his heart can but kindle up while he exclaims, 'what God has wrought!' [T]he savage has left the ground for civilized man; the rich prairie, from bringing forth all its strengths to be burned, is now receiving numerous enclosures, and brings a harvest of corn and wheat to feed the church" (287). This is an example of the conjunction of Christian rhetoric with the celebration of nature so typical of breadbasket patriotism, but for William Apess it is also an example of the way Americans conflate control over nature with removal of the Indians.

Philip Freneau's earlier poem "On the Emigration to America, and Peopling the Western Country" (1784) also draws connections between a prosperous white America, Indian removal, and the glories of nature, as we can see from these two stanzas:

> What charming scenes attract the eye,
> On wild Ohio's savage stream!
> There Nature reigns, whose works outvie
> The boldest pattern art can frame;
> There ages past have rolled away,
> And forests bloomed but to decay.
>
> From these fair plains, these rural seats,
> So long concealed, so lately known,
> The unsocial Indian far retreats,
> To make some other clime his own,
> When other streams, less pleasing flow,
> And darker forest round him grow.
> (quoted in McMichael, 527)

Freneau makes the Ohio River "savage" in the sense of unharnessed, while his "unsocial" Indian quietly decamps, seeking a place in nature, even if "less pleasing," that is beyond the sphere of entrepreneurial development. One of the key arguments for the Europeans' right to take over Indian lands hinged on the fact that the Indians did not change and develop their territory; thus, according to one view, deriving from John Locke, such land could not be called true property because it had not been "improved." In this poem Freneau applauds land use in terms similar to those of Reverend Gold.

William Apess shows that he was familiar with the rhetorical flourishes here exemplified by Freneau and others, but he wished to reverse them by presenting the Indian not as the waster of natural resources (burning the prairies, allowing the forests simply to decay without turning the wood to use) but as the paradigm of natural intelligence, a vital resource itself wasted by whites. He was certainly not alone in using this strategy, but Apess is the only writer to combine so effectively the three main elements of American national rhetoric—Christianity, nature, and liberty—in a personification of America as an Indian.

In the "Eulogy," for instance, he juxtaposes Washington and King Philip to suggest that nature may succeed where civilized strategies fail. In retelling the story of Philip's escape from the swamp where he was surrounded by Puritan soldiers, he remarks: "We may look upon this move of Philip's to be equal, if not superior, to that of Washington crossing the Delaware. For while Washington was assisted by all the knowledge that art and science could give, together with all the instruments of defense and edged tools to prepare rafts and the like helps for safety across the river. Philip was naked as to any of these things, possessing only what nature, his mother, had bestowed upon him; and yet makes his escape with equal praise" (297). It seems unlikely that Philip was without any "edged tools," but the important point is that this is another example of transpositional discourse in which an Indian and a white man mirror one another causing the reader to acknowledge the Indian rather than the white man as the true American hero.

Having introduced this comparison, Apess then juxtaposes two captures, one in which a white lad is taken but released by the compassionate Indians and another in which an old Indian is captured and then executed by the ruthless Puritans. This juxtaposition—plus

Apess's comments concerning Philip's equal distribution of his own wampum among his men, which he compares favorably to Washington's payment of the soldiers in the Revolutionary War with worthless "continental" money—multiplies the mirroring effect. In each of these cases the Indians appear superior to the traditional American heroes, and superior precisely because they embody the values America wishes to claim as its own, here liberality of spirit and egalitarianism. Nature may even turn out to be a better nursery for citizenship than English culture, Apess suggests, because those who emerge from it are more likely to be generous and free.

The third of the three terms Apess recontextualizes in this essay is liberty. If Christianity and nature figure largely in American national rhetoric, liberty plays a role equally great or greater. For example, Freneau's poem, quoted in part above, envisions the West as the site in which America's true spirit will unfold because it embodies the principle of liberty:

> While virtue warms the generous breast,
> There heaven-born freedom shall reside,
> Nor shall the voice of war molest,
> Nor Europe's all-aspiring pride—
> There Reason shall new laws devise,
> And order from confusion rise. (527)

Freedom (liberty) is an element which many writers in both the eighteenth and nineteenth centuries present as essential to America's vision of itself, an element seen as lacking in the Old Order of Europe. Liberty is not merely a value instilled during the Revolutionary Era; it is presented as intrinsic to the New World landscape. Though it seems (as in this poem) to come with the territory, however, it must also be preserved (as we can see at the end of this stanza) by new laws generated in the new context.

Pursuing his aim of subverting and redeploying American national rhetoric, William Apess dwells at length upon Philip as a figure for liberty. Ironically, the Puritans function by contrast as the first supporters of slavery in America. Thus, Apess insists that his white audience revise the direction of their filial piety by taking seriously the threat to American ideals represented by these early settlers. Addressing his audience concerning this issue, Apess insists: "Only look at it; then stop and pause: My fathers came here for liberty themselves, [you will say], and then they must go and chain the mind, that image they professed to serve, not content to rob and cheat the poor ignorant Indians but [they] must take one of the king's sons and make a slave of him. Gentleman and ladies, I blush at these tales, if you do not, especially when they professed to be a free and humane people" (301).

His main point is clear. The Puritans professed to be a free and humane people but they were not. In contrast, King Philip, the so-called savage, is both benevolent and unrestricted by the need to pay homage to any power but the God of Nature. Even when the whites try to force him to abide by their laws and customs, he maintains his independent spirit and refuses to do their bidding for a long time. "When the governor finds that His Majesty [King Philip] was displeased, he then sends messengers to him and wishes to know why he would make war upon him (as if he had done all right), and wished to enter into a new treaty with him. The king answered them thus: 'Your governor is but a subject of King Charles of England; I shall not treat with a subject; I shall treat of peace only with a king, my brother; when he comes, I am ready'" (294).

Apess, quoting Daniel Gookin from Drake, praises Philip as "a man of good understanding and knowledge in the best things" (306). Philip represents Christian forbearance, natural wisdom and dignity, independence and free self-respect. His talents, however, were wasted on the vicious Puritans whom Americans now revere as their founding fathers. Apess says that no true American should celebrate the landing of the Pilgrims (which for some reason he dates as occurring on December 22, 1622) or the Fourth of July, because "a foundation was laid in the first Legislature to enslave our people, by taking from them all rights, [a pattern] which has been strictly adhered to ever since. Look at the disgraceful laws, disenfranchising us as citizens. Look at the treaties made by Congress, all broken" (306).

It was common in the nineteenth century for American patriotic writers to trace the beginnings of the nation back to the time of the

Pilgrims and Puritans.[12] For example, Daniel Webster's "Discourse Delivered at Plymouth, on the 22nd of December, 1820"[13]—which Apess no doubt has in mind to refute—eulogizes the Pilgrims as bringing with them the seeds of liberty that later grew into the United States. Webster claims: "At the moment of their landing, therefore, they possessed institutions of government, and institutions of religion: and friends and families, and social . . . institutions, framed by consent, founded on choice and preference, how nearly do these fill up our whole idea of country!" (quoted in Montgomery, 246). O'Connell sees Apess responding to Webster both by redeploying his national rhetoric and by putting King Philip in the same league as George Washington. "Apess's elegy, knowingly I think, borrows the form most associated with a commemoration of the Fathers' unqualified virtues and inserts Philip among them" (xxi).

As against Webster's personification of America in the figure of George Washington, Apess claims King Philip, asserting: "as a man of natural abilities, I shall pronounce him the greatest man that was ever in America; and so it will stand, until he is proved to the contrary, to the everlasting disgrace of the Pilgrims' fathers" (308). Webster's claims were also sweeping. In his speech on the completion of the Bunker Hill monument, he pulled out all the stops, insisting that Washington's character alone justified American institutions: "I claim him for America. . . . To him who denies or doubts whether our fervid liberty can be combined with law, with order, with the security of property, with the pursuits and advancement of happiness; to him who denies that our forms of government are capable of producing exaltation of soul, and the passion of true glory; to him who denies that we have contributed anything to the stock of great lessons and great examples;—to all these I reply by pointing to Washington!" (Montgomery, 416–17).

Webster predicted that future generations would be inspired by the Bunker Hill Monument to cry out: "Thank God, I—I also—AM AN AMERICAN!" (Montgomery, 417). For him, George Washington was produced by the institutions of America and embodied its spirit of liberty, Christianity, and "our long contest with unreclaimed nature and uncivilized man" (Montgomery, 416). Webster's task was to elevate the nation so that it could assume its rightful place among the nations of Europe. "Uncivilized man" had no place in this process.

For William Apess the task was to assert "I—I also—AM AN AMERICAN" and to elevate his (Indian) people so that they could take their appropriate place among Americans of all description, protected by the laws and exercising the rights of full citizens. O'Connell remarks: "His appeal to republicanism, common enough in the history of American dissent, asserts the rights of Native Americans as Americans, as full participants in a democratic polity" (lxxv).

In some ways this task demanded the use of transpositional rhetoric, of mirroring as a device to reveal to his audience the similarity of Indian and white claims. "And while you ask yourselves, 'What do they, the Indians, want?' you have only to look at the unjust laws made for them and say, 'They want what I want,' in order to make men of them, good and wholesome citizens" (310). This is indeed a stunning moment in the history of Native American oratory, a utopian instance of vision and universalism unanswerable by the hegemonic discourse on savagery, because it so clearly calls to mind the words of the Declaration of Independence: "We hold these truths to be self-evident, that all men are created equal, that they are endowed by their Creator with certain unalienable Rights, that among these are Life, Liberty, and the pursuit of Happiness."

The force of this argument is so powerful that the comments with which he ends must strike us as deeply ironic: "Having now closed, I would say that many thanks is [*sic*] due from me to you, though an unworthy speaker, for your kind attention; and I wish you to understand that we are thankful for every favor." Indeed, almost immediately he reverses this subjugated thrust with a transpositional dig: "and you and I have to rejoice that we have not to answer for our fathers' crimes; neither shall we do right to charge them one to another. We can only regret it, and flee from it; and from henceforth, let peace and righteousness be written upon our hearts and hands forever, is the wish of a poor Indian" (310). A "poor Indian" indeed!

William Apess gave the "Eulogy on King Philip" twice before white audiences in Boston. The second version was considerably shorter than the first, but the repeat performance seems to have been generated by dissatisfaction on the part of his first audience concerning his views on missionaries. Promotional literature claimed he would spell these out in more detail on the second occasion.

We don't know what his audiences thought about the main thrust of the lecture, but its incendiary implications remain clear in both versions. America has not acted in conformity with its ideals. The nation is not what it claims to be. If it were, there would be no need for power to assert itself in destructive "uncivil" wars. As it stands now, the nation is in need of transformation.

What, then, is to be done? Let every friend of the Indians now seize the mantle of Liberty and throw it over those burning elements that has [*sic*] spread with such fearful rapidity, and at once extinguish them forever. It is true that now and then a feeble voice had been raised in our favor. Yes, we might speak of distinguished men, but they fall so far short in the minority that it is heard but at a small distance. We want trumpets that sound like thunder, and men to act as though they were going at war with those corrupt and degrading principles that robs [*sic*] one of all rights, merely because he is ignorant and of a little different color. Let us have principles that will give everyone his due; and then shall wars cease, and the weary find rest. (307)

In this example of blistering *ressentiment,* we must finally acknowledge the convergence of transpositional and subjugated discourse, as Apess insists that politics—the hope of those who are subjugated—must take up the banner unfurled by visionary poetics, the *domaine imaginaire* of transposition. America must become both a white and an Indian nation, the nation of true liberty, respect for nature, and genuine Christian charity it has failed for so long actually to be.

The Gift Outright

The land was ours before we were the land's.
She was our land more than a hundred years
Before we were her people. She was ours
In Massachusetts, in Virginia,
But we were England's, still colonials,
Possessing what we still were unpossessed by,
Possessed by what we now no more possessed.
Something we were withholding made us weak
Until we found out that it was ourselves
We were withholding from our land of living,
And forthwith found salvation in surrender.
Such as we were we gave ourselves outright
(The deed of gift was many deeds of war)
To the land vaguely realizing westward,
But still unstoried, artless, unenhanced,
Such as she was, such as she would become.

Robert Frost

9. Native American Literature
and Nineteenth-Century Nationalisms

Of course, William Apess overstated the case when he implied that Indians simply wanted what Euro-Americans wanted, to be taken seriously as American citizens. In fact, many Indians wished instead to be left alone; the only nations they recognized were those that had nurtured them and their ancestors in tribal polities appropriate to their geographical circumstances, religious beliefs, habits of social interaction, and physical needs. American citizenship was no guarantee that any of these basic aspects of Native American life would be addressed in a manner superior to what they had known prior to contact with whites. In fact, many rightly suspected that the opposite was the case.

Nevertheless, all the Indian narratives we have examined in this study—even the life of Black Hawk—affirm that Indian nations would be better off if they achieved a stable political arrangement with the U.S. government and most therefore advocate American citizenship for Native Americans. In the process of reflecting upon the conflicts that plagued Indian-white relations in the nineteenth century, they also interrogate American nationalist rhetoric, providing a critique of many of its essential features and an alternative vision of nationhood. Let us now consider in summary form the elements of that critique and alternative vision.

Manifest Destiny

The ideology of Manifest Destiny (a term coined by the influential Democrat John L. O'Sullivan in an editorial in 1845) brings together the elements of nationalist rhetoric most abhorrent to Native Americans. As America began to define itself in the early years of the nineteenth century, it focused attention on the conjunction between "open lands" and opportunity for its people. In *Empire for Liberty* Wai-Chee Dimock notes that even "the word 'freedom' came to be a code word for America's continental expansion" (9), what Frost calls "the land vaguely realizing westward." We have already seen that the notion of an unbounded frontier ("the West") was an essential component of American thinking, though it did not originate in the nineteenth century. Philip Freneau celebrates it in his poem "On the Emigration to America, and Peopling the Western Country" (1784), which makes European ambitions for the New World synonymous with movement west. Even a century and a half earlier, William Bradford noted the steady push of settlers into the western parts of Massachusetts, a hunger for outlying lands that eventually contributed to the violence of King Philip's War. Some historians have even proposed that the dominance of Puritanism itself was possible only because of the "safety valve" presented by western expansionism. However, such a safety valve was only provisionally effective, for wherever whites pushed out into areas previously unsettled by Europeans, they encountered the indigenous population who eventually resisted encroachment and pushed back.

Nevertheless, Americans forged ahead with a mixed policy of "buying" new lands, trading "security" for new territories, or taking them by force. By the nineteenth century the success of what some called the "American Empire" seemed indistinguishable from the process of annexing all the land "from sea to shining sea." Patriotic rhetoric concerning America's mandate to dominate the continent and subjugate the Indians may be considered under four headings: "Manifest Destiny" itself, America as the home of God's "chosen people," the renewal of America through "just wars," and the relegation of Indians to the category of "vanishing Americans." Each of these terms inspired Native Americans to mount counterarguments and to envision alternative possibilities in their search for a more just and inclusive conception of nationhood.

O'Sullivan's view of America's mission was straightforward. The American claim to new territory was "by the right of our manifest destiny to overspread and to possess the whole of the continent which Providence has given us for the development of the great experiment of liberty and federative self government entrusted to us. It is a right such as that of the tree to the space of air and earth suitable for the full expansion of its principle and destiny of growth" (quoted in Weinberg, *Manifest Destiny*, 145). The naturalizing of the imperial project represented by the comparison of the nation to a tree is striking. The air (Indian territory) is simply an opening; it presents no resistance to the growth of the tree (the nation). "The land was ours before we were the land's."

Also implicit in this vision is a hierarchy of humans and of nations in which white America, because of its "great experiment of liberty and federative self government," stands at the top. Or as Charles Bancroft put it in *The Footprints of Time* (1879): "America stands a model which other nations will carefully copy, in due time, as they can adapt themselves and change their institutions" (quoted in Montgomery, 6).

There was disagreement, of course, in terms of how America should achieve her "Manifest Destiny," whether by aggression or accretion. The former ("paternal") model emphasized imposition of authority; the latter ("maternal") model insisted that simply through time and accretion, "others" would be passively incorporated into the mass. In this model, as Dimock describes it, "the conflict between whites and Indians over land possession ceased to appear as conflict, and became instead a painless story of growth" (18), "the land vaguely realizing westward."

The aggressive model often hid its aggression against Indians in the language of "fathers" and "children." President Andrew Jackson was the Great Father who simply desired his Indian "children" to behave. Of course, if they didn't, he was ready to punish them severely, for children must not be allowed to determine their own course or obstruct the plans of their parents.

The passive model seems at first its binary opposite. As Charles Bancroft describes it in *The Footprints of Time*, the course of history travels westward "to New and Free America. There the Englishman, the German, the Frenchman, the Italian, the Scandinavian, the Asiatic, and the African all meet as equals. There they are free to speak, to think, and to act. . . . So America adopts the children of all lands only to return a manhood enobled by a sense of dignity through the practice of a system of self-government which improves the condition and promotes the interest of each while it produces harm to none" (quoted in Montgomery, 8).

The multiple illusions of this vision of America are striking. Blacks, whites, and Asians are equally free to speak, to think, to act. Note, however, that the Native American is missing, as is all organized resistance to American expansionism. America has become an abstraction, absorbing all, redeploying all. In 1850 Daniel Webster, distressed at threats of secession by the South, was equally sanguine concerning America's innocence and practical idealism. "In all its history, it has been beneficent; it has trodden down no man's liberty; it has crushed no state" (quoted in Greenfeld, 474). In such visions, based in deep denial, even the possibility of effective resistance is muted by a belief in the inexorable force of history and the inevitable recognition of the superiority of white models of social organization. On some issues "fathers" and "mothers" agree: the Indian can offer no serious challenge to American conceptions of the nation.

Horace Greeley put it most baldly:

But the Indians are children. Their arts, wars, treaties, alliances, habitations, crafts, properties, commerce, comforts, all belong to the very lowest and rudest ages of human existence. Some few of the chiefs have a narrow and short-sighted shrewdness, and very rarely in their history, a really great man, like Pontiac or Tecumseh, has arisen among them; but this does not shake the general truth that they are utterly incompetent to cope in any way with the European or Caucasian race. Any band of schoolboys, from ten to fifteen years of age, are quite as capable of ruling their appetites, devising and upholding a public policy, constituting and conducting a state or community, as an average Indian tribe. (quoted in Black and Weidman, 130)

From this point of view, Manifest Destiny is a kind of boon to Native Americans, releasing them from the responsibilities of pretending to organize their people into self-sufficient nations.

In the texts we have been examining, however, a serious challenge to these assumptions was mounted. In the first place, in a work such as *The Life of Black Hawk*, the Indian nation (the Sauk and Fox) is represented in many respects as superior to the United States. Indian leaders serve for life, not just for four-year terms, and therefore unlike American presidents are able to grow in wisdom and effectiveness. The nation (before white encroachment and whiskey) is able to provide justice, protection, stability, and harmony in family relations, unlike American culture which, for Black Hawk, is deficient in these respects. The primary aim of Indian warriors is to succeed in battle with minimal loss of life to one's own forces. (Indian wars killed comparatively few people.) Hostile or uncongenial "others" (remember Black Hawk's proposal for the negroes that they be "managed" by redistribution of the population) are either pushed out of the territory or adopted into the tribe. In all these areas, Black Hawk confronts America with a jaundiced eye.

The point here is not whether Black Hawk gives an accurate picture of the way his nation functioned before it was decimated by alcohol, disease, and American military force. Instead, the point to be recognized is that the autobiography calls into serious question two assumptions of the doctrine of Manifest Destiny: the movement west as "natural and inevitable" and the belief in a hierarchy of cultures, ultimately recognized by all, that places whites above Indians. Like O'Sullivan, Black Hawk invokes nature. But in his mind, the God of Nature, while giving life to all, enshrines diversity and territorial divisions rather than preparing a single nation to dominate the continent. If God had wished the Indians to be like the whites, he says, He would have created us all alike. Furthermore, the Great Spirit has allocated each group its own space. Black Hawk admires the eastern mountain peoples who are content with what the Great Spirit has given them and "prefer living in their *own* country, to coming out to *ours,* and driving us from it" (144). Black Hawk clarifies in unmistakable terms the injustice of the doctrine of Manifest Destiny, and he does so by means of a transpositional argument in which Americans and Indians are evaluated evenhandedly, not *always* (and this is important) giving the edge to the Indian any more than to the white.

Another Native American who confronts the assumptions of Manifest Destiny head-on is George Copway. On the issue of fathers and children, Copway says: "The government and its agents style us 'My children.' The Indians are of age—and believe they can think and act for themselves. The term 'My children' comes with an ill grace from those who seem bent on driving them from their fathers' houses" (*Traditional History,* 201). As we have seen, Copway proposed creating a permanent state for the Indians in Dakota so that they would not be threatened, as they so often were, by continual "removals." Furthermore, Copway has many good things to say about traditional Ojibwa culture which he renders in some places the equal or superior of white culture. Where he discusses the principles of government that operate within the tribe, he concludes: "The law of the nation, like that of ancient Greece, has been enacted with a view to the health of its subjects" (*Traditional History,* 53). As he reflects upon the promise of America as a nation for both whites and Indians, he insists that it too should be ruled by laws enacted with a view to the health of (all) its subjects.

In another passage in praise of native language, he asserts: "After reading the English language, I have found words in the Indian combining more expressiveness. There are many Indian words which when translated into English lose their force, and do not convey so much meaning as the original does in one word" (*Traditional History,* 124–25). Like John Rollin Ridge, however, George Copway not only criticized American nationalist rhetoric but also internalized the hierarchical assumptions later articulated in the doctrine of Manifest Destiny. Even as spokesmen for the kind of universalism implicit in some versions of this doctrine, however, Copway and Ridge unsettle the certainties of American nationalism. For instance, though Copway foresaw English becoming "the universal language of all lands" (*Traditional History,* 260–61), he notes the superiority of Ojibwa for some purposes. Thus, he dislodges the illusion of a white "national identity"—that is, the notion that white culture is in all respects superior—upon which so much American rhetoric is based.

Because Copway and Ridge insist upon their status as Americans, while at the same time locating that "Americanness" within an Indian context, the abstraction that America too often becomes in the rhetoric of Manifest Destiny is deconstructed. We come to see that national identity is a fiction. As Étienne Balibar writes: "*All identity is individual,* but there is no individual identity that is not historical, or, in other words, constructed within a field of social values, norms of behavior and collective symbols" (94). Copway and other Native American writers draw attention to the way fictions of national identity in the republic differ because the histories, social values, and collective symbols upon which they are based are not the same.

Considering these Native American texts, we might be led to conclude that nationalism itself is the culprit, but "there is always a 'good' and a 'bad' nationalism" (Balibar and Wallerstein, 47). The cases of Copway and Ridge, both of whom gravitated to urban spaces, illustrate the dangers of assuming that those who have been dislodged from traditional certainties are inevitably better off. The problem with Homi Bhabha's celebration of "the otherness of the people-as-one" ("Mimicry," 301) is that, as Leslie Marmon Silko (Laguna Pueblo) puts it, questions of power remain unresolved where you have neither identity nor any way of knowing how an "identity" might be created. In choosing to personify America in the dislocated and internally divided character of Joaquín Murieta, Ridge suggests that lack of integration, lack of a sense of community (such as we see also in his frontier towns) is dangerous; that is, it reduces the capacity of individuals to resist oppressive power effectively. In fact, Murieta dies in the end because, like Ridge, he has "separated himself from the main body of his men."

In his poem on Mount Shasta, Ridge appeals to the doctrine of Manifest Destiny by offering a spatial perspective representing by analogy a succession of temporal phases. Where the hills "in the long review of distance / Range themselves in order grand," we see Ridge's belief in the evolution of human cultures. Mount Shasta, with its cold, white summit, towers over all. Parins tells us that Ridge "had confidence in the working out of America's Manifest Destiny" (124). However, change is not accomplished painlessly in Ridge's poem. Unlike Euro-Americans who, by dispersing geographical conflict along a temporal axis and thus making it seem a process of natural evolution, sought to minimize recognition of the suffering produced by the clash of cultures (see Dimock, 18–19), Ridge (reversing the equation and rendering time as space) conveys in his poem's concluding lines a terrifying sense of the price of working out this national destiny. Pity's tears freeze upon the mountain summit, and even "deep sympathy," when faced with the absolute law of historical progression, fails to alleviate the human suffering thereby created. In all these instances, Manifest Destiny is not the happy coincidence of a chosen people with a landscape equal to their imagination but instead an ideology rooted in terror and cultural arrogance, the "tower of pride" epitomized by the "imperial" Mount Shasta.

Chosen People

In O'Sullivan's 1845 editorial laying out the doctrine of Manifest Destiny, he argues that "Providence has given us" the breadth of the continent "for the great experiment of liberty and federative self government entrusted to us" (Weinberg, 145). Americans are God's chosen people, or as Richard Frothingham would put it, in *The Rise of the Republic of the United States* (1890): "The vast region which the flag of the United States protects was, two centuries and a half ago, the roaming ground of tribes of Indians. . . . It was virtually a waste awaiting, in the order of Providence, the magic influence of an incoming race, embued with the spirit of a new civilization" (Montgomery, 1). Euro-Americans' belief that the Christian God marked out the North American continent to be the domain of white people, consigning its native population to an inferior status or extinction, is well illustrated in a book edited by Joseph Allan Montgomery and published by the American Christian Constitution Press called *The Christian History of the Constitution of the United States of America* (1960). The preface by its compiler, Verna Hall, concludes with a quotation from I Peter 2:9: "Ye are a chosen generation, a royal priesthood, an holy nation, a peculiar people, that ye should show forth the praises of Him who hath called you out of darkness into His marvellous light" (vi).

Perhaps it is true, as Balibar argues in "The Nation Form: History and Ideology," that all nationalism includes the idea of a chosen people. But the intensity of America's belief that European Christians were singled out for a special providence, giving them the right to occupy territory inhabited by Native Americans and the responsibility to change the ways of indigenous peoples to make them conform to white standards, was particularly evident in the nineteenth century when this version of history was being challenged in literature and on the frontier. (*The Christian History of the Constitution of the United States*, though it makes its argument in 1960, is mostly an anthology of nineteenth-century documents.)

Several of the Native American writers we have examined—William Apess, George Copway, and Sarah Winnemucca—were Christians, but one and all they contest the idea that God has foreordained the ruthless treatment of Native Americans undertaken in the name of American nationalism. William Apess, as we have seen, is particularly scathing in his denunciation of Christian racism, and he further derides "that wise, learned, and humane politician, Andrew Jackson" for his belief that Indians "ought to be driven to the wilds of the Far West" (225).

In his document on the Mashpee rebellion, Apess even converts John Winthrop's famous image of the city on a hill to his purposes. Repeatedly quoted in support of Americans' belief in their mission as a chosen people, this speech of 1630 claims: "we shall be as a city upon a hill, the eyes of all people are upon us. So that if we shall deal falsely with our God in this work we have undertaken, and so cause Him to withdraw His present help from us, we shall be made a story and a by-word through the world" (quoted in McMichael, 67). When Apess greets the Christian missionary at Mashpee, he finds that the congregation are all "pale faces" because religion has not been made agreeable to the native population. Apess says, "Recovering a little from my astonishment, I entered the house with the missionary. It had the appearance of some eminent monument set upon a hilltop, for a landmark to generations to come" (170). In this transposition of Winthrop's "Model of Christian Charity," Apess implies a new vision of the nation and the house of God, one in which people of all races will be welcomed and treated fairly. He and the white missionary go together into the house on the hill.

George Copway also, knowingly or unknowingly, taps into this image when he recommends the creation of an Indian state within the United States, to be governed by the law of necessity, the law of common interest, and the law of love, where "one good man would be like a light-house in a storm, who would warn and guide the rest" (*Traditional History*, 271). Implicit in all these Native American texts is a personification of the national character. As Immanuel Wallerstein claims, "The history of nations, beginning with our own, is always already presented to us in the form of a narrative which attributes to these entities the continuity of a [human being, or] subject" (Balibar and Wallerstein, 86). But the "human subject" metanarrative of American nationalism goes further here than claiming for the state a continuous history unfolding and reinforcing basic attributes. It enshrines a conception of ethnic essence as well.

For Euro-Americans, George Washington, Andrew Jackson, and Abraham Lincoln summed up certain basic aspects of the American character. However, just as Frederick Douglass used Madison Washington, an escaped slave, to give form to African American aspirations in the terms of both American national rhetoric and black culture, Indians, for their part, emblematized the nation in Native American figures who represented the virtues of both Christian morality, that essential feature of white nationalism, and traditional tribal wisdom. In his reflections on the nation, even Black Hawk praises not only Sauk practices but also the principle of Christian charity (which in his textual practice he himself represents): do unto others as you would have them do unto you. Sarah Winnemucca and William Apess also reexamine the Golden Rule in an Indian context. In contrast to the conceptions of many Euro-Americans, the "chosen people" in Indian texts are often the individuals singled out by the Great Spirit for uncommon responsibilities as mediators between Indians and whites: Massasoit, Pocahontas, William Penn, and, just as often, these writers themselves.

Sarah Winnemucca is an especially good example of this, since she believed her family to be "chosen" for uncommon service and sacrifice. From her early training by her grandfather in the singing of "The Star-Spangled Banner," her life, it seems, was destined to embroil her in the duties and trials of "translation." Among her own people, she advocated adjustment to the ways of the white man by learning English and undertaking systematic agriculture. In *Life Among the Piutes,* her address to the whites, she sought to bring the nation (in particular, the members of Congress) to a sense of its responsibility with regard to native populations. Like Apess, she challenges Americans concerning their interpretation of Christian principles and their belief in their status as a "chosen people." In her direct address to her readers, she chides:

Oh, for shame! You who are educated by a Christian government in the art of war; the practice of whose profession makes you natural enemies of the savages, so called by you. Yes, you, who call yourselves the great civilization; you who have knelt upon Plymouth Rock, covenanting with God to make this land the home of the free and the brave. Ah, then you rise from your bended knees and seizing the welcoming hands of those who are owners of the land, which you are not, your carbines rise upon the bleak shore. (207)

If anyone other than a member of her family or Sarah herself emerges as a positive personification of American ideals in *Life Among the Piutes,* it is the good agent Samuel Parrish, who is apparently removed from his job because he is *not* a Christian. In Sarah Winnemucca's experience, the Christian reservation agents were the worst, exerting brutal authority over the natives and defending it by alleging that the Indians were heathens and savages. Sarah aims to recall America to its Christian ideals of justice, mercy, and equality by revealing the horrors inflicted upon Native Americans in the reservation system and the frontier wars. Who should be the chosen? According to Sarah Winnemucca, Apess, and Black Hawk, the chosen (who may become chiefs) are those who distinguish themselves by their capacity for self-sacrifice.

Just Wars

Though some explanations of America's manifest destiny muted the possibilities of conflicts with indigenous populations, others sought to justify American aggression by claiming that wars against Indians were necessary not only for purposes of security but also to develop in American manhood a spirit of sacrifice and a sense of national community. In Robert Frost's poem "The Gift Outright," salvation and surrender to our responsibilities as Americans involved "many deeds of war." As Richard Slotkin has argued in *Regeneration through Violence*, such attitudes have a long history in North America. In 1676 Increase Mather published *A Brief History of the War with the Indians in New England*, arguing that such wars were trials sent by God in order to reform second-generation Puritans who had strayed from the path of righteousness. Mather had no doubts about the "chosen people" and their right to inflict damage upon the indigenous population. "That the Heathen People amongst whom we live, and whose Land the Lord God of our Fathers hath given to us for a rightfull Possession, have . . . been planning mischievous devices against that part of the English Israel which is seated in these goings down of the sun, no Man that is an Inhabitant of any considerable standing, can be ignorant" (quoted in Slotkin, 84). In his mind, such mischievous devices justified violent repression.

In the nineteenth century, Henry Trumbull's *History of the Discovery of America*, a popular anthology of Indian war narratives, was published and republished over a forty-year period. Like many historians of this period, Trumbull traced the essential character of America back to the seventeenth-century Puritans. Like Mather, he presented the conflicts with the Indians as an important step for the chosen people, because they "destroyed or dispersed a horde of fierce and blood thirsty *Savages*" — they introduced order and symmetry by the assistance of the instruments of art . . . and thus the new world like the old became subject to man" (Slotkin, 433). Though Trumbull did not believe that America's Manifest Destiny should carry expansionism beyond Kentucky, he concurred with those who argued that wars with the Indians, in the eastern third of the continent at least, were beneficial and just.

The romance of the War of Independence still overshadowed much of the nineteenth century and suggested that American mettle, when tested in the fires of military confrontation, emerged stronger for the experience. In keeping with this view, a doctrine of muscular Christianity developed in which Americans congratulated themselves on achieving the spread of civilization where none had existed before, invoking a divine plan as justification for what in many cases were simply massacres.

One such defender of "just wars" was Senator Thomas Hart Benton. In 1846 he made the following remarks in a speech on the Oregon question in which he argued in favor of western expansion:

> For my part, I cannot murmur at what seems to be the effect of divine law. I cannot repine that this Capitol has replaced the wigwam—this Christian people, replaced the savages—white matrons, the red squaws—that such men as Washington, Franklin and Jefferson, have taken the place of Powhatan, Opechonecanough, and other red men, howsoever respectable they may have been as savages. Civilization or extinction has been the fate of all people who have found themselves in the track of the advancing Whites, and civilization, always the preference of the Whites, has been pressed as an object, while extinction has followed as a consequence of resistance. The Black and the Red Races have often felt their ameliorating influence. (quoted in Meigs, 309–10)

Similarly, in 1838, during the period of Cherokee resistance, a working man contributed the following remarks to the *Southern Banner:* "The white man is the only real, legal, moral, and civil proprietor of this country and state. . . . By white men alone was this continent discovered; by the prowess of white men alone (though not always properly and humanely exercised [!]) were the fierce and active Indians driven occidentally. And if swarms and hordes of infuriated red men pour down now" (Greenfeld, 457), this writer warned, white men alone will defend the state and even its blacks against them.

Such direct expressions of racial bias bring to mind Étienne Balibar's remark that "in the historical 'field' of nationalism, there is always a reciprocity of determination between [nationalism] and racism" (52). Balibar goes on to say: "It cannot be by chance that the genocide of the Indians became systematic immediately after the United States—the 'first of the new nations' in [H. M.] Lipset's famous expression—achieved independence" (53).

However, if massacres were sanctioned in the years immediately after the Revolutionary War, the policy of "subjugation or extermination" was considerably expanded after the Civil War. According to Slotkin, "The Indian wars of the post–Civil War period, particularly the war on the southern plains in 1867–69, were provoked, often deliberately and officially, by the whites in order to justify the expropriation of Indian lands for use by the railroads and their associated land companies" (562). During this three-year period two and a half million buffalo were deliberately slaughtered in order to starve out those tribes who resisted placement on reservations. These are the years of the massacres of the Cheyenne, the Nez Perce, the Sioux. The Commissioner of Indian Affairs explained the policy clearly in 1889: "The Indians must conform to 'the white man's ways,' peaceably if they will, forcibly if they must. They must adjust themselves to their environment, and conform their mode of living substantially to our civilization. This civilization may not be the best possible, but it is the best the Indian can get. They cannot escape it, and must either conform to it or be crushed by it" (Lincoln, *Renaissance*, 21). Liah Greenfeld argues that the Civil War "marked the line between the dream of nationality and its realization" (480). Many felt that the birth of the nation as a unitary reality occurred by means of this "just war" and were ready to see America engage in other military adventures to keep the muscle of American nationalism taut. And indeed, many Indian fighters of the latter part of the century had fought first in the Civil War.

Though wars were no rare occurrence among Indian nations, the Native American texts under consideration here call into question not only the justice of American genocidal wars but, in some cases, the nobility of war itself. As we have seen, William Apess refuses to praise King Philip simply as a warrior because, as he tells us, he does not believe in war. It is interesting to note that while some Euro-Americans were bent on combining a reading of Christianity with a policy of military intervention, Apess insists that war is justifiable only as a defense against hostility, because "Power was not given us to abuse each other, but . . . delegated to us by the King of heaven, a weapon of defense against error and evil" (279).

If whites admire the leaders of the American Revolution, Apess argues, they must be ready to respect equally those seventeenth-century Indians who resisted tyranny and enslavement by taking arms in their own defense. Apess holds a mirror up to whites to show that Americans treat Indians as savages when they resist white encroachment while at the same time, should some outside group try to take over the Americans' land, they are ready to defend it to the death.

In Governor Blacksnake's memoirs, Red Jacket confronts Americans at the time of the Revolutionary War with a national narrative of "father" and "children" that draws attention to the parallels between English tyranny over the colonies and American tyranny over the Indians. In both cases the "covenant chain of Peace" is broken despite promises of lasting cordiality between the two groups. At this point Red Jacket refuses to enter either side of the conflict, concluding his remarks, in Williams's awkward translation, with this airy *au fin:* "it is true that all the Indians Nations has nothing to Do with your father children quarrels we are therefore take upon the consideration with your opinion and with ours agreeable and we take your advise and we shall stand Notual [neutral]" (56). Summing up the Revolutionary War as a "father-children quarrel"—even if Blacksnake's memory of this speech was by the middle of the nineteenth century a little clouded—serves to deflate many of the pretensions of American nationalist rhetoric.

Several of these Native American texts retell the stories of Indian-white conflicts in terms that seriously undermine the claim that they were just wars. Black Hawk's whole aim in the autobiography was to show that he and his people were dealt with unfairly. Land sales were made by Indians who did not represent the tribe, and who were made intoxicated by liquor at the time, but all the Indians were subsequently expected to honor these agreements. During the uprising Indian women and children were massacred, which Black Hawk claims he never allowed his warriors to do. When some of his men raised white flags and attempted to surrender, they were butchered. In fact, so persuasive was Black Hawk's account of the war that it caused many white people to acknowledge American wrongdoing in this conflict.

John Rollin Ridge's portrayal of the violence in American society suggests that aggression breeds counteraggression and destabilizes the whole foundation of the state. More than any other text, *The Life and Adventures of Joaquín Murieta* challenges the notion that there is a core of authenticity at the heart of the nation. His protagonist, who is at once a Mexican and a figure for America, is created by the sociopolitical conditions affecting the state. He is the victim of racism himself, but he and his henchmen also engage in massacres of the nonresisting Chinese. Toward the end of his life, he kills an innocent Indian simply on the suspicion that the Indian might betray him. America seems here a free-for-all in which "frontier justice" means that no one gets a fair trial. Mexicans are harassed and killed and many others are simply hanged in the middle of the night.

It is the war of all against all, with those who do not fight back (the Chinese and, in Ridge's essays, the Digger Indians) becoming the victims of brutal aggression. Murieta himself is told that he cannot be an American (cannot earn a living and hold property) because of his Mexican background. The pervasive racism in the novel invites us to agree with Balibar that "By seeking to circumscribe the common essence of nationals, racism thus inevitably becomes involved in the obsessional quest for a 'core' of authenticity that cannot be found, shrinks the category of nationality and destabilizes the historical nation" (59). Ridge's work draws particular attention to the problems with doctrines emphasizing racial purity as the basis for national identity. Though Murieta's desire for revenge is understandable, Ridge hints early on that doctrines of racial purity contribute to violence through the process of totalization (which is itself an act of violence) where he says of Joaquín: "He had contracted a hatred to the whole American race, and was determined to shed their blood, whenever and wherever an opportunity occurred" (14).

Vanishing Americans

The very term "Manifest Destiny" implies that history is already in place. In fact, history seems an illusion since what is to be is already known, clear, manifest. In like terms the fate of the Indians was not in doubt for many nineteenth-century Americans. They were destined to disappear, to vanish, a metaphor that implies the same gradual and inevitable sequence of events, the same *derealization*, as Manifest Destiny itself. In Robert Frost's "The Gift Outright," Indians have been completely erased from the process of "possessing" the land. Elbert Smith's epic poem in celebration of Black Hawk also captures this sense of an effortless process where he apostrophizes Pontiac:

> Live on, O mighty prince of Ottawa!
> Live in thy people's hearts, while they remain—
> Until they fall, and dwindle out of sight. (37)

Even those who were sympathetic to the Indians believed that Native Americans must inevitably vanish, either because their purity, associated with nature, could not survive the spread of European-style culture, or because their savagery must be eliminated to make room for civilization. Not until late in the century did the "Indian Problem" come to mean how to save and make prosper those who were left. In *The Vanishing American* Brian Dippie places the arrival of this new construction—Manifest Destiny as the white man's burden—in the late 1880s.

Yet for a half century Native American writers had been challenging the view that Indians were predestined to die out. In the "Eulogy on King Philip," William Apess directly attacks the "deep-rooted popular opinion in the hearts of many that Indians were made, etc., on purpose for destruction, to be driven out by white Christians, and they to take their places; and that God decreed it from all eternity" (287). In his view the nation must accommodate people of all races. He asks simply: "Why are we not protected in our persons and property throughout the Union?" (156). George Copway also attacks the doctrine of the vanishing American. In his *Traditional History and Characteristic Sketches of the Ojibway Nation*, he retorts: "The pale face says that there is a fate hanging over the Indian bent on his destruction. Preposterous! They give him liquors to destroy himself with, and then charge the great Good Spirit as the author of their misery and mortality" (93–94).

After the massacre at Wounded Knee in 1890, which marked the end of Indian military resistance, there seemed little hope that Native American culture could be kept from vanishing. At the Chicago World's Fair in 1893, Simon Pokagon, an old Potawatomi chief, opened the fair on Chicago Day by ringing the new Liberty Bell. He offered a "plain and clear" answer to the question of what can be done for the remnant of the Indian population. "We *must* give up the pursuits of our fathers. . . . We must teach our children to give up the bow and arrow . . . and, in place of the gun, we must take the plow, and live as white men do. . . . Our children *must* learn that they owe no allegiance to any clan or power on earth except the United States. They must learn to love the Stars and Stripes, and, at all times to rejoice that they are American citizens" (emphasis in original, Dippie, 204).[1] National ideology, it would seem, had triumphed at the expense of a multicultural vision of the nation.

However, as we now know, this was premature. Pokagon himself was not entirely the white man's Indian as he has been portrayed. His seemingly accommodationist speech on Chicago Day was preceded by an extraordinary birch-bark document ("The Red Man's Rebuke") which he also handed out at the Columbian Exposition. In this document, he begins by proclaiming: "In behalf of my people, the American Indians, I hereby declare to you, the pale faced race that has usurped our lands and homes, that we have no spirit to celebrate with you the great Columbian Fair now being held in this Chicago city, the wonder of the world" (see appendix for complete document). Though pessimistic about the future of Native Americans, Pokagon calls into question the predestined passing away of the red man, presenting a vision of divine retribution in which God will reverse the power relations of Indians and whites in the afterlife. His rebuke contains a detailed discussion of the history of Native American oppression by Europeans and concludes with a vision out of Revelation in which those whites who have engaged in oppressive acts are, like the biblical Beast, cast down into an endless abyss.

In 1992 *boundary 2* published a special issue, edited by Karl Kroeber, entitled *1492–1992: American Indian Persistence and Resurgence;* among other points, it directly called into question the idea that Native Americans would in time simply vanish from the face of the earth. For this journal issue, the poet Wendy Rose included a poem, "Retrieving Osceola's Head, Okemah, Oklahoma, June 1985," that ends with the following challenge:

We are the dust that settles on the heart.
We are the twin deer drinking in the temple.
We are the whirlpool of blood stealing the books.
We are the apricots dancing and bursting in summer.
We are her and we are him.
We are all of the murders returning. (239)

The truth of the matter is that Native Americans did not vanish and, in fact, are growing in numbers, according to the census, faster than any other ethnic group in America.[2] Of course, the conception of self-determination for tribes within the larger polity of the United States, which George Copway, William Apess, John Rollin Ridge, and Sarah Winnemucca all championed, is still being worked out today. In *The Nations Within: The Past and Future of American Indian Sovereignty* (1984), Vine Deloria Jr. and Clifford M. Lytle discuss some of the difficulties of maintaining control over the Indian communities when they exist within the larger legal polity of the United States. They insist that "Indians have preserved the idea of nationhood or peoplehood throughout their period of contact with the non-Indian world but have had great difficulty communicating the essence of what they believe to the larger society" (263).

Nevertheless, it remains true that nineteenth-century Native American literature contains a discussion about those very matters. As we might expect, the conversation is not a monologue. Writers disagree about the nature of Indian identity, the proper construction of the nation, the right relation between Indian nations and the United States, the advisability of preserving traditional cultural practices, and the appeal of Euro-American life.

Those, such as Black Hawk and Sarah Winnemucca, who favor transpositional discourse emphasize the fundamental equality of Indians and whites. Those, such as George Copway and John Rollin Ridge, who favor adopting the white man's ways, resort more often to subjugated discourse and seem afflicted by what Nietzsche called *ressentiment*, helpfully defined by Liah Greenfeld as "a psychological state resulting from suppressed feelings of envy and hatred (existential envy) and the impossibility of satisfying these feelings" (15).

As we look a little further into *ressentiment*, however, we can see that it comprehends attitudes belonging to both transpositional and subjugated discourse. "The first condition (the structural basis of envy itself) is the fundamental comparability between the subject and the object of envy, or rather the belief on the part of the subject in the fundamental equality between them, which makes them in principle interchangeable. The second condition is the actual inequality (perceived as not fundamental) of such dimensions that it rules out practical achievement of the theoretically existing equality" (Greenfeld, 15–16). The result of this "unbearable inconsistency between several aspects of reality" is the kind of "anomie," or destabilization, that seems to have afflicted all of these writers at some time during their lives.[3]

In Greenfeld's discussion of *ressentiment*, we can see that the two discursive modes we have been exploring come together. It is now time to return to my proposition, given in chapter 1, to deconstruct the binary they represent. To some degree, the distinction between transpositional and subjugated discourse is arbitrary because acknowledgement of subjugation in the interests of raising consciousness concerning injustice is always both political (the domain of subjugated discourse) and utopian (the domain of transpositional discourse); all the writers we have analyzed here are operating to some degree in both modes. This should not surprise us, as *ressentiment* shows that a recognition of fundamental equality and a degree of hatred and envy concerning the superior position of the dominant group are both likely in situations of political oppression. Even to imagine a world of egalitarian reciprocity contradicts the hierarchies of oppression and is potentially a political act. Furthermore, subjugated discourse not infrequently incorporates transpositional arguments, as where William Apess talks about the degradation, prostitution, and misery of Indian communities and then adds that "there is no people in the world but who may be destroyed in the same way" (156). Therefore, though for purposes of rhetorical analysis I have separated the two modes—subjugated and transpositional—we can see that they come together in many of these works as Native American writers attempt to work out appropriate ways of conceptualizing the idea of nation.

However, it should be clear that, despite convergence on many fronts, these texts are not all making the same arguments or doing the same things with that idea. In fact, Black Hawk, William Apess, and Sarah Winnemucca (the writers who use transpositional discourse most often) offer a fundamentally democratic notion of nation that emphasizes broad discussion of political issues and consensus in decision making. George Copway and John Rollin Ridge, the two who more often fall into subjugated patterns of discourse, are preoccupied with the constitution of elite groups and more likely to favor a top-down mode of political organization. It is important to recognize that both models were available in Indian communities (as well as in American society more generally).

According to Liah Greenfeld's *Nationalism: Five Roads to Modernity,* the notion of America as a multicultural society in which individuals carry a dual identity based on both nationalism and ethnicity did not enter American culture until the end of the nineteenth century. Similarly we are used to thinking of cultural relativism as an effect of cosmopolitanism and the work of anthropologists such as Franz Boas. Nevertheless, one effect of reading these Native American texts is that we can see these "modern" views embodied much earlier in works which argue for a "native" America, an Indian nation. Though their contributions have long gone unrecognized, these writers not only wrestled with ideas of nationalism but affected the discourse about nation to some degree, since all their works were, at least briefly, popular with some segments of the white American population, and even those who would oppose these ideas had to take them into account.

What has it meant to be an Indian in a non-Indian culture, to be "the outsider inside"? As Kenneth Lincoln puts it: "This confusion, this challenge, *is* an Indian identity in America, as much as the call for harmonies in the old ways or tribal integrities" (*Renaissance,* 105). It is time to recognize that the American character has always been a contested matter. Perhaps we should say that there is no American character outside of the history of these contestations, which took place far earlier and across a broader spectrum of the American population than many of us once believed.

Retrieving Osceola's Head
Okemah, Oklahoma
June 1985

Dr. Weedon was an unusual man. . . He used to hang the head of Osceola on the bedstead where his three little boys slept and leave it there all night as a punishment. — Weedon's granddaughter, quoted by Peter Mathiessen in *Indian Country*

Hotter than the comet that skims the earth,
wilder than the wild winds of earth that blow into our lungs,
we burn, burn, sweeping clean the holy ground with spring
bobbing on the flood that rises within, submerging and breaking
into sunlight with glittering eyes. We remember something
inevitable as biting insects and tricky as the black swamp.

> We have learned
> to keep our heads.
> Just use the umbilical string
> uprooted from the ashes,
> stretch it as far as you can
> and hold it with one hand.
> Wipe from your back and nipples
> the sand, turn around, speak
> directly to the perpetrator
> or risk becoming him.

We are the dust that settles on the heart.
We are the twin deer drinking in the temple.
We are the whirlpool of blood stealing the books.
We are the apricots dancing and bursting in summer.
We are her and we are him.
We are all of the murders returning.

Wendy Rose

Appendix

"The Red Man's Rebuke"

I am grateful to the Southwest Museum Library of Los Angeles for allowing me to reprint from the birch-bark document this fascinating defense of Native American claims by Simon Pokagon. Pokagon published many essays and was known as the "Longfellow of his race." He is generally credited with writing the first novel about Native Americans by a Native American, *Queen of the Woods* (1899). In Brian Dippie's *The Vanishing American: White Attitudes and U.S. Indian Policy,* he describes Pokagon as "the white man's kind of Indian," calling him "humble, earnest, and, above all, progressive" (204), but what follows here shows that he was far from the docile spokesman for progress that Dippie makes him. Pokagon was angered by the lack of representation of Native American views at the World's Fair. After the opening of the fair, he apparently wrote "The Red Man's Rebuke" to protest this exclusion, and the mayor of Chicago, Carter Harrison, then took up his cause, offering him the chance to speak on Chicago Day, October 10, 1893. Dippie claims that Pokagon sold copies of his "address" at the fair. "He most impressed fair-goers by parading as the representative of a vanishing race and selling copies of his address, printed on birch bark and titled *The Red Man's Greeting*" (204). However, what he sold at the fair was not his speech but his earlier, more pessimistic, document.

I first encountered "The Red Man's Greeting" in the Alderman Library at the University of Virginia where it was available only on very murky microfiche. After a long and seemingly fruitless search for the original birch-bark document (which proclaimed itself "The Red Man's Greeting" in the Alderman Library version but which contained no passages recognizable from the World's Fair speech), I discovered "The Red Man's Rebuke" at the Southwest Library. It was identical to the Alderman Library's "Red Man's Greeting" except for the title. Pokagon's speech at the World's Fair was also entitled "The

Red Man's Greeting," and in C. H. Engle's "publisher's notes" at the front of *Queen of the Woods,* he too mentions a birch-bark document entitled "Red Man's Greeting," so I suspect that Dippie confused the speech, the "address," with the birch bark document. In any case, this difficult-to-find piece of Native American literature is certainly worth resuscitating. Engle clarifies that Pokagon wrote it *before* the speech (and may therefore have changed its name in future editions to avoid confusion). On May 1, 1893, the opening day of the fair, the chief had watched with great sorrow as other nations were recognized but not "the original Americans." He went home in great distress. "It was in such a frame of mind he was inspired to write 'The Red Man's Greeting,' fitly termed by Professor Swing of Chicago, 'The Red Man's Book of Lamentations.' It was published in a booklet made from the manifold bark of the white birch tree. The little unique rustic book has been read with great interest, and highly complimented by the press, both in this country and in Europe, for its wild, rough imagery and native eloquence" ("publisher's notes," *Queen of the Woods,* 10). A review from the daily *Inter Ocean,* included by Engle, calls it "a cry from the Indian heart" and proclaims: "No one can read it without realizing the 'other' side of the Indian question" (11). It appears here complete for the first time since 1893.

The Red Man's Rebuke

by Chief Pokagon (Pottawattamie Chief)

"Shall not one line lament our forest race,
For you struck out from wild creation's face?
Freedom—the self same freedom you adore,
Bade us defend our violated shore."

In behalf of my people, the American Indians, I hereby declare to you, the pale-faced race that has usurped our lands and homes, that we have no spirit to celebrate with you the great Columbian Fair now being held in this Chicago city, the wonder of the world.

No; sooner would we hold high joy-day over the graves of our departed fathers, than to celebrate our own funeral, the discovery of America. And while you who are strangers, and you who live here, bring the offerings of the handiwork of your own lands, and your hearts in admiration rejoice over the beauty and grandeur of this young republic, and you say, "Behold the wonders wrought by our children in this foreign land," do not forget that this success has been at the sacrifice of *our* homes and a once happy race.

Where these great Columbian show-buildings stretch skyward, and where stands this "Queen City of the West," once stood the red man's wigwam; here met their old men, young men, and maidens; here blazed their council-fires. But now the eagle's eye can find no trace of them. Here was the center of their wide-spread hunting-grounds; stretching far eastward, and to the great salt Gulf southward, and to the lofty Rocky Mountain chain westward; and all about and beyond the Great Lakes northward roamed vast herds of buffalo that no man could number, while moose, deer, and elk were found from ocean to ocean; pigeons, ducks, and geese in near bow-shot moved in great clouds through the air, while fish swarmed our streams, lakes, and seas close to shore. All were provided by the Great Spirit for our use; we destroyed none except for food and dress; had plenty and were contented and happy.

But alas! the pale-faces came by chance to our shores, many times very needy and hungry. We nursed and fed them—fed the ravens that were soon to pluck out our eyes, and the eyes of our children; for no sooner had the news reached the Old World that a new continent had been found, peopled with another race of men, than, locust-like, they swarmed on all our coasts; and like the carrion crows in spring, that in circles wheel and clamor long and loud, and will not cease until they find out and feast upon the dead, so these strangers from the East long circuit made and turkey-like they gobbled in our ears, "Give us gold, give us gold"; "Where find you gold? Where find you gold?"

We gave for promises and "gewgaws" all the gold we had, and showed them where to dig for more; to repay us, they robbed our homes of fathers, mothers, sons, and daughters; some were forced across the sea for slaves in Spain, while multitudes were dragged into the mines to dig for gold, and held in slavery there until all who escaped not, died under the lash of the cruel task-master. It finally passed into their history that, "the red man of the West, unlike the black man of the East, will die before he'll be a slave." Our hearts were crushed by such base ingratitude; and, as the United States has now decreed, "No Chinaman shall land upon our shores," so we then felt that no such barbarians as they, should land on *ours.*

In those days that tried our fathers' souls, tradition says: "A crippled, grey-haired sire told his tribe that in the visions of the night he was lifted high above the earth, and in great wonder beheld a vast spider-web spread out over the land from the Atlantic Ocean toward the setting sun. Its net-work was made of rods of iron; along its lines in all directions rushed monstrous spiders, greater in strength, and larger far than any beast of earth, clad in brass and iron, dragging after them long rows of wigwams with families therein, out-stripping in their course the flight of birds that fled before them. Hissing from their nostrils came forth fire and smoke, striking terror to both fowl and beast. The red men hid themselves in fear, or fled away, while the white men trained these monsters for the war path, as warriors for battle."

The old man who saw the vision claimed it meant that the Indian race would surely pass away before the pale-faced strangers. He died a martyr to his belief. Centuries have passed since that time, and we now behold in the vision as in a mirror, the present net-work of railroads, and the monstrous engines with their fire, smoke, and hissing steam, with cars attached, as they go sweeping through the land.

The cyclone of civilization rolled westward; the forests of untold centuries were swept away; streams dried up; lakes fell back from their ancient bounds; and all our fathers once loved to gaze upon was destroyed, defaced, or marred, except the sun, moon, and starry skies above, which the Great Spirit in his wisdom hung beyond their reach.

Still on the storm-cloud rolled, while before its lightning and thunder the beasts of the field and the fowls of the air withered like grass before the flame—were shot for love of power to kill alone, and left to spoil upon the plains. Their bleaching bones now scattered far and near, in shame declare the wanton cruelty of pale-faced men. The storm unsatisfied on land swept our lakes and streams, while before its clouds of hooks, nets, and glistening spears the fish vanished from our waters like the morning dew before the rising sun. Thus our inheritance was cut off, and we were driven and scattered as sheep before the wolves.

Nor was this all. They brought among us fatal diseases our fathers knew not of; our medicine-men tried in vain to check the deadly plague; but they themselves died, and our people fell as fall the leaves before the autumn's blast. To be just, we must acknowledge there were some good men with these strangers, who gave their lives for ours, and in great kindness taught us the revealed will of the Great Spirit through his Son Jesus, the mediator between God and man. But while we were being taught to love the Lord our God with all our heart, mind, and strength, and our neighbors as ourselves, and our children were taught to lisp, "Our Father who art in heaven, hallowed be thy name," bad men of the same race, whom we thought of the same belief, shocked our faith in the revealed will of the Father, as they came among us with bitter oaths upon their lips, something we had never heard before, and cups of "fire-water" in their hands, something we had never seen before. They pressed the sparkling glasses to our lips and said, "Drink and you will be happy." We drank thereof, we and our children, but alas! like the serpent that charms to kill, the drink-habit coiled about the heart-strings of its victims, shocking unto death, friendship, love, honor, manhood—all that makes men good and noble; crushing out all ambition, and leaving naught but a culprit vagabond in the place of a man.

Now as we have been taught to believe that our first parents ate of the forbidden fruit, and fell, so we as fully believe that this fire-water is the hard cider of the white man's devil, made from the fruit of that tree that brought death into the world, and all our woes. The arrow, the scalping knife, and the tomahawk used on the war-path were *merciful* compared with it; *they* were used in our defense, but the accursed drink came like a serpent in the form of a dove. Many of our people partook of it without mistrust, as children pluck the flowers and clutch a scorpion in their grasp; only when they feel the sting, they let the flowers fall. But Nature's children had no such power; for when the viper's fangs they felt, they only hugged the reptile the more closely to their breasts, while friends before them stood pleading with prayers and tears that they would let the deadly serpent drop. But all in vain. Although they promised so to do, yet with laughing grin and steps uncertain like the fool, they still more frequently guzzled down this hellish drug. Finally, conscience ceased to give alarm, and, led by deep despair to life's last brink, and goaded by demons on every side, they cursed themselves, they cursed their friends, they cursed their beggar babes and wives, they cursed their God, and died.

You say of us that we are treacherous, vindictive, and cruel; in answer to the charge, we declare to all the world with our hands uplifted before high Heaven, that before the white man came among us, we were kind, outspoken, and forgiving. Our real character has been misunderstood because we have resented the breaking of treaties made with the United States, as we honestly understood them. The few of our children who are permitted to attend your schools, in great pride tell us that they read in your own histories, how William Penn, a Quaker, and a good man, made treaties with nineteen tribes of Indians, and that neither he nor they ever broke them; and further, that during seventy years, while Pennsylvania was controlled by the Quakers, not a drop of blood was shed nor a war-whoop sounded by our people. Your own historians, and our traditions, show that for nearly two hundred years, different Eastern powers were striving for the mastery in the new world, and that our people were persuaded by the different factions to take the war-path, being generally led by white men who had been discharged from prisons for crimes committed in the Old World.

Read the following, left on record by Peter Martyr, who visited our forefathers in the day of Columbus.

"It is certain that the land among these people is as common as the sun and water, and that 'mine and thine,' the seed of all misery, have no place with them. They are content with so little, that in so large a country they have rather a superfluity than a scarceness: so that they seem to live in the golden world without toil, living in open gardens not intrenched with dykes, divided with hedges, or defended with walls. They deal truly one with another, without laws, without books, without judges. They take him for an evil and mischievous man, who taketh pleasure in doing hurt to another, and albeit they delight not in superfluities, yet they make provision for the increase of such roots whereof they make bread, content with such simple diet whereof health is preserved, and disease avoided."

Your own histories show that Columbus on his first visit to our shores, in a message to the king and queen of Spain, paid our forefathers this beautiful tribute:—

"They are loving, uncovetous people: so docile in all things that I swear to your majesties there is not in the world a better race or a more delightful country. They love their neighbors as themselves, and their talk is ever sweet and gentle, accompanied with smiles; and though they be naked, yet their manners are decorous and praiseworthy."

But a few years passed away, and your historians left to be perused with shame, the following facts:—

"On the islands of the Atlantic coast and in the populous empires of Mexico and Peru, the Spaniards, through pretense of friendship and religion, gained audience with chiefs and kings, their families and attendants.

They were received with great kindness and courtesy but in return they most treacherously seized and bound in chains the unsuspecting natives; and as a ransom for their release demanded large sums of gold, which were soon given by their subjects. But instead of granting them freedom as promised, they were put to death in a most shocking manner. There [*sic*] subjects were then hunted down like wild beasts, with bloodhounds, robbed and enslaved while under pretext to convert them to Christianity, the rack, the scourge, and the fagot were used. Some were burned alive in the thickets and fastnesses for refusing to work the mines as slaves."

Tradition says these acts of base ingratitude were communicated from tribe to tribe throughout the continent, and that a universal wail as one voice went up from all the tribes of the unbroken wilderness: "We must beat back these strangers from our shores before they seize our land and homes, or slavery and death are ours."

Reader, pause here, close your eyes, shut out from your heart all prejudice against our race, and honestly consider the above records penned by the palefaced historians centuries ago; and tell us in the name of eternal truth and by all that is sacred and dear to mankind, was there ever a people without the slightest reason of offense, more treacherously imprisoned and scourged than we have been? And tell us, have crime, despotism, violence, and slavery ever been dealt out in a more wicked manner to crush out life and liberty; or was ever a people more mortally offended than our forefathers were?

Almighty Spirit of humanity, let thy arms of compassion embrace and shield us from the charge of treachery, vindictiveness, and cruelty, and save us from further oppression! And may the great chief of the United States appoint no more broken down or disappointed politicians as agents to deal with us, but may he select good men that are tried and true, men who fear not to do the right. This is our prayer. What would remain for us if we were not allowed to pray? All else we acknowledge to be in the hands of this great republic.

It is clear that for years after the discovery of this country, we stood before the coming strangers, as a block of marble before the sculptor, ready to be shaped into a statue of grace and beauty; but in their greed for gold, the block was hacked to pieces and destroyed.

Child-like we trusted in them with all our hearts; and as the young nestling while yet blind, swallows each morsel given by the parent bird, so we drank in all they said. They showed us the compass that guided them across the trackless deep, and as its needle swung to and fro only resting to the north, we looked upon it as a thing of life from the eternal world. We could not understand the lightning and thunder of their guns, believing they were weapons of the gods; nor could we fathom their wisdom in knowing and telling us the exact time in which the sun or moon should be darkened; hence we looked upon them as divine; we revered them—yes, we trusted in them, as infants trust in the arms of their mothers.

But again and again was our confidence betrayed, until we were compelled to know that greed for gold was all the balance-wheel they had. The remnant of the beasts are now wild and keep beyond the arrow's reach, the fowls fly high in air, the fish hide themselves in deep waters. We have been driven from the homes of our childhood and from the burial places of our kindred and friends, and scattered far westward into desert places, where multitudes have died from homesickness, cold, and hunger, and are suffering and dying still for want of food and blankets.

As the hunted deer close chased all day long, when night comes on, weary and tired, lies down to rest, mourning for companions of the morning herd, all scattered, dead, and gone, so we through weary years have tried to find some place to safely rest. But all in vain! Our throbbing hearts unceasing say, "The hounds are howling on our tracks." Our sad history has been told by weeping parents to their children from generation to generation; and as the fear of the fox in the duckling is hatched, so the wrongs we have suffered are transmitted to our children, and they look upon the white man with distrust as soon as they are born. Hence our worst acts of cruelty should be viewed by all the world with Christian charity, as being but the echo of bad treatment dealt out to us.

Therefore we pray our critics everywhere to be not like the thoughtless boy who condemns the toiling bees wherever found, as vindictive and cruel, because in robbing their homes he once received the poisoned darts that nature gave for their defense. Our strongest defense against the onward marching hordes, we fully realize is as useless as the struggles of a lamb borne high in air, pierced to its heart, in the talons of an eagle.

We never shall be happy here any more; we gaze into the faces of our little ones, for smiles of infancy to please, and into the faces of our young men and maidens, for joys of youth to cheer advancing age, but alas! instead of smiles of joy we find but looks of sadness there. Then we fully realize in the anguish of our souls that their young and tender hearts, in keenest sympathy with ours, have drank in the sorrows we have felt, and their sad faces reflect it back to us again. No rainbow of promise spans the dark cloud of our afflictions; no cheering hopes are painted on our midnight sky. We only stand with folded arms and watch and wait to see the future deal with us no better than the past. No cheer of sympathy is given us; but in answer to our complaints we are told the triumphal march of the Eastern race westward is by the unalterable decree of nature, termed by them "the survival of the fittest." And so we stand as upon the sea shore, chained hand and foot, while the in-coming tide of the great ocean of civilization rises slowly but surely to overwhelm us.

But a few more generations and the last child of the forest will have passed into the world beyond—into that kingdom where Tche-ban-you-booz, the Great Spirit, dwelleth, who loved justice and mercy, and hateth evil; who has declared the "fittest" in his kingdom shall be those alone that hear and aid his children when they cry, and that love him and keep his commandments. In that kingdom many of our people in faith believe he will summon the pale-faced spirits to take position on his left, and the red spirits on his right, and that he will say, "Sons and daughters of the forest, your prayers for deliverance from the iron heel of oppression through centuries past are recorded in this book now open before me, made from the bark of the white birch, a tree under which for generations past you have mourned and wept. On its pages silently has been recorded your sad history. It has touched my heart with pity and I will have compassion."

Then turning to his left he will say, "Sons and daughters of the East, all hear and give heed unto my words. While on earth I did great and marvelous things for you—I gave my only Son, who declared unto you my will, and as you had freely received, to so freely give, and declare the gospel unto all people. A few of you have kept the faith; and through opposition and great tribulation have labored hard and honestly for the redemption of mankind, regardless of race or color. To all such I now give divine power to fly on lightning wings throughout my universe. Now, therefore, listen; and when the great drum beats, let all try their powers to fly. Only those can rise who acted well their part on earth to redeem and save the fallen."

The drum will be sounded, and that innumerable multitude will appear like some vast sea of wounded birds struggling to rise. We shall behold it, and shall hear their fluttering as the rumbling of an earthquake, and to our surprise shall see but a scattering few in triumph rise, and hear their songs re-echo through the vault of heaven as they sing, "Glory to the highest who hath redeemed and saved us."

Then the Great Spirit will speak with a voice of thunder to the remaining shame-faced multitude: "Hear ye: it is through great mercy that you have been permitted to enter these happy hunting-grounds. Therefore I charge you in presence of these red men that you are guilty of having tyrannized over them in many and strange ways. I find you guilty of having made wanton wholesale butchery of their game and fish, I find you guilty of using tobacco, a poisonous weed made only to kill parasites on plants and lice on man and beast. You found it with the red men, who used it only in smoking the pipe of peace, to confirm their contracts, in place of a seal. But you multiplied its use, not only in smoking, but in chewing, snuffing, thus forming unhealthy, filthy habits, and by cigarettes, the abomination of abominations, learned little children to hunger and thirst after the father and mother of palsy and cancers.

"I find you guilty of tagging after the pay agents sent out by the great chief of the United States, among the Indians, to pay off their birth-right claims to home, and liberty, and native lands, and then sneaking about their agencies by deceit and trickery, cheating and robbing them of their money and goods, thus leaving them poor and naked. I also find you guilty of following the trail of Christian missionaries into the wilderness among the natives, and when they had set up my altars, and the great work of redemption had just begun, and some in faith believed, you then and there most wickedly set up the idol of man-tchi-man in-to (the devil), and there stuck out your sign, SAMPLE ROOMS. You then dealt out to the sons of the forest a most damnable drug, fitly termed on earth by Christian women, 'a beverage of hell,' which destroyed both body and soul, taking therefore, all their money and blankets, and scrupling not to take in pawn the Bibles given them by my servants.

"Therefore know ye, this much abused race shall enjoy the liberties of these happy hunting grounds, while I teach them my will, which you were in duty bound to do while on earth. But instead, you blocked up the highway that led to heaven that the car of salvation might not pass over. Had you done your duty, they as well as you would now be rejoicing in glory with my saints with whom you, fluttering, tried this day in vain to rise. But now I say unto you, Stand back! you shall not tread upon the heels of my people, nor tyrannize over them any more. Neither shall you with gatling gun or otherwise disturb or break up their prayer-meetings in camp any more. Neither shall you practice with weapons of lightning and thunder any more. Neither shall you use tobacco in any shape, way or manner. Neither shall you touch, taste, handle, make, buy, or sell anything that can intoxicate any more. And know ye, ye cannot buy out the law or skulk by justice here; and if any attempt is made on your part to break these commandments, I shall forthwith grant these red men of America great power, and delegate them to cast you out of Paradise, and hurl you headlong through its outer gates into the endless abyss beneath—far beyond, where darkness meets with light, there to dwell, and thus shut you out from my presence and the presence of angels and the light of heaven forever and ever."

The End

Notes

1. I use the term "America" here to represent the United States as a symbolic construct, because this is the usage implicit in most of the texts I quote. However, I am fully aware that many have interpreted the term "America" either more broadly, to include territory and people north and south of the U.S. borders, or more narrowly, to refer to the U.S. government and its actions. In Benedict Anderson's influential work *Imagined Communities: Reflections on the Origins and Spread of Nationalism* (1991), he sees nationalism developing from "Creole Pioneers" in both English North America and Spanish South America. He states, "People all over Spanish America thought of themselves as 'Americans,' since this term denoted precisely the shared fatality of extra-Spanish birth" (63). My narrower usage of the term "America" is purely pragmatic and not intended to challenge more liberal interpretations. For an excellent discussion of the vagaries of this term in connection with "American Literature," see Carolyn Porter, "What We Know We Don't Know: Remapping American Literary Studies."

2. This term comes from Lauren Berlant, who writes, "We are bound together because we inhabit the *political* space of the nation, which is not merely juridical, territorial (*jus soli*), genetic (*jus sanguinis*), linguistic, or experiential, but some tangled cluster of these. I call this space the 'National Symbolic,'" (*The Anatomy of National Fantasy,* 4–5).

3. See Albert Gelpi, ed., *The Poet in America,* 597.

4. In *Keywords* Williams uses the following set of abbreviations: eC as early or first period (third) of century, mC as middle period (third), and lC as last third or end of century. I should point out here that Benedict Anderson, whose *Imagined Communities* has been very influential in discussions of nationalism, contests the idea that racism is an essential component of the rise of nationalism. It was, however, a key ingredient in the rise of North American nationalism, as we will see further on.

5. This phrase is from Benedict Anderson. He defines "nation" as "an imagined community—and imagined as both inherently limited and sov-

ereign" (6). Though most people do not know each other in the nation, they imagine they share an identity "always conceived as a deep, horizontal comradeship" (*Imagined Communities,* 7).

6. At first, Native Americans had no conception of race as nineteenth-century Europeans came to define it. They did distinguish between whites and peoples of color as we will see in the chapters on Apess, Black Hawk, and Sarah Winnemucca, but color was not coded hierarchically until white interpretations intervened.

7. In the "memorials" that the Cherokee presented to Congress at the time of debate over their removal from Georgia, they spoke of their "nation" in terms that clearly reflect the influence of Euro-American models of nationhood. See Krupat, "Figures and the Law" in *Ethnocriticism,* 164–72, where he reprints the 1829 and 1830 memorials in full.

8. In "Mapping Identities: Literature, Nationalism, Colonialism," Reiss takes issue with a number of contemporary theorists—Terry Eagleton, Edward Said, Homi Bhabha, Eric Cheyfitz—who he claims fall victim to a series of disabling binaries: metropolitan vs. indigenous, novel vs. epic, nation vs. tribe. Reiss insists that the true state of affairs was always much more complex. Reiss sees some ground for hope in cross-cultural comparisons. Like Aimé Cesaire who declares "exchange is oxygen" (and Gerald Vizenor who looks to the mixed-blood commentator), Reiss wishes to resist "imposing ideas of otherness and not only to come to terms with difference (yet in self-protective guise) but to welcome the hybrid" (675).

9. The Cherokee confronted Congress with their alternative views about nations at several key points (see Krupat, "Figures and the Law" in *Ethnocriticism,* and Priscilla Wald). Sarah Winnemucca's work was circulated to members of Congress by Elizabeth Peabody. George Copway addressed petitions to Congress concerning the creation of an Indian state. John Rollin Ridge went to Washington after the Civil War to negotiate terms for the Cherokee.

10. For an interesting discussion of the Statue of Liberty as a form of personification, see Berlant, 22 ff.

11. For a helpful survey of historical issues relating to these challenges, see Pauline Turner Strong and Barrik van Winkle, "Tribe and Nation: American Indians and American Nationalism." The section of their article entitled "Imagining and Appropriating an Identity: The Indian as Symbolic Resource for American Nationalism" condenses more detailed discussions in Berkhofer, Slotkin, and Pearce.

12. In *Empire for Liberty* Wai-Chee Dimock examines the use of national

personification in the work of Herman Melville. However, she sees Melville's preoccupation with Manifest Destiny as part of his own imperialistic authorial desires. Sometimes Indians (e.g., George Copway) also seem driven by such motives, but this is not typical of Indian writing.

13. See Murray, 27.

14. For example, see Dimock, "Nation, Self, and Personification," 3–41.

15. See Lincoln, *Native American Renaissance,* and Basso, *Portraits of "The Whiteman,"* though the latter is not about written texts but about oral linguistic practices.

16. I assume that most of my readers will not be fluent in Indian languages, as I am not, and therefore I have opted for the Anglicized versions of these Indian names.

17. Arnold Krupat's discussion of metaphorical discourse in "Figures and the Law" is similar in some respects to what I am calling transpositional discourse. See *Ethnocriticism,* 157 ff.

18. In *I Am a Man: The Indian Black Hawk,* Cyrenus Cole reports, "According to the accounts of white men, the meeting was dramatic. For a few moments the two grizzled warriors stood facing each other in silence. It was the red warrior who spoke first. 'I am a man and you are another' is what he said" (246).

19. By "writing team" I mean the three people who most directly participated in the production of Black Hawk's biography: Antoine LeClaire (the translator), J. B. Patterson (the editor), and Black Hawk himself.

20. Keokuck (c. 1780–1848), whose name means "the man who has been everywhere," became an important rival to Black Hawk because of his great skill in persuasive oratory. Black Hawk himself was not a great public speaker but a man who spoke with deeds. His autobiography is a departure from his usual practice as it chooses words instead.

21. For an extended discussion of the issues raised by Spivak and Bhabha, see Rey Chow, "Where Have All the Natives Gone?"

22. This passage will be further discussed in chapter 5.

23. See Roland Barthes's "The Death of the Author" in *Image, Music, Text* and Michel Foucault's "What Is an Author?" in *The Foucault Reader.* For my response to these texts, see my essay "Feminist Literary Criticism and the Author" in *Critical Inquiry.* In that essay I express my reservations about the sweeping use of "death-of-the-author" criticism as though it were somehow improper even to mention the author or the circumstances of composition of a given text. Though I do not subscribe to such views, I have found useful some of the theoretical challenges to earlier conceptions of authorship.

2. Writing Indians

1. For discussions of the use of Indians as national symbols, see Berkhofer Jr., *The White Man's Indian;* E. McClung Fleming, "Symbols of the United States: From Indian Queen to Uncle Sam"; Lester C. Olson, *Emblems of American Community in the Revolutionary Era;* Rayna Green, "The Pocahontas Perplex: The Image of Indian Women in American Culture"; and Carroll Smith-Rosenberg, "Subject Female: Authorizing American Identity."

2. Though actually Dippie completed his dissertation on this subject in 1970, prior to the publication of Slotkin's and Rogin's works.

3. I say that Fisher *may* provide such a context of reconsideration because his argument in *Hard Facts* is not always clear. The passive voice consistently redirects attention away from human actors toward large impersonal forces.

4. See, for example, T. J. Jackson Lears's essay "The Concept of Cultural Hegemony: Problems and Possibilities." For an example of an argument directly related to Native Americans, see Arnold Krupat's thoughts on hegemony in *Ethnocriticism:* "I return, again and again to Raymond Williams's sense of the way in which the very nature of cultural hegemony is such that it cannot help but permit breaks, blanks, holes, areas weakly (or un-) colonized, with room, thus, for 'residual' and 'emergent' elements to have a certain play" (78).

5. For instance, Herman Melville was openly critical of Parkman's views on Indians. When he reviewed *The Oregon Trail* in 1849, Melville wrote, "We are all of us—Anglo-Saxons, Dyaks, and Indians—sprung from one head and made in one image. If we reject this brotherhood now, we shall be forced to join hands hereafter" (quoted in Maddox, 72). Sandra Zagarell considers nonhegemonic views of nation in her essay "Expanding 'America': Lydia Sigourney's *Sketch of Connecticut* and Catharine Sedgwick's *Hope Leslie.*"

3. The Irony and Mimicry of William Apess

1. In 1992 University of Massachusetts Press published *On Our Own Ground: The Complete Writings of William Apess, A Pequot,* edited and introduced by Barry O'Connell. Though individual works (the eulogy and *Nullification,* for instance) were available prior to this, O'Connell's edition is an important contribution to American literature because it brings together all

of Apess's published work and thus provides the reader with an opportunity to compare these fascinating texts one with another.

2. See A. LaVonne Ruoff's "Three Nineteenth-Century American Indian Autobiographers"; Krupat's *The Voice in the Margin*, *Ethnocriticism*, and *Native American Autobiography;* H. David Brumble III's *American Indian Autobiography;* and David Murray's *Forked Tongues.*

3. In *Ethnocriticism* Krupat begins by noting that Apess has introduced the text with a passage about the Indians' loss of their land and tribal authority (their nation, in effect), but he sees the plot of this narrative building toward compensation. By joining the Christian throng, Apess eventually constructs a new tribe, a new family, for himself in which the earthly concept of nation dissolves into a broader union of souls. "The tribe to which he would now belong, defining himself by his membership, is that of 'the followers of the most high' " (224).

4. On the subject of the reliability of Indian memory in a preliterate culture, see John C. Ewer's foreword to *Two Leggins*, ix–x.

5. For helpful discussions of the use of the language of "fathers" and "children" in relations between Indians and whites, see Pearce, Rogin, and Berkhofer. As will be discussed in chapter 4, Indians often used the term "father" to refer to the white official in charge of trade relations, whether he was French, Spanish, English, or American. When whites appropriated this terminology, however, they tended to infantilize the Indians. "Indians were rendered helpless and placed in situations where they behaved, from the white point of view, irrationally. Their actions were then attributed to their 'inveterate,' 'improvident,' childlike character. Indians were not forced to act in regressed and childlike ways; they were children" (Rogin, *Fathers and Children*, 231).

6. Barry O'Connell speculates that William Apess might have some African American ancestors since he so consistently connects Indians and blacks, a connection not typical (as we shall see) of other Native American writers.

7. There is some question, however, as to how much of this document Apess wrote himself and how much was added by other writers. O'Connell concludes: "*Indian Nullification* is an odd book. Directly or indirectly, it is the work of many hands, more a documentary of the controversy than a singular account" (165).

8. Murray says: "It is the complex relation between on the one side the Christian civilised Indian, affirmer of white values, and on the other the Indian proud of his heritage and bitterly critical of white actions which is most interesting in his work" (57).

9. At many places in Apess's work, as I will note again further on, I am reminded of Melville and forced to wonder if Melville knew of these texts. Here the story of the lions and the carvers brings to mind the sternpiece of Castile and Leon in "Benito Cereno" where the masked satyr has his foot on the prostrate neck of a writhing figure connected later to the flag of Spain described as figuring a closed castle and a white lion rampant.

10. See, for example, the Fourth of July speeches by Frederick Douglass ("What to the Slave is the Fourth of July") and by John Quinney (Mahican), usually called simply "Quinney's Speech," both available in *The Heath Anthology of American Literature*, vol. 1, edited by Paul Lauter, et al.

4. Black Hawk and the Moral Force of Transposition

1. See my discussion of Ziff in chapter 1.

2. Wallace tries to argue that Patterson puts Black Hawk before his audience as a defeated hero, the best of his kind, but even as a "superior Indian," a man unable to join white society due to his otherness. "That is, although Black Hawk is capable of seeing through the behavior of whites, the voice that emerges in the text consistently presents itself as incapable of understanding the complexity of white 'civilized' behavior" (490). One of Wallace's best points concerns the translation of alcohol as "bad medicine," of cities as "big villages," of Euro-American women as "squaws," and of journalists as "village criers." He comments, "There is no good reason to translate Black Hawk's words into this fake, Indian-colloquial English; a more accurate word would serve just as well. Translating certain words this way, then must be seen as a method of stressing Black Hawk's cultural separateness" (491). Though I agree with this point, I think the text—due to its transpositional argument—gives a more complicated sense of Black Hawk's cultural critique.

3. Page numbers in this chapter refer to the widely used Prairie State Books edition published by the University of Illinois Press in 1990.

4. It is useful in this context to compare John Tanner's autobiography (recently republished as *The Falcon*). Growing up on the frontier in a Euro-American family, Tanner was abducted by the Indians at the age of nine and adopted into a Chippewa tribe. When he was middle-aged, he tried to reconnect to white society but was never able to do so, though the autobiography is a result of this attempt. In it Tanner (with the help of his white editor) recounts stories of scalping and the scalp dance with no negative commen-

tary, demonstrating that whites could themselves play the role of unregenerate Other under certain circumstances. The issue is culture not color.

5. For example, he once entertained the idea of offering the United States
the lead mines in which the Indians worked for part of each year in return
for being allowed to stay in the general area if not in Saukenuk, Black
Hawk's village on the Rock River in Illinois.

6. The treaty was signed under questionable circumstances and certainly
exchanged a much larger amount of land for a much smaller amount of
money than was usually the case. According to Black Hawk, four Indians
with the good wishes of the Sauk and Fox nation went to Saint Louis to
retrieve an Indian prisoner being held in the stockade for murder. While
there they were given alcohol and made to sign papers whose content they
did not fully understand. At the end of the "celebration," the prisoner was
sent out from the fort but shot dead before he could reach safety. Black
Hawk claimed, "This was all myself or nation knew of the treaty of 1804. It
has been explained to me since. I find, by that treaty, all our country, east of
the Mississippi, and south of the Jeffreon, was ceded to the United States for
one thousand dollars a year! [In 1804 President Jefferson claimed that more
than $2,000 had already been given.] I will leave it to the people of the
United States to say, whether our nation was properly represented in this
treaty? or whether we received a fair compensation for the extent of country
ceded by those *four* individuals? I could say much about this treaty, but I will
not, at this time. It has been the origin of all our difficulties" (61–62). In
italicizing the word four, attention is drawn to the fact that normally such a
treaty would have required the participation of the whole tribe and long
discussion by a tribal council.

7. In "Masculinity and Self-Performance in *The Life of Black Hawk*," Timothy Sweet concludes that "gender is constructed [by the Sauk] according
to a paradigm more complex than that of Western patriarchy, in which
'woman' is marked (only) as object and 'man' (only) as subject: for the Sauk
man, both subject and object positions are occupied at once" (484). Thus,
Sweet takes Black Hawk to be representative, comparing his *individual*
views with the *structure* of patriarchy. However, one could argue that Sweet
(by concentrating on Black Hawk) overemphasizes the fluidity of gender
roles in Sauk culture and underrates the way patriarchy in the West is
similarly lived by individuals in highly various ways, with some men refusing the models of male behavior purveyed by the culture.

8. Black Hawk's commentary about this treaty in the autobiography is
typically bitter, "Here for the first time, I touched the goose quill to the

treaty—and not knowing, however, that, by that act, I consented to give away my village. Had that been explained to me, I should have opposed it, and never would have signed their treaty, as my recent conduct will clearly prove. What do we know of the manner of the laws and customs of white people? They might buy our bodies for dissection, and we would touch the goose quill to confirm it, without knowing what we are doing" (98–99).

9. Note that Black Hawk's view of the reliability of the British differs markedly from Cornplanter's view of them as "deceivers."

10. An example of Black Hawk's use of irony is the following:

A short time after the Pottowatomies left, a party of thirty braves, belonging to our nation, from the *peace camp* on the Missouri, paid us a visit. They exhibited *five scalps*. . . . Myself and braves then showed the two we had taken. . . .

They recounted to us all that had taken place—the number that had been killed by the *peace party*, as they were called and recognized—which far surpassed what our warriors, who had joined the British, had done! The party came for the purpose of joining the British! I advised them to return to the peace party. (76)

11. Many descriptions of Black Hawk in the last years of his life note that he was wearing Western clothing. The portrait by J. O. Lewis reproduced in Jackson's 1955 edition shows him "in the red-collared blue coat, with brass buttons, that he wore home from Fortress Monroe" (169). William Armiger Scripps, a London publisher who encountered Black Hawk on board a steamer, described him as "dressed in a short blue frock coat, white hat and red leggins tied around below the knee with garters. . . . His nose [was] perforated very wide between the nostrils, so as to give it the appearance of the upper and under mandibles of a hawk. He wears light colored leather gloves, and a walking stick with a tassel" (Jackson 1955 ed., 17). Black Hawk enjoyed his frock coat, in which he was buried, and particularly valued the medals he had received from the government which he wore around his neck. None of these adornments seems to have troubled him with thoughts of acculturation, however. Nothing could change his fundamental loyalties to his own people, and thus he apparently saw no contradiction in his untraditional garb which he assumed for the purpose of "dressing up," rather than as a sign of his acceptance of white supremacy.

12. See also Vizenor's description in *Manifest Manners* of the Black Hawk mannikins used to promote the *Encyclopedia Britannica* in shopping centers. "The sculptured simulations [of Black Hawk, Pontiac, Cochise, Massasoit, and others] were stationed in a diorama more than a decade ago to promote one of the most celebrated encyclopedias, but the unusual feature of the

exhibition was that few of the names of the plastic figures were entered in the reference books published by the sponsors of the simulations. The want of manifest manners had excused or abandoned the entries of tribal names in the encyclopedia of dominance" (39).

5. The Terms of George Copway's Surrender

1. It is interesting that much of the Copway material excerpted in the *Heath Anthology of American Literature* (vol. 1) focuses on the sections of the autobiography where he waxes eloquent about his early experiences with nature. To present this as a representative taste of the autobiography very much reduces the complexity and confusion of the text, as though in the interest of reconstructing Copway as an "Indian"—the son of the forest he tried so hard not to be.

2. Knobel states, "The American Indian was useful to nativists in making contrasts. Even the Indians ('interesting relics of Oriental races' as their friends, much less their detractors, called them) were more suitable candidates for citizenship than European-born Roman Catholics. Remarkable as it seems, this rhetorical use of the Indian was not artificial nor strained but fit neatly within the larger pattern of nativist thought" (192). It is ironic, however, that *Copway's American Indian* carried notices of the Improved Order of Red Men, which was a fertile seedbed for nativist ritual and organization but which did not admit Indians to membership.

3. Apparently Clark allowed him to publish the poem under his own name in order to raise money for an Indian school, ever the declared focus of Copway's fundraising. The only parts of the text actually written by Copway were an introduction, a short poem to his wife, and some endnotes.

4. Actually Copway published and republished his works under different titles adding material as padding but reusing some passages a number of times.

5. This poem goes as follows:

> O had our Indian fathers known
>> What prophets told of Christ and heaven!
> For them, we drop a tear and mourn,
>> But weep for joy, our sins forgiven.

This poem (whose source I have not been able to locate) no sooner introduces the forbidden subject of the unregenerate past than it hurries on to celebrate present indications of salvation.

6. For an expression of similar views concerning the use of the term "children" to designate Native Americans, see the remarks of the Otoe chief Medicine Horse to the Indian Commissioner Edward P. Smith in 1873 (quoted in Nabokov, *Native American Testimony*, 137): "We are not children. We are men," etc.

7. For example, he tells a conversion story about one Indian in the autobiography who empties the contents of his medicine bag after becoming a Christian. In context it seems that Copway approves of this exorcism of the past, but in other places, when he emphasizes the importance and sacredness of the medicine bag to the people, he invites us to respect the pouch as a powerful cultural artifact. Again, Black Hawk represents a clear contrast. He never suggests that the medicine bag that he inherits is anything other than sacramental.

6. John Rollin Ridge and the Law

1. See Kenneth Lincoln's *Native American Renaissance;* A. LaVonne Ruoff's *American Indian Literatures* and "American Indian Authors, 1774–1899"; and Louis Owens's *Other Destinies: Understanding the American Indian Novel.* In *American Indian Novelists* Owens and Tom Colonnese list Simon Pokagon's *Queen of the Woods* as the first Indian novel, not mentioning Ridge.

2. Elias Boudinot Sr., like his cousin Rollin Ridge's father, was educated in the North at an Indian school founded by whites. He took the name of the benefactor of the school and was the first editor of the *Cherokee Phoenix* founded in 1824 which published a weekly paper, about three-fourths of which was in English and one-fourth in Cherokee. (Sequoyah had created a Cherokee syllabary in 1821 making possible the representation of the Cherokee language in eighty-six characters.) His son, Elias Cornelius Boudinot, studied and practiced law but also did editorial work, first on the *Arkansian* and later in Little Rock as the editor-in-chief of the *True Democrat.* Rollin Ridge kept in touch with his cousin but broke with him over money near the end of his life.

3. No one has published a genealogy of the Ridge family though this family included a number of distinguished individuals. Major Ridge got his name from fighting for the Americans in the Creek War. His nephew, Elias Boudinot (1803–39), was one of the founding editors of the *Cherokee Phoenix*, and Stand Watie (1806–71), Elias's younger brother, was a brigadier general in

the Confederate forces, one of the last to surrender, on June 23, 1865. Elias Cornelius Boudinot (1835–90) studied law and was admitted to the bar in 1856. Like his father he was also a journalist, doing editorial work first on the *Arkansan* and later as the editor-in-chief of the Little Rock *True Democrat*. A lieutenant-colonel under Stand Watie, he lived in Washington for many years due to his effort to claim damages for his tobacco factory which had been suddenly seized by the government after the war. He came to know many illustrious people in Washington and was highly regarded in political circles.

4. Marshall is often represented as the "bad guy" in Indian legislation, but in fact his attitudes toward Indians were complex and in some ways quite progressive. As early as 1784 he and Patrick Henry had authored a bill to encourage intermarriage between Indians and whites. Each mixed-race couple would receive a stipend, and their children would be educated by the American government free of charge between the ages of ten and twenty-one. The bill survived its first two readings but failed on the third, causing Marshall to comment: "Our prejudices oppose themselves to our interests and operate too powerfully for them." Furthermore, Marshall undertook cases, shunned by his colleagues, to defend the freedom of children born to Indian mothers and slave fathers on the grounds that legally the child follows the mother's status and therefore should be free, a conception of the case often ignored by slaveholders (see Jean Smith, *John Marshall: Definer of a Nation* New York: Holt, 1996).

5. Many of the prosperous Cherokees owned slaves, including Major Ridge, his son John, and John Ross. Perdue states: "In 1835 John Ross, David Vann and John Ridge owned nineteen, thirteen, and twenty-one slaves respectively, and possessed estates that were fairly typical of the large slaveholders" (59). Rollin Ridge inherited two slaves, one of whom, Wacooli, accompanied him to California. Rollin supported Stephen Douglas against Abraham Lincoln and took Douglas's position on slavery, advocating that the states themselves decide whether to be slave or free. Though he opposed many racial distinctions, he felt that blacks were presently inferior to whites. He believed in Manifest Destiny. His biographer, James Parins, comments: "This myth of progress, along with its accoutrements—cultural imperialism, colonialism, and inherent racism—was widely accepted in nineteenth-century Britain and America. It is not surprising that one with Ridge's education and background would accept these ideas as truth" (124–25).

6. The distinction between "Mexicans"—many of whom claim descent

from indigenous peoples—and "Indians" is not always clear, and many contemporary Chicano/as—refusing alliance with the Spanish who colonized Mexico and South America—dislike being called "Hispanics," seeing themselves as historically connected to tribal peoples instead. However, the situation in Ridge's day was complex. American Indians did not necessarily see themselves as allied to "Mexicans" whom they sometimes regarded as their enemies. Therefore, we cannot simply conclude that Ridge (or his readers) would have found the substitution of Mexicans for Native Americans a natural one.

7. One source I looked at claims that Murieta was killed by William T. Henderson. Though I have not been able to confirm this, it shows how confusing the "facts" about Murieta are.

8. Interestingly, Neruda includes an Indian, Rosendo Juárez, who joins Murieta's band to fight against white oppression. (There is no such Indian character in Ridge's novel.) His lines, which Neruda says he took from Jill L. Cossley-Batt's *The Last of the California Rangers*, sound as manufactured as the files of the San Francisco *Call* upon which Cossley-Batt (an Englishwoman) based her version of Murieta's life (see Jackson ed., xli–xliii). The Indian says, "If the white gringo wished to live peacefully with his Indian brother, he could do so. All men are brothers and the earth is mother of us all" (131). For a revealing study of similarly invented Indian oratory, see Rudolf Kaiser's "Chief Seattle's Speech(es): American Origins and European Reception."

9. This is the title of a rewriting of the various Murieta tales—both Ridge's and the pirated version in the *California Police Gazette*—by Walter Noble Burns in 1932. Jackson says the book "did more than any writing about Murieta since Ridge himself to crystallize the Murieta story in the minds of Americans" (xlv). It was bought by Hollywood for a movie script.

10. In a commentary on the bargain struck with Joaquín by the young man from Arkansas, Ridge says: "If they had a right to purchase their lives at the price of silence, they had an equal right, and not only that, but were morally bound, to stand up to their bargain. It were well if men were never forced into such a position, but society has no right, after it has happened, to wring from them a secret which belongs to *them* and not to the world. In such matters God is the only judge" (79–80).

11. In *Iron Cages* Ronald Takaki reminds us that the Chinese were lumped together with both blacks and Indians. "What they all had in common was made clear in the 1854 California Supreme Court decision in the case of *People v. Hall.* 'No black, or mulatto person, or Indian shall be allowed to

give evidence in favor of, or against a white man,' the court declared. 'Held, that the words, Indian, Negro, Black, and White are generic terms, designating races. That, therefore, Chinese and all other people not white, are included in the prohibition from being witnesses against whites.' Thus, like blacks and Indians, the Chinese were 'not white' " (220).

12. For instance, women are subject to rape (Rosita is raped and Rosalie is threatened with rape, though Murieta denounces such practices, saying, "I would have no woman's person without her consent"). However, the women in the band frequently dress up as men, ride hard, and even fight. When Gonzales is killed, his wife takes a second husband, the brutal Guerra who beats her. She is about to slit his throat when Murieta intervenes. Nevertheless, Guerra is found dead several days later, and the narrator explains that "his affectionate wife" poured a tiny bit of hot lead in his ear while he was asleep, killing him in such a way that the cause of his death is never discovered.

13. In his essay "The Cherokees—Their History—Present Condition and Future Prospects" Ridge blames the misery of his people on "the stern denial of justice by the Supreme Court of the United States in 1831" (50). Clearly the government has been guilty of serious acts of violence against the Five Civilized Tribes. Nevertheless, Ridge goes on to say that the confusion within the Cherokee community which has created a "furious banditti" will continue to exist "until a strong arm is extended over them—I mean the laws of the United States[.] I would advocate a measure therefore, which looks to the event of making the Cherokee nation an integral part of the United States, having Senators and Representatives in Congress, and possessing all the attributes, first of a territorial government, and then of a sovereign State" (52). Ridge seemed to believe that the nation of the United States as an "imagined community" transcended the experiential polity whose actions at both the federal and the state levels were deeply unjust.

14. The school he had attended in Arkansas proposed in its mission statement: "The great distinctive principles of civil and religious liberty, on which depends the durability of our Republican Institutions, shall be carefully inculcated" (Parins, 41). In 1861 Ridge published an "Ode to the National Flag," identifying it as a national emblem signifying liberty. For other Indian appropriations of the American flag, see Herbst and Kopp, *The Flag in American Indian Art*.

15. Hollinger used this terminology at a seminar he gave at the Scripps College Humanities Institute (September 17, 1996) to talk about the contrary impulses of provincialism and cosmopolitanism.

7. Sarah Winnemucca's Mediations: Gender, Race, and Nation

1. See also Catherine S. Fowler's statement: "I would like to suggest in the light of 20th century ethnohistoric and ethnographic hindsight that Sarah's position on assimilation, perhaps more than any other single factor, has led scholars, and to a certain degree her own people, to diminish her contributions to Native American scholarship" (33).

2. In her biography of Crazy Horse, Mari Sandoz also focuses upon the destructive effects caused by inadequate or corrupt translators. One of the delights of Sarah Winnemucca's feisty presentation of her people's woes is that she insists upon naming names and giving the addresses of those who have worked against her. In the case of one such, "Captain Dave," she writes: "No man can be a leading man among Indians, unless he is honorable and brave. Dave is neither. On the contrary, he has no character whatever, and could always be hired to do a wicked thing. He is my own cousin" (98). Eventually Captain Dave (or Numana) became the head man at the Pyramid Lake Reservation.

3. In 1875 the Cheyennes were similarly massacred on the Sappa (Black) River, and the babies in their baskets thrown into the fire. A policy of extermination was then in effect concerning Native Americans who were resisting white authority (see Sandoz, 1993).

4. Canfield lists them as follows: Providence, Hartford, New York City, Newburgh and Poughkeepsie (New York), Philadelphia, Dorset (Vermont), Boston, Salem, Cambridge, and Germantown (Massachusetts). In Baltimore, she spoke sixty-six times in a variety of venues.

5. For a discussion of these matters, see Jorge Noriega's "American Indian Education in the United States: Indoctrination for Subordination to Colonialism." See also Laura Wexler, "Tender Violence: Literary Eavesdropping, Domestic Fiction, and Educational Reform."

6. Even Gae Whitney Canfield has no explanation for Sarah's death. She and her sister had eaten a large dinner and consumed some chokecherry wine, after which Sarah collapsed and died. The local coroner ascribed her death to "too much wine" (259), but that seems unlikely. She may have been suffering from pneumonia, valley fever, cholera, malaria, or even hepatitis, and it seems more likely that, however much wine she drank, it was a combination of the alcohol with her lingering disease that killed her. One source lists her death as due to the tuberculosis that killed Lewis Hopkins four years earlier, but since quinine seemed to help her, some form of fever seems more plausible.

7. The photographs provided here allow one to see the contrast between the haughty photograph she sent to her brother in 1878 and these publicity photos which make her look docile and pleading. The photographs of the young Indian students that Laura Wexler includes show a similar transformation from challenging and resistant to domestic and demure.

8. There are marriage records for Sarah Winnemucca and three white men: Edward Bartlett (1871) who was an alcoholic and whom she left after a year, divorcing him in 1876 so she could marry Joseph Satwaller, with whom she was no longer living by 1878, though we don't know why. In 1881 she married Lewis Hopkins with whom she seems to have been deeply in love. Though he accompanied her on the speaking tours, did research for her in several libraries, and often introduced her lectures, he did her the most harm because, while she was bringing in all the income and saving money to take home to the Paiutes, he was giving people promissory notes on her bank account for his gambling debts, which eventually led to bankruptcy. He caused rifts between Sarah and her family, her people, and the white friends who might otherwise have loaned her money for her Indian projects. Sarah also claimed that she had been briefly married to an Indian who beat her. Canfield identifies this Indian as D. R. Jones, but says, "If Sarah was living with an Indian at this period in her life, she may have married him in an Indian ceremony, but not with any white formality" (82), as she was still officially married to Bartlett.

9. During the Ghost Dance period, a Paiute named Jack Wilson (or Wovoka) claimed that in 1888 he had had a vision of a future in which Indians would be restored to their lands and white people would fade away. Without any use of force, there would be peace among people of all colors and nations. These Ghost Dances were quickly modified by various tribes and took on a tone threatening to whites. They were subsequently banned by the American government, but many Indians continued to hold Ghost Dances until the movement faded in the 1890s.

10. "The New Colossus" was written and published in 1883, the same year as Sarah's book, though it was not inscribed on the Statue of Liberty until after Lazarus's death in 1887.

11. Benedict Anderson seems to argue to the contrary in his *Critical Inquiry* essay "Exodus" in which he discusses the way nationalist politics (for instance, in the Middle East) has now moved out to the diaspora who can keep in touch with the hub through jet travel and computer technology. Of course, this postmodern situation has little bearing on the examples we are considering here.

8. Personifying America: Apess's "Eulogy on King Philip"

1. I say "all but forgotten" though it is certainly worth wondering whether Herman Melville somehow came upon a copy of this sermon and chose the name of the *Pequod* in *Moby Dick* with an intention of reminding his readers of heroic qualities run amuck in the figure of Philip, a precursor of Ahab to the extent that his otherwise enlightened instincts are eventually maddened into a lust for revenge. Philip was not actually a Pequot, though Apess claims him as such. No one, to my knowledge, has made a compelling argument as to why Melville named the ship after this tribe; a better argument could be made if Melville had mistakenly believed that King Philip (or Metacom) was a Pequot. (Apess also spells Pequot as Pequod though he is not alone in so doing.) Furthermore, Melville like Apess uses the name "Philip of Mount Hope" when mentioning King Philip in *The Confidence Man*. I know of no piece of historical writing other than Apess's that uses this designation for the Indian leader.

2. Barry O'Connell has recently turned up obituaries in New York journals indicating that Apess died there of alcoholism in 1839.

3. In *New England Frontier* Alden T. Vaughan claims that the Pequots, who themselves had been almost wiped out by the Puritans in an earlier conflict, contributed to the final defeat of King Philip's forces by fighting on the side of the whites (314). It is beyond dispute that the Wampanoags and the Pequots were distinct tribes though they both belonged to the much larger Algonquian group. In *A Son of the Forest* Apess claims that his grandmother was the king's granddaughter, which may have been true whether or not King Philip was the chief of the Pequots.

4. Frederick Douglass uses the same strategy in setting up his character Madison Washington in *The Heroic Slave*.

5. At the end of the essay Apess says, "Let every friend of the Indians now seize the mantle of Liberty and throw it over those burning elements that has [*sic*] spread with such fearful rapidity, and at once extinguish them forever" (307). Here the burning elements seem to be frontier wars between Indians and whites. The earlier passage is less clear as to the nature of these "burning elements." Since they appear in connection with the shining out of "brilliant talents" and since the metaphor seems to be one of smothering, the initial reference to the Puritans' inability to put out Indian fires may be designed to be read as something to be celebrated.

6. "Who shall stand?" makes an allusion to Malachi 3:2: "But who may abide the day of his coming? and who shall stand when he appeareth? for he is like a refiner's fire, and like fuller's soap."

7. Though I will concentrate on the essay's argument as it relates to Native Americans, Apess consistently widens his range of reference, as where he calls upon "every man of color" to "wrap himself in mourning" rather than celebrate the landing of the Pilgrims and the Fourth of July. Slavery comes in for an especially virulent attack further on.

8. It has been estimated that one out of every eight colonial families suffered a loss due to the war.

9. By the time Lydia Maria Child came to publish her "Appeal for the Indians" in 1868, her view of King Philip was patterned on the now established tradition that Philip went to war to defend his territory rather than, as Alden T. Vaughan claims, that the Indian leader after repeatedly selling off his own tribe's hunting grounds saw the need to take a stand in a situation of diminishing Indian influence (*New England Frontier*, 312). The parallel Child makes between Philip and European monarchs, however, may owe more to Apess than to European-American historians. Child writes, "King Philip, driven to desperation by the continual encroachments of white men, went to war to defend his territories from invaders, just as white monarchs do" (*Hobomok, and Other Writings*, 222). She is not, of course, representative of mainstream white views of Indians at this time.

10. Sentences that could be improved by editing are especially prevalent on pp. 301–2. The following is an example: "And there is no manner of doubt but that all my countrymen would have been enslaved if they had tamely submitted. But no sooner would they butcher every white man that come in their way, and even put an end to their own wives and children, and that was all that prevented them from being slaves; yes, *all*" (301).

11. Quite a few Indians in later texts take issue with the term "savage." I am indebted to Colin Thompson for reminding me that Montaigne's essay on cannibals raises the question of who the real savages are: those of the New World or those of the Old who murdered each other in numerous religious wars. Roger Williams, of whom Apess speaks appreciatively, also compared (civilized) Europeans disadvantageously to (so-called uncivilized) Native Americans (see Williams's "A Key into the Language of America"). For further discussion of Montaigne on this issue, see Eric Cheyfitz, *The Poetics of Imperialism*.

12. See also George Bancroft's *History of the United States* and Edward Eggleston's *The Beginners of a Nation* (1896).

13. Note the similarity of the date of this speech celebrating the Pilgrims' arrival to the date Apess chooses for the landing at Plymouth: December 22 instead of December 16.

9. Native American Literature and Nineteenth-Century Nationalisms

1. Despite the abject tone of these remarks, Pokagon remained unreconciled to the fate of the American Indian. See "The Red Man's Rebuke" (appendix).

2. Of course, one does not know precisely what these figures indicate since many people are now calling themselves Indians who are not recognized by people whose families have lived as Native Americans for centuries.

3. Frantz Fanon's essay "On National Culture" in *The Wretched of the Earth* and Alfred Memmi's essays on the psychology of colonized peoples are very insightful about these matters.

Works Cited

Abler, Thomas, editor. *Chainbreaker: The Revolutionary War Memoirs of Governor Blacksnake.* As told to Benjamin Williams. Lincoln: University of Nebraska Press, 1989.

Anderson, Benedict. "Exodus." *Critical Inquiry* 20 (1994): 314–27.

——. *Imagined Communities: Reflections on the Origins and Spread of Nationalism.* Revised edition. London: Verso, 1991.

Apess, William. *On Our Own Ground: The Complete Writings of William Apess, A Pequot.* Edited and introduction by Barry O'Connell. Amherst: University of Massachusetts Press, 1992.

Appiah, Kwame Anthony. *In My Father's House: Africa in the Philosophy of Culture.* New York: Oxford University Press, 1992.

Balibar, Étienne, and Immanuel Wallerstein. *Race, Nation, and Class.* Translated by Chris Turner. London: Verso, 1991.

Bancroft, George. *History of the Formation of the Constitution of the United States of America.* New York: Appleton, 1882.

——. *History of the United States of America: From the Discovery of the Continent.* 10 vols. Boston: Little Brown, 1861–75.

Barthes, Roland. "The Death of the Author." In *Image, Music, Text.* Translated by Stephen Heath, pp. 142–48. New York: Hill and Wang, 1977.

Basso, Keith. *Portraits of "The Whiteman": Linguistic Play and Cultural Symbols Among the Western Apache.* Cambridge: Cambridge University Press, 1979.

Bataille, Gretchen M., and Kathleen Mullen Sands. *American Indian Women: Telling Their Lives.* Lincoln: University of Nebraska Press, 1984.

Berkhofer, Robert F., Jr. "Clio and the Culture Concept: Some Impressions of a Changing Relationship in American Historiography." In *The Idea of Culture in the Social Sciences.* Edited by Louis Schneider and Charles M. Bonjean, pp. 77–100. Cambridge, Mass.: Harvard University Press, 1973.

——. *The White Man's Indian: Images of the American Indian from Columbus to the Present.* New York: Knopf, 1978.

Berlant, Lauren. *The Anatomy of National Fantasy: Hawthorne, Utopia and Everyday Life.* Chicago: University of Chicago Press, 1991.

Bhabha, Homi K. "Of Mimicry and Man: The Ambivalence of Colonial Discourse." *October* 28 (spring 1984): 125–33.

——, editor. *Nation and Narration*. London: Routledge, 1993.

Black, Nancy B., and Bette S. Weidman. *White on Red: Images of the American Indian*. Port Washington, N.Y.: Kennikat, 1976.

Black Hawk, *Autobiography of Ma-Ka-Tai-Me-She-Kia-Kiak, or Black Hawk*. Edited by J. B. Patterson. Oquawka, Ill., 1882. Revised edition. Notes added by James D. Riskell. Rock Island, Ill.: American Publishing, 1912.

——. *Black Hawk, An Autobiography* (1833). Edited and introduction by Donald Jackson. Urbana: University of Illinois Press, 1955, 1990.

Braschi, Giannina. *Empire of Dreams.* Translated by Tess O'Dwyer. New Haven: Yale University Press, 1994.

Brumble, H. David, III. *American Indian Autobiography*. Berkeley: University of California Press, 1988.

Bush, Clive. *The Dream of Reason: American Consciousness and Cultural Achievement from Independence to the Civil War*. New York: St. Martin's, 1977.

Canfield, Gae Whitney. *Sarah Winnemucca of the Northern Paiutes*. Norman: University of Oklahoma Press, 1983.

Catlin, George. *North American Indian Portfolio*. London, 1844.

Cheyfitz, Eric. *The Poetics of Imperialism: Translation and Colonization from "The Tempest" to "Tarzan."* New York: Oxford University Press, 1991.

Child, Lydia Maria. *Hobomok, and Other Writings on Indians*. Edited by Carolyn Karcher. New Brunswick, N.J.: Rutgers University Press, 1986.

Chow, Rey. "Where Have All the Natives Gone?" In *Displacements: Cultural Identities in Question*. Edited by Angelika Bammer, pp. 125–51. Bloomington, Ind.: Indiana University Press, 1994.

Cole, Cyrenus. *I Am a Man: The Indian Black Hawk*. Iowa City: State Historical Society, 1938.

Copway, George. *The Life History, and Travels of Kah-Ge-Ga-Gah-Bowh (George Copway)*. Albany: Weed and Parsons, 1847.

——. *The Traditional History and Characteristic Sketches of the Ojibway Nation*. London: Charles Gilpin, 1850.

Crèvecoeur, J. Hector St. John de. *Letters from an American Farmer* (1782). New York: Dutton, 1957.

Deloria, Vine, Jr., and Clifford M. Lytle. *The Nations Within: The Past and Future of American Indian Sovereignty*. New York: Pantheon, 1984.

Dimock, Wai-Chee. *Empire for Liberty: Melville and the Poetics of Individualism*. Princeton: Princeton University Press, 1989.

Dippie, Brian W. *The Vanishing American: White Attitudes and U.S. Indian Policy*. Middletown, Conn.: Wesleyan University Press, 1982.

Douglass, Frederick. *The Heroic Slave*. In *Three Classic African-American Novels*. Edited by William L. Andrews, pp. 25–69. New York: Penguin, 1990.

Drake, Benjamin. *The Life and Adventures of Black Hawk*. Cincinnati: George Conclin, 1849.

Drake, Samuel G. *Biography and History of the Indians of North America* (1832). 10th ed. Boston: Benjamin B. Mussey, 1848. Also published as *The Aboriginal Races of North America*.

———. *The Old Indian Chronicles*. Boston: Antiquarian Institute, 1836. (Includes *Chronicles of the Indians of America from Its First Discovery to the Present Time*).

Drinnon, Richard. *Facing West: The Metaphysics of Indian-Hating and Empire-Building*. Minneapolis: University of Minnesota Press, 1980.

Eastman, Charles. *From the Deep Woods to Civilization: Chapters in the Autobiography of an Indian* (1916). Lincoln: University of Nebraska Press, 1977.

Edwards, Jonathan. *Basic Writings*. Edited by Ola Elizabeth Winslow. New York: New American Library, 1966.

Eggleston, Edward. *The Beginners of a Nation*. New York: Appleton, 1896.

Fanon, Frantz. *The Wretched of the Earth*. New York: Grove, 1968.

Farmer, David, and Rennard Strickland, editors. *A Trumpet of Our Own: Yellow Bird's Essays on the North American Indian*. San Francisco: Book Club of California, 1981.

Fisher, Philip. *Hard Facts: Setting and Form in the American Novel*. New York: Oxford University Press, 1987.

Fleming, E. McClung. "Symbols of the United States: From Indian Queen to Uncle Sam." In Browne et al., *Frontiers of American Culture*, pp. 1–24.

Foucault, Michel. "What Is an Author?" Translated by Josué Harari. In *The Foucault Reader*. Edited by Paul Rabinow, pp. 101–20. New York: Pantheon, 1984.

Fowler, Catherine S. "Sarah Winnemucca." In *American Indian Intellectuals*, pp. 33–42. St. Paul: West Publishing, 1970.

Gelpi, Albert, editor. *The Poet in America*. Lexington, Mass.: Heath, 1973.

Ginsberg, Allen. "America." In *Howl and Other Poems*, pp. 31–34. San Francisco: City Lights, 1956.

Green, Rayna. "The Pocahontas Perplex: The Image of Indian Women in American Culture." In *Unequal Sisters: A Multi-Cultural Reader in U.S. Women's History.* Edited by Ellen Carol DuBois and Vicki L. Ruiz, pp. 15–21. New York: Routledge, 1990.

Greenfeld, Liah. *Nationalism: Five Roads to Modernity.* Cambridge: Harvard University Press, 1992.

Hawthorne, Nathaniel. *The Scarlet Letter* (1850). Edited by Ross C. Murfin. *Case Studies in Contemporary Criticism.* Boston: Bedford–St. Martin's, 1991.

Herbst, Toby, and Joel Kopp. *The Flag in American Indian Art.* Seattle: University of Washington Press, 1993.

(Hopkins), Sarah Winnemucca. *Life Among the Piutes: Their Wrongs and Claims.* Edited by Mrs. Horace Mann. Boston: Cupples, Upham, 1883. (*Reprint* 1994, University of Nevada Press.)

Hughes, Langston. "I, Too." In *The Poet in America.* Edited by Albert Gelpi, pp. 43. Lexington, Mass.: Heath, 1973.

Jaimes, M. Annette, editor. *The State of Native America: Genocide, Colonization, and Resistance.* Boston: South End Press, 1992.

Jaimes, M. Annette, and Theresa Halsey. "American Indian Women: At the Center of Indigenous Resistance in North America." In Jaimes, *The State of Native America,* pp. 311–44.

Jameson, Fredric. "Third World Literature in the Era of Multi-National Capitalism." *Social Text* 15 (fall 1986): 65–88.

Jennings, Francis. *The Invasion of America: Indians, Colonialism, and the Cant of Conquest.* New York: Norton, 1975.

Kaiser, Rudolf. "Chief Seattle's Speech(es): American Origins and European Reception." In Krupat and Swann, *Recovering the Word,* pp. 497–536.

Knobel, Dale T. "Know-Nothings and Indians: Strange Bedfellows?" *Western Historical Quarterly* 15 (1984): 175–98.

Kroeber, Karl, editor. *1492–1992: American Indian Persistence and Resurgence.* Special issue. *boundary 2* 19 (fall 1992).

Krupat, Arnold. *Ethnocriticism: Ethnography, History, Literature.* Berkeley: University of California Press, 1992.

——. *For Those Who Come after: A Study of Native American Autobiography.* Berkeley: University of California Press, 1985.

——. "Scholarship and Native American Studies: A Response to Daniel Littlefield, Jr." *American Studies* 34 (1993): 81–100.

——. *The Voice in the Margin.* Berkeley: University of California Press, 1989.

———, editor. *Native American Autobiography*. Madison: University of Wisconsin Press, 1994.

Krupat, Arnold, and Brian Swann, editors. *Recovering the Word: Essays on Native American Literature*. Berkeley: University of California Press, 1987.

Lears, T. J. Jackson. "The Concept of Cultural Hegemony: Problems and Possibilities." *American Historical Review* 90 (1985): 567–93.

Least Heat Moon, William. *PrairyErth (a deep map)*. Boston: Houghton Mifflin, 1991.

Lincoln, Kenneth. *Native American Renaissance*. Berkeley: University of California Press, 1983.

Maddox, Lucy. *Removals: Nineteenth-Century American Literature and the Politics of Indian Affairs*. New York: Oxford University Press, 1991.

Martin, Calvin, editor. *The American Indian and the Problem of History*. New York: Oxford University Press, 1987.

McMichael, George, editor. *Anthology of American Literature*. Vol. 1. New York: Macmillan, 1989.

Meigs, William Montgomery. *The Life of Thomas Hart Benton*. Philadelphia: Lippincott, 1904.

Melville, Herman. *The Confidence Man: His Masquerade* (1857). Edited by Stephen Matterson. New York: Penguin, 1990.

———. *Moby Dick, or The Whale* (1850). Introduction by Andrew Delbanco. Notes by Tom Quirk. New York: Penguin, 1992.

Memmi, Albert. *The Colonizer and the Colonized*. Translated by Howard Greenfield. Boston: Beacon, 1967.

Montgomery, Joseph, editor. *Christian History of the Constitution of the United States of America*. Introduction by Felix Morley. Compiled by Verna M. Hall. San Francisco: American Christian Constitution Press, 1960.

Morse, Jedediah, D. D., and Rev. Elijah Parish, A.M. *A Compendious History of New England Designed for Schools and Private Families*. Charlestown: Samuel Etheridge, 1804.

Murray, David. *Forked Tongues: Speech, Writing, and Representation in Native American Texts*. Bloomington, Ind.: Indiana University Press, 1991.

Nabokov, Peter, editor. *Native American Testimony*. Foreword by Vine Deloria Jr. New York: Penguin, 1991.

———. *Two-Leggings: The Making of a Crow Warrior*. New York: Thomas Crowell, 1967.

Neruda, Pablo. *Splendour and Death of Joaquín Murieta*. Translated by Ben Belitt. New York: Farrar, Straus, 1972.

Nichols, Roger L. *Black Hawk and the Warrior's Path*. Arlington Heights, Ill.: Harlan Davidson, 1992.

Noriega, Jorge. "American Indian Education in the United State: Indoctrination for Subordination to Colonialism." In Jaimes, *The State of Native America*, pp. 371–402.

Olson, Lester C. *Emblems of American Community in the Revolutionary Era*. Washington, D.C.: Smithsonian Institution Press, 1991.

Owens, Louis. *Other Destinies: Understanding the American Indian Novel. American Indian Literature and Critical Studies Series*. Norman: University of Oklahoma Press, 1992.

Owens, Louis, and Tom Colonnese. *American Indian Novelists: An Anotated Critical Bibliography*. New York: Garland, 1985.

Parins, James W. *John Rollin Ridge*. Lincoln: University of Nebraska Press, 1991.

Pearce, Roy Harvey. *Savagism and Civilization*. 2d ed. Baltimore: Johns Hopkins University Press, 1953, 1965.

Perdue, Theda. *Slavery and the Evolution of Cherokee Society: 1540–1866*. Knoxville, Tenn.: University of Tennessee Press, 1979.

Pokagon, Simon. *O-Gi-Maw-Kwe Mit-I-Gwa-Ki* or *Queen of the Woods*. Hartford, Mich.: C. H. Engle, 1899. (With a "biography of the chief, by the publisher.")

———. "The Red Man's Rebuke." Hartford, Mich.: C. H. Engle, 1893. Also called "The Red Man's Greeting."

Porter, Carolyn. "What We Know That We Don't Know: Remapping American Literary Studies." *American Literary History* 9 (1994): 467–526.

Reiss, Timothy J. "Mapping Identities: Literature, Nationalism, Colonialism." *American Literary History* 4 (1992): 649–77.

Ridge, John Rollin (Yellow Bird). *The Life and Adventures of Joaquín Murieta, the Celebrated California Bandit* (1853). Introduction by Joseph Henry Jackson. Norman: University of Oklahoma Press, 1955.

———. *A Trumpet of Our Own: Yellow Bird's Essays on the North American Indian*. See Farmer and Strickland.

Rogin, Michael. *Fathers and Children: Andrew Jackson and the Subjugation of the American Indian*. New York: Knopf, 1975.

Roscoe, Will. *The Zuni Man-Woman*. Albuquerque: University of New Mexico Press, 1991.

Rose, Wendy. "The Great Pretenders: Further Reflections on White Shamanism." In Jaimes, *The State of Native America*, pp. 403–22.

———. "Retrieving Osceola's Head, Okemah, Oklahoma, June 1985." *boundary 2* 19 (1992): 238–39.

Ruoff, A. LaVonne Brown. "American Indian Authors, 1774–1899." In *Critical Essays on Native American Literature*. Edited by Andrew Wiget, pp. 191–211. Boston: G. K. Hall, 1985.

———. *American Indian Literatures: An Introduction, Bibliographic Review, and Selected Bibliography*. New York: Modern Language Association, 1990.

———. "Three Nineteenth-Century American Indian Autobiographers." In *Re-Defining American Literary History*. Edited by A. LaVonne Brown Ruoff and Jerry W. Ward Jr., pp. 250–69. New York: Modern Language Association, 1990.

Said, Edward. *Culture and Imperialism*. New York: Knopf, 1993.

Samuels, Shirley, editor. *The Culture of Sentiment: Race, Gender, and Sentimentality in Nineteenth-Century America*. New York: Oxford University Press, 1992.

Sandoz, Mari. *Cheyenne Autumn*. Lincoln: University of Nebraska Press, 1953.

Schmitz, Neil. "Captive Utterance: Black Hawk and Indian Irony." *Arizona Quarterly* 48 (1992): 1–18.

Slotkin, Richard. *Regeneration through Violence: The Mythology of the American Frontier 1600–1860*. Middletown, Conn.: Wesleyan University Press, 1973.

Smith, Anna Deveare. *Fires in the Mirror*. Boston: WGBH Educational Foundation, 1993.

Smith, Donald B. "The Life of George Copway or Kah-ge-ga-gah-bowh (1818–1869)—and a Review of His Writings." *Journal of Canadian Studies* 23, no. 3 (1988): 5–38.

Smith, Elbert H. *Ma-Ka-Tai-Me-She-Kia-Kiak; or Black Hawk and Scenes in the West, A National Poem*. New York: Edward Kearny, 1848.

Smith-Rosenberg, Carroll. "Subject Female: Authorizing American Identity." *American Literary History* 5 (1993): 481–511.

Spivak, Gayatri. "Can the Subaltern Speak?" In *Marxism and the Interpretation of Culture*. Edited Cary Nelson and Lawrence Grossberg, pp. 271–313. Urbana: University of Illinois Press, 1988.

Stiffarm, Lenore A., and Phil Lane Jr. "The Demography of Native North America: A Question of American Indian Survival." In Jaimes, *The State of Native America*, pp. 23–54.

Stowe, Harriet Beecher. *Uncle Tom's Cabin* (1852). Introduction by Alfred Kazin. New York: Bantam, 1981.

Strong, Pauline Turner, and Barrik van Winkle. "Tribe and Nation: American Indians and American Nationalism." *Social Analysis* 33 (September 1993): 9–26.

Sweet, Timothy. "Masculinity and Self-Performance in the *Life of Black Hawk.*" *American Literature* 65 (1993): 475–99.

Takaki, Ronald. *Iron Cages: Race and Culture in Nineteenth-Century America.* Revised edition. New York: Oxford University Press, 1979, 1990.

Tanner, John. *The Falcon: A Narrative of the Captivity and Adventures of John Tanner during Thirty Years Residence among the Indians in the Interior of North America* (1830). Introduction by Louise Erdrich. New York: Penguin, 1994.

Turner, Frederick. "On the Revision of Monuments." In Martin, *The American Indian*, pp. 114–19.

Vaughan, Alden T. *New England Frontier: Puritans and Indians 1620–1675.* Revised edition. New York: Norton, 1965, 1979.

Viola, Herman J. *After Columbus: The Smithsonian Chronicle of the North American Indians.* Washington, D.C.: Smithsonian Books, 1990.

Vizenor, Gerald. *Manifest Manners: Postindian Warriors of Survivance.* Hanover, N.H.: Wesleyan University Press, 1994.

Wagner, Francis, with Christina Wagner-Jones. *Nation-Building in the United States: The American Idea of Nationhood in Retrospect.* Center Square, Penn.: Alpha Publications, 1985.

Wald, Priscilla. "Terms of Assimilation: Legislating Subjectivity in the Emerging Nation." In Kroeber, *1492–1992*, pp. 77–104.

Walker, Cheryl. "Feminist Literary Criticism and the Author." *Critical Inquiry* 16 (1990): 551–71.

Wallace, Mark. "Black Hawk's *An Autobiography:* The Production and Use of an Indian Voice." *American Indian Quarterly* 18 (1994): 481–94.

Weinberg, Albert Katz. *Manifest Destiny: A Study of Nationalist Expansionism and American History.* Baltimore: Johns Hopkins University Press, 1935.

Wexler, Laura. "Tender Violence: Literary Eavesdropping, Domestic Fiction, and Educational Reform." In Samuels, *The Culture of Sentiment*, pp. 9–38.

Williams, Raymond. *Keywords: A Vocabulary of Culture and Society.* Fontana, U.K.: Croom Helm, 1976.

Winnemucca, Sarah. See (Hopkins), Sarah Winnemucca.

Wise, Gene. " 'Paradigm Dramas' in American Studies: A Cultural and Institutional History of the Movement." *American Quarterly* 31 (Bibliography Issue, 1979): 293–337.

Zagarell, Sandra A. "Expanding 'America': Lydia Sigourney's *Sketch of Connecticut*, Catharine Sedgwick's *Hope Leslie*." *Tulsa Studies in Women's Literature* 6 (1987): 225–45.

Ziff, Larzer. *Writing in the New Nation: Prose, Print, and Politics in the Early United States.* New Haven: Yale University Press, 1991.

Index

Abler, Thomas, 48–49

African Americans, xv, 1, 3, 51, 52, 68, 74–76, 152, 158–59, 187–88, 189, 194, 197, 225 n.6, 231 n.5, 232–33 n.11. *See also* Douglass, Frederick; Hughes, Langston; Slavery; Smith, Anna Deveare

Alcohol, 27, 45, 68, 69, 72, 96–97, 99, 105, 138, 155, 156–57, 189, 213–14, 220, 226 n.2, 227 n.6, 234 n.6, 236 n.2

Americanization, 1, 10, 16, 27, 103–4, 112–16, 131, 136, 139, 198, 202, 228 n.11, 234 n.1

American Studies, 28–40

Anderson, Benedict, 4, 6, 11, 45–46, 221 n.1, n.4, n.5, 235 n.11

Apess, William, 8, 13, 14, 21–22, 24, 41–59, 90, 93, 94, 122, 131, 139, 141, 152–53, 158, 161, 185, 193, 194, 198–99, 203–5, 222 n.6, 224–25 n.1, 225 n.3, n.6, n.7, 226 n.9; *A Son of the Forest*, 41–47, 50–52, 66, 165, 236 n.3; "Eulogy on King Philip," 41, 164–81, 201, 224 n.1, 236 n.1, n.5, 237 n.7, n.9, n.10, n.11, n.13; "Indian's Looking Glass," 41, 52–53, 172; *Nullification*, 41, 54–59, 224 n.1, 225 n.7

Appiah, Kwame Anthony, 14

Atkinson, Henry, 72–73

Authenticity, xii–xiv, 8–9, 20, 46, 61–63, 85, 105–6, 200

Balibar, Étienne, 190–91, 192, 197, 200

Bancroft, Charles, 187–88

Bancroft, George, 30, 237 n.12

Bannock War, 145, 153, 155–56

Barthes, Roland, 22, 223 n.23

Basso, Keith, 76, 223 n.15

Benton, Thomas Hart, 197

Berdache, 155

Berkhofer, Robert, 24, 25–27, 29, 33, 222 n.11, 224 n.1, 225 n.5

Berlant, Lauren, 3, 221 n.2, 222 n.10

Bhabha, Homi, xiv, 19–20, 51, 53, 85, 94–95, 106–7, 119, 191, 222 n.8, 223 n.21

Biddle, Nicholas, 7–8

Black Elk Speaks, xi

Black Hawk (Sauk), xv, 12–13, 17–18, 21, 24, 54, 56, 60–83, 84, 88, 90, 95, 96, 107, 111–12, 122, 127, 135, 139, 151, 161, 162, 188–89, 194, 195, 199, 203, 205, 222 n.6, 223 n.19, n.20, 226 n.2, 227 n.5, n.6, n.7, n.8, 228–29 n.9, n.10, n.11, n.12, 230 n.7

Black Hawk War, 17–18, 61, 65, 69, 75, 77, 79–80, 82–83

Blacksnake, Governor (Seneca), 14, 47–50, 199

Cheryl Walker is Richard Armour Professor of Modern Languages at Scripps College and Director of the Scripps Humanities Institute. She is also the author of three books on American woman poets.

Library of Congress Cataloging-in-Publication Data

Walker, Cheryl

Indian nation : Native American literature and nineteenth-century nationalisms /
Cheryl Walker.

p. cm. — (New Americanists)

Includes bibliographical references and index.

ISBN 0-8223-1950-0 (cloth : alk. paper). — ISBN 0-8223-1944-6 (pbk. : alk. paper)

1. American literature—Indian authors—History and criticism. 2. Literature and
anthropology—United States—History—19th century. 3. Literature and society—
United States—History—19th century. 4. American literature—19th century—History
and criticism. 5. Indians of North America—Civilization—Historiography. 6. National
characteristics, American, in literature. 7. Nationalism—United States—History—19th
century. 8. United States—Civilization—Indian influences. 9. Ethnic relations in
literature. 10. Nationalism in literature. 11. Indians in literature. I. Title. II. Series.

PS153.I52W35 1997

810.9'897—dc20   96-43795   CIP